3,000 MORE QUESTIONS AND ANSWERS

ISBN 0 00106210 7
First published 1984
Copyright © 1984 Plantagenet Somerset Fry
Printed in Great Britain
by William Collins Sons & Co. Ltd.

Line illustrations by Jason Lewis

PLANTAGENET SOMERSET FRY'S

3,000 MORE QUESTIONS AND ANSWERS

COLLINS

Contents

What is a cathedral?
A cathedral is a church that contains a bishop's throne. The word comes from *kathedra*, the classical Greek for seat, and the throne is generally to be found by a cathedral's choir stalls. The area over which a bishop presides is known as a see, which also means seat.

Who manages a cathedral?
Generally, it is run by a chapter, which is a body of priests headed by a dean, or in the case of cathedrals associated with monasteries (where the abbot was also the bishop), a body of monks.

Which is the smallest cathedral in the world?
Probably it is the Little Metropole, in Athens in Greece. Known also as *Panayia Gorgoepikoos* (the Virgin who grants requests quickly), it is one of the oldest cathedrals as well. It was founded in the 8th century but the building that has survived is mainly of the 12th and 13th centuries. It is only about 11.5 m × 7.5 m (38 ft × 25 ft) overall.

Which is the largest medieval cathedral in Europe?
The cathedral at Seville in southern Spain, whose overall horizontal dimensions are about 130 m × 76 m (430 ft × 250 ft) which is over two acres. Seville Cathedral has no domes and only one tower – the huge Renaissance belfry called the Giralda. Inside the nave is 39.5 m (130 ft) tall. The remains of Columbus were brought back from the West Indies at the end of the 19th century and buried in the cathedral.

Is St Peter's at Rome a cathedral?
Strictly speaking, it is not a cathedral, but a church. And it is the largest church in the world. It stands over what is believed to be the place where St Peter, one of the twelve disciples, was buried.

Which is the largest medieval cathedral in Britain?
York Minster, which was built on cruciform plan between 1220 and 1475.

What is a basilica?
It is a building plan based on a plan of a rectangle divided lengthwise into a central nave with one aisle, or two aisles, on either long side, and with an apse at the shorter eastern end. At the shorter western end is the entrance chamber, generally called the narthex. The word basilica comes from the Greek *basileus*, (king), because the plan was originally used for a king's throne room.

What is Romanesque style?
It is an architectural style in Europe based on classical Roman models, and it was used in cathedrals and church architecture from the end of the 5th century to the end of the 13th century. One of its main features is strict adherence to proportion, using rounded arches and solid columns, with relatively small window area.

Where did Gothic style first appear?
In France, especially in the area known as the Île de France. Here, in the mid-12th century, cathedrals began to rise, which became some of the loveliest cathedrals ever built. They include Notre Dame in Paris, and the cathedrals at Amiens, Chartres, Laon and Rheims. A slightly earlier Gothic church was the abbey church of St Denis, also in Paris.

Which cathedral tower, now 97m (319ft) tall, was meant to rise to about 168m (550ft)?
The tower of St Rombout's cathedral at Malines (Mechelen) in Belgium. It was built between 1452 and 1578, and though short of the intended height is very impressive. It has 558 steps from the ground to the top.

Which, or in which cathedral:

was Thomas à Becket murdered?
Canterbury.

did the central tower collapse to be replaced by a famous octagon tower?
Ely.

was Nelson buried?
St Paul's.

was Charles VII of France crowned in 1429?
Reims.

is there what is regarded as the most exquisite stained glass in the world?
Chartres.

is the church of the Order of the Golden Fleece?
St Michael's, Brussels.

are there five towers with pyramid tops, all of the same height?
Tournai.

began as a Catholic cathedral, became a Protestant cathedral and was then returned to the Catholic Church?
s'Hertogenbosch, Holland.

has its west end separated by an open space from the rest of the building?
Utrecht.

has a steeple known as 'Old Steve'?
St Stephan, Vienna.

was Charlemagne buried?
Aachen. (See also p 150.)

escaped destruction by the Tatars in the mid-13th century because it was (and is) on an island?
Trogir, Yugoslavia. (See also p 96.)

has the tallest cathedral tower and spire in the world 161 m (528 ft)?
Ulm.

was Erasmus buried?
Basel.

did Albert Schweitzer redesign the organ, in the 1920s?
Aarhus.

is the largest in Scandinavia?
Trondheim.

houses the Byzantine bronze cross carried into battle by El Cid?
New Salamanca.

contains the bones of the disciple, James?
Santiago de Compostela, Spain.

has battlements round the top of the building?
Se Velha, Coimbra, Portugal.

Ely Cathedral

What is heraldry?

Strictly speaking, it is the art, or science, of armorial bearings. These arose in the Middle Ages as devices, or marks, designed to distinguish one armoured warrior from another in battle, in the tournament or on state and other important occasions. Kings, princes, lords and knights chose devices with some thought, and the devices were frequently intended to symbolize individual characteristics, or beliefs, or even the bearer's name in some way, which they portrayed on their shields.

Where did heraldry begin?

It appears to have started simultaneously in most countries of Western Europe some time in the second quarter of the 12th century. That is the dating of the earliest evidence so far found which actually describes the use of heraldic devices on warriors' shields, or in some other form. This was the shield given by Henry I of England (1100–1135) to Geoffrey Plantagenet, Count of Anjou, when he married the king's daughter Matilda in 1128. The shield was described by Geoffrey's biographer.

What is a coat of arms?

Warriors of the age when heraldry began used to wear their armour over a shirt or vest. They also wore a surcoat, a loose flowing garment on which were embroidered the devices emblazoned, or painted, on their shields. The surcoat came to be called a coat of arms, and in time this phrase was used to mean the full scheme of the devices which the holder was entitled to wear.

What is the College of Arms?

Otherwise known as the Heralds' College, it is an English body of men who today supervise the granting of arms to those entitled to them, to check that those who claim to bear arms are in fact so entitled, and to advise generally on all matters concerned with heraldry and genealogy (family trees).

When was the College of Arms founded?

It was founded by King Richard III in 1484. Their official headquarters, the Heralds' College, was given to the heralds in 1558 by Queen Mary I, and these are located in Queen Victoria Street, near Blackfriars Station.

Who are the Heralds?

In order of precedence, they are (in England): Garter King-of-Arms, Clarenceux King-of-Arms, Norroy King-of-Arms. These are the senior members of the college. They are followed by six heralds, namely, Chester, Lancaster, Richmond, Windsor, York and Somerset. Under them are four pursuivants, Rouge Dragon, Portcullis, Rouge Croix, Bluemantle. In Scotland, the head of the heralds is the Lyon King-of-Arms, who is assisted by three heralds, Albany, Ross and Rothesay, and three pursuivants, Carrick, March and Unicorn. There is also a Wales Herald Extraordinary.

What is an escutcheon?

It is a word used to express the entire coat of arms, or just the field on which the arms are painted. The field is the surface of the shield.

What is a crest?

Originally, it was a personal device worn by a warrior on his helmet. It was made of wood or metal, and its design was part of the warrior's armorial bearings. Crests were often elaborate, and might represent particular achievements of the holder. They might be birds in flight, beasts on their hind legs, monsters in angry posture, or they might be human figures such as a Saracen's head. Many crests were portrayals of a human arm encased in armour, with the hand wielding a sword, dagger, mace or axe.

What is a tincture?
It is the heraldic term for a colour, which is used on a shield or coat of arms.

What are the heraldic colours?
They are: metals – gold and silver (often shown as yellow or white in painting) colours – red, blue, black, green, purple, orange or brown, blood red, purple-red, the last three of which are not often used furs – ermine (black spots on white, white spots on black, black spots on gold, gold spots on black, vair (white and blue shapes variously arranged).

What is a lion rampant?
The lion is the king of the heraldic beasts, and was used perhaps more than any other beast. It therefore became necessary to vary the posture of the lion more widely than other animals. One of the best known attitudes is the lion rampant, which shows him erect, one hind paw on the ground, the other three raised, the lion looking forward, with his tail erect. The lion in the Royal Arms of Scotland is a rampant lion.

What is the fleur-de-lis?
This is the emblem of France, and it first appeared on a royal seal of King Louis VII (1137–1180).

What is a difference?
All members of a family entitled to bear arms have the same bearings, but to distinguish the various male members from the head, signs were devised to represent the relationship of each member to the head. These are called differences.

What is a lozenge in heraldic terms?
It is a diamond-shaped figure (not rectangular) on which the arms of females are displayed.

What is meant by baton sinister?
It is a narrow bar that is used on a coat of arms to indicate that the bearer of the arms is an illegitimate descendant of the head of the family, particularly in the case of royal families. It is called sinister because the baton or bar proceeds from the top left (Latin, *sinister*) side of the shield down towards the right (*dexter*) bottom.

What is an achievement?
It is defined as the 'complete display of armorial bearings', and consists of the coat of arms, the crest, the supporters, badges, motto and coronet (if it applies).

What is a tabard?
It is a coat, with or without sleeves, worn by a herald and is emblazoned with the arms of the king.

Little Quiz 1

Here are the first lines of twenty famous poems. What are the poems and who wrote them?

1. I sprang to the stirrup, and Joris, and he;
2. At Flores in the Azores Sir Richard Grenville lay
3. In Xanadu did Kubla Khan,
4. White founts falling in the courts of the sun,
5. The curfew tolls the knell of parting day,
6. Quinquereme of Nineveh from distant Ophir
7. Tiger! Tiger! burning bright
8. The Jackdaw sat on the Cardinal's chair!
9. Not a drum was heard, not a funeral note,
10. Scots, wha hae wi' Wallace bled,
11. O what can ail thee, knight-at-arms,
12. I met a traveller from an antique land,
13. Once more unto the breach, dear friends, once more;
14. When I consider how my light is spent,
15. I wandered lonely as a cloud
16. Slowly, silently, now the moon
17. If I should die, think only this of me:
18. What is this life, if full of care,
19. He did not wear his scarlet coat
20. The Assyrian came down like the wolf on the fold

When did Hollywood become the centre of the American film industry?
Before World War I, probably as early as 1910.

Where were the first experiments made with sound films?
In Japan in 1913 and 1914. Live actors performed alongside moving pictures.

For what films is the American pioneer director, D. W. Griffith, best remembered?
His two masterpieces were *Birth of a Nation* (1915) and *Intolerance* (1916).

Who was Leni Riefenstahl?
Born in 1902, she was an actress turned film-maker who made several propaganda films for the Nazi régime in Germany before and during World War II.

Who inaugurated the screen newsreel?
Charles Pathé, a French film pioneer, first in France in 1909, then in America in 1910. Britain had its first newsreel in 1911.

Who was regarded as the great 'screen lover' of the 1920s?
Rudolph Valentino.

Julius, Leonard, Arthur and Herbert were the first names of four famous comedy brothers. Who were they?
The Marx brothers – Groucho, Chico, Harpo and Zeppo.

In what film did Charlie Chaplin first speak on the screen?
The Great Dictator (1939) in which he aped Hitler.

Why is an Oscar called an Oscar?
The name is said to have come from an exclamation uttered by a girl secretary in the office of the American Academy of Motion Pictures. On seeing the gilt bronze statuette made in 1927 for the first award, she cried out, 'It's like my Uncle Oscar!'

What composition was used as theme music for the Noel Coward directed film *Brief Encounter?*
Rachmaninov's Second Piano Concerto.

Which British film of 1949 based on a story by Graham Greene featured theme music played on a zither?
The Third Man. The music was composed by the zither player, Anton Karas.

What made William Wyler's *The Best Years of Our Life* noteworthy?
It was regarded as one of the best films to portray the effects of World War II on the ordinary American man and woman.

What was *Rashomon?*
The title of a Japanese film of 1951 by Akira Kurosawa which won the Grand Prix at the Venice Film Festival of that year, and thus enabled Japanese films to break into the Western World.

John Williams wrote the music for two American 'blockbuster' films of recent times. What were they?
ET and *Star Wars.*

Who first produced moving pictures?
Dr Etienne Marey (1830–1904), a French physiologist in Paris who in 1888 produced a camera capable of taking a sequence of photographs on a continuous strip of film.

Who was the first Indian film director to achieve a major international reputation?
Satyajit Ray (b 1921), who began to make films of international interest in the 1950s. He won the Cannes Film Festival Grand Prix award in 1956 for *Pather Panchali,* based on a Bengali childhood.

Who founded the Columbia Picture Corporation?
Harry Cohn (1891–1958), whose studios produced numerous remarkable pictures in the 1930s and after World War II.

What kind of films is the French director Claude Chabrol (b 1930) famous for?
Psychological studies of murder and its results in families. He is a 'disciple' of the great thriller film director Alfred Hitchcock. Among Chabrol's films are *Les Biches* and *Le Boucher*.

Could you have seen a full-length feature film in colour prior to the outbreak of World War I?
Feature films in colour even in the 1930s were rare. Yet, it is a little known fact that as early as 9 April 1914, a five-reel melodrama in colour, *The World, the Flesh and the Devil*, opened at the Holborn Empire in London. This film was produced in Kinemacolor, a process developed by a Brighton man, George Albert Smith, as early as 1906. However, it was not until 1965 that the number of colour films released in Britain exceeded that of black-and-white films.

Did the composer Jerome Kern have any connection with films?
By 1924, Kern was acknowledged the leading American composer of show music. However, many of his stage shows were in turn filmed – *Show Boat*, for which he wrote the score in 1927, on three occasions. Amongst the lyricists he collaborated with were Oscar Hammerstein II, Johnny Mercer and Ira Gershwin. His last complete film score was *Centennial Summer*, released in 1946 a year after his death.

In which film did Ronald Reagan appear as General George Custer?
In *Santa Fé Trail*, in 1940.

Who was born William Claude Dukenfield?
W. C. Fields, the American actor, in Philadelphia, 1880.

Whose real name was Larushka Skikne?
The British actor Laurence Harvey, born in Lithuania in 1927.

Strictly speaking, *The Magnificent Seven* **had eight starring actors. Can you name them all?**
Yul Brynner, Eli Wallach, Steve McQueen, Charles Bronson, Horst Buchholz, James Coburn, Brad Dexter, Robert Vaughn.

Where did film festivals begin?
The first film festival was held as part of a wider festival – a Biennale – at Venice in 1932. Judging on this occasion was by popular vote, official awards being first instituted at the second festival there two years later.

Little Quiz 2
   Who murdered?
   1. Jean Marat
   2. Robert Kennedy
   3. Thomas Becket
   4. Lord Darnley
   5. George, Duke of Buckingham
   6. Edward II of England
   7. Martin Luther King
   8. Julius Caesar
   9. Mahatma Gandhi
   10. Dr Verwoerd, prime minister of South Africa
   11. James I of Scotland
   12. Aldo Moro, prime minister of Italy
   13. Pyotr Stolypin, prime minister of Russia
   14. William the Silent, Prince of Orange
   15. Abraham Lincoln

What happened to Actaeon?
He was a hunter who spied on the goddess Artemis (Diana) while she was bathing. She turned him into a stag, whereupon his own hounds set on him and tore him to pieces.

Who won Atalanta's Race?
Atalanta was a huntress. Suitors who challenged her to a race lost their lives if they did not win. The runner Milanion, however, took with him three golden apples and dropped them during the contest. Atalanta stopped to pick them up, one by one, which allowed Milanion to win.

What happened to Daedalus and Icarus?
Daedalus was a Greek craftsman who built the famous labyrinth at the palace of Minos in Crete. When he fled from Crete, he took his son Icarus with him. He achieved his escape by making wings which he fixed to himself with wax, and did likewise with Icarus. But when they got near the Sun, the wax melted on Icarus, his wings dropped off and the boy was drowned.

Why did Oedipus put out his own eyes?
Abandoned as a baby on the mountains by his parents and brought up by shepherds, Oedipus later unknowingly killed his father and married his mother. On learning the truth his mother hanged herself and Oedipus put out his own eyes.

What was the chimaera?
A mythological monster with a lion's head, a goat's body and a dragon's tail.

What were Scylla and Charybdis?
Scylla was a nymph who was changed into a collection of dangerous rocks between Italy and Sicily. Charybdis was another nymph, who was changed into a whirlpool off the coast of Sicily.

Who was the messenger of the gods?
Mercury (Roman name), or Hermes (Greek). He is generally portrayed wearing winged sandals.

Who was Cuchullain?
The legendary hero of Irish mythology, who was son (or nephew) of Conchobar, king of Ulster.

Who sulked in his tent at the battle of Troy?
Achilles.

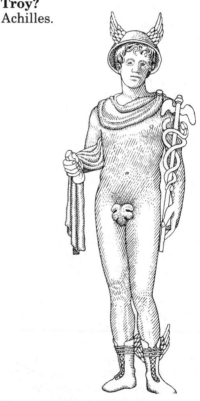

Mercury the Messenger

Who were the Argonauts?
They were the heroes who accompanied Jason on his journey to fetch the Golden Fleece, and were so called because they travelled in a ship called the *Argo*.

Who killed Fafnir the dragon?
Sigurd slew him with the magic sword of Odin.

What do we mean by an Achilles heel?

The demi-god Achilles was washed by his mother when a boy in the river Styx to make him immortal. Unfortunately, she held him by one heel which remained dry. Achilles was eventually slain at the battle of Troy when an arrow shot by Paris pierced his heel. An Achilles heel today means a weak point in a person's character.

Which Norse god had his lips sewn up for telling lies?

Loki, the god of strife.

Where are the Elysian Fields?

This is another name for Paradise, or the Islands of the Blessed, to which those who were favoured by the gods went after they died.

Who was the legendary commander-in-chief of the Greek forces at the battle of Troy?

Agamemnon, king of Mycenae. His prize in the war was one of the Trojan king Priam's daughters, Cassandra. When he got home to Mycenae, however, he was murdered by his wife Clytemnestra.

What happened to Persephone?

Persephone (or Proserpina in Roman mythology) was the daughter of Zeus (Jupiter) and Demeter (Ceres). She was kidnapped by the underworld god, Pluto who eventually agreed that she should spend half the year with him and the other half on Earth.

What is *The Golden Bough*?

It is a work on mythology and comparative religion which first appeared in 1890. It was written by Sir James George Frazer (1854–1941), a Scottish folklorist and social anthropologist. The golden bough was a branch broken by Aeneas from a tree in the sacred grove of Nemi. There are twelve volumes of the work and an abridged version was published in 1922.

What was the shirt of Nessus?

Nessus was a centaur, whom Heracles (Hercules) shot with a poisoned arrow. In revenge, the beast told Deianeira, Heracles' wife, to soak a piece of cloth in its blood; she was to dress Heracles in this if he ever ceased to love her. Following her husband's unfaithfulness with Iole, Deineira sent him a new shirt made from the poisoned cloth. Upon dressing himself in it, Heracles found that it stuck to his skin in an agonizing fashion and that he was unable to remove it. In remorse, Deianeira committed suicide; her husband built a funeral pyre for himself which was then lit by one of his servants, and he was taken up into the sky to join the immortals upon Olympus.

Little Quiz 3

What do the following Americanisms mean?

1. Attorney
2. Faucet
3. Wash rag
4. Wad
5. Gas, gasoline
6. Suspenders
7. Cracker
8. Patrolman
9. Garbage can
10. Rubbers
11. Pavement
12. Speakeasy
13. Derby
14. Bill
15. Subway
16. Bully
17. Knock
18. Street car
19. Elevator
20. Candy

When was the first artificial satellite launched into space?
Sputnik I was sent up by the USSR on 4 October 1957.

Which was the first animal sent into space?
A dog, Laika, which was sent up in the USSR's second satellite, on 3 November 1957.

Who was the first American astronaut to go into orbit round the earth?
Colonel John Glenn, in the Mercury capsule Friendship 7, on 20 February 1962.

What was Telstar?
Telstar was the first active communications satellite sent into space on 10 July 1962 and which began to relay live television programmes from 23 July.

What objective did the spacecraft Mariner 2 achieve on 14 December 1962?
It flew past the planet Venus after a voyage of over three months.

What did Mariner 4 achieve in 1965?
It flew past the planet Mars and photographed Martian craters. The journey took from 28 November 1964 to 14 July 1965.

Who was the first man in space?
Yuri Gagarin, the Soviet cosmonaut, who made a two-hour orbital flight in Vostok I on 12 April 1961.

Who was the first woman in space?
Second Lieutenant Valentina Vladimirovna Tereshkova, aged 26, of the Soviet Air Force. She spent 2 days, 22 hours, 50 minutes orbiting the Earth alone aboard Vostok 6 in June 1963.

Which country achieved the first
unmanned spacecraft flight round the moon and brought the craft back to Earth?
The USSR, in September 1968. The vehicle was Zond 5.

Which country achieved the first soft landing on the moon?
The USSR, with Luna 9, a spacecraft which photographed the surface, on 3 February 1966.

What was the Apollo–Soyuz Test Project?
It was a joint American–Russian mission on which the US astronaut Thomas Stafford and the USSR cosmonaut Alexei Leonov met and shook hands in the interconnecting hatch of the Apollo–Soyuz complex, that is, the two spacecraft linked in space, 17 July, 1975.

What other nations apart from the USA and the USSR have launched satellites into space?
France (1965), Britain (1969), China (1970), Japan (1970), India (1980).

When was the first soft landing on Venus?
On 17 August 1970, by the USSR, when a capsule from Venera 7 settled on the surface. The craft was of course unmanned.

What was Lunokhod I?
This was the world's first remote-controlled lunar roving vehicle. It was landed successfully on the moon by the USSR on 17 November 1970.

Who sent up the first orbiting space station?
The USSR sent up Salyut I on 19 August 1971, and it remained in space until early the following October.

Which spacecraft took the first close-

up pictures of Saturn's rings?
Voyager I (USA) in November 1980.

Who was the first man to land on the moon's surface?
Colonel Neil Armstrong of the USA. He
was followed closely by Edwin Aldrin,
and both stepped out onto the surface on
20 July 1969.

What were Colonel Armstrong's words when he stepped down onto the moon?
'That's one small step for a man, one
giant leap for mankind.'

What did Helios I achieve?
This space probe launched jointly by the
USA and West Germany, went as close
as 45 million km (28 million miles) to the
Sun. This was in 1974.

Which spacecraft made the first return trip into space?
The space shuttle orbiter Columbia. It
first blasted into orbit on 12 April 1981.
It made a return journey on 12 November
1981.

Who was the first spaceman to die of natural causes?
Colonel Pavel Ivanovich Belyayev of the
Soviet Air Force, who had commanded
the Voskhod 2 flight in March 1965. He
died of a stomach complaint in January
1970.

Where is Tyuratam?
Tyuratam, originally referred to as
Baikonur, is the USSR equivalent of
Cape Canaveral. It lies in Kazakshtan, to
the east of the Aral Sea.

What lunar fly-by mission almost ended in disaster?
That of Apollo 13 in April 1970.
Following an explosion aboard the
service module, the crew of three were
able to use the lunar module as a refuge
which saved their lives.

Who was the first Western European to travel in space?
French astronaut Jean-Loup Chrétien,
who accompanied a Soviet commander
aboard Soyuz T-6 in June 1982.

Who has made the most flights into space?
John Watts Young, who made his first
flight into space in 1965 and his fifth in
1981.

Who was the first man to die during a space mission?
Colonel Vladimir Mickhailovich
Komarov of the Soviet Air Force, who
died aboard Soyuz I when it crashed to
Earth in April 1967. According to the
official Russian account, the accident was
due to parachute failure.

Little Quiz 4
  **In which countries do these rivers
  mainly flow?**
  1. Irrawaddy
  2. Ganges
  3. Po
  4. Tagus
  5. Scheldt
  6. Rhone
  7. Tay
  8. Taff
  9. Liffey
  10. Test
  11. Red
  12. Flinders
  13. Dnieper
  14. Maranon
  15. Xingu
  16. Yukon
  17. Yangtze
  18. Orange
  19. Clutha
  20. Menderes

?ism

What is populism?
A doctrine whose advocates believe they represent the common people irrespective of political persuasions.

What is capitalism?
It is the economic system based on private or corporate ownership of the means of production of wealth, the distribution of whose goods depends upon competition in a free market.

What would it mean if you were a communist and were accused by your colleagues of deviationism?
It means that you had a tendency to think, speak or act contrary to the orthodox communist line.

What is Post-Impressionism?
It is the term used to describe French art styles of the very late 19th century and the early 20th century, immediately following those of the impressionists. Notable exponents of post-impressionism were Cézanne, Gauguin and Van Gogh.

What is a mechanism?
It is a system or process made up from components which work together and function like a machine.

What is holism?
It is the belief that some wholes are greater than the sum of their component parts.

What is atavism?
It means reverting to primitive instincts from Latin *atavus* a great-great-great-grandfather.

Is atheism a religion?
No, it is the refusal to accept the existence of God, or of any supernatural being, past or present.

What is an aphorism?
It is a short and pithy saying.

What is a euphemism?
The use of a mild word or phrase in place of a harsh or offensive one, for example, 'a stranger to the truth' instead of 'liar'.

What has Castroism to do with Fidel Castro?
It has everything to do with him. When Castro overturned the US-backed government of General Batista in Cuba in 1959, he set up a new communist state in the island, in which the communist ideas were tempered with the traditional Latin-American revolutionary aims of giving the peasants and industrial workers a fair deal.

What is an organism?
It is a living being, plant or animal, with components that work together.

What is metabolism?
A word describing the continuous processes of the building up and breaking down of cells in living organisms, which accounts for the sustaining of life and growth.

What is pantheism?
This has two meanings. It means the worship of, or belief in, many gods, as in ancient civilizations. It also means belief that one god is everything and everything is that god.

What is transvestism?
It means the habit of wearing the clothes of the sex opposite to that of the wearer.

What is Zionism?
It is the movement for establishing and maintaining a national community for the Jews in Palestine. It is also the belief that such a home is the destiny of Jews.

What does syllogism mean?
It is a logical argument constructed from two propositions, one following another, and a conclusion arrived at.

What is Fabianism?
It is an early socialist philosophy developed in Britain in the later 19th century, which stated that the changes required in society would be better and more permanent if they were achieved slowly instead of by violent revolution.

What is prognathism?
It is the state of being prognathous, that is, having a projecting jaw.

What is a micro-organism?
Any organism which is extremely small, such as a bacterium, virus or tiny cellular structure like an amoeba.

In what play is there a character called Miss Prism?
The Importance of Being Earnest, by Oscar Wilde.

What is a malapropism?
A misapplication of a word with humorous, or even ludicrous results. The name derives from a character, Mrs Malaprop, in Sheridan's comedy *The Rivals*, a lady given to such misuse of English.

What is Zoroastrianism?
A religion founded in Persia by the prophet Zoroaster in the 6th century BC. Its holy book is known as the Avesta, its supreme god is referred to as Akura Mazda. Most of its adherents now live in and around Bombay.

What is Lamaism?
The name for the form of the Buddhist faith developed in Tibet. Its spiritual leader, the Dalai Lama, is considered to be divine; however, the present holder of this position was forced by the Chinese occupation of his land to flee to a life of exile in India in 1959.

What is Arianism?
This was a Christian heresy, first expressed by one Arius of Alexandria in the 4th century. This denied the full divinity of Christ. It was condemned by the Council of Nicaea. After remaining dormant for over a millennium, Arianism enjoyed a limited following in 17th and 18th century England and had some influence in the development of Unitarian thought.

What is Wahabism?
This was a movement within Islam that was developed in Arabia in the 18th century by Muhammad ibn Abd-el-Wahhab. Since Saudi Arabia achieved statehood following World War I, Wahabism has been the official creed of that country.

What is deism?
The belief that there is a god, but that he (or she) has not revealed himself (or herself) except in the normal courses of nature and history.

Little Quiz 5
What are the capital cities of:
1. West Germany
2. Burma
3. South Africa
4. Ecuador
5. Bolivia
6. Mexico
7. Cuba
8. Trinidad
9. Northern Ireland
10. Iceland
11. Uruguay
12. Chile
13. Egypt
14. Israel
15. Sudan
16. Bulgaria
17. Malta
18. Albania
19. Malawi
20. Malagasy

What is a *de facto* ruler?
A monarch who rules not because he is the legitimate successor of the previous monarch but because he has seized power by a coup d'état or by war. Henry VII of England was *de facto* king by virtue of having won the throne at the battle of Bosworth in 1485 from the rightful king, Richard III who was killed.

What do we mean when we say 'do something pronto!'?
Pronto is Spanish for quickly.

Would you find it advantageous to be given *carte blanche* in a new job?
Yes, for it means virtually that you can do what you like in the position, though there would obviously be some limits. *Carte blanche* means white card or sheet, and the term comes from the idea of giving someone a blank sheet of paper and allowing them to write out their own terms.

What is *parvenu*?
Parvenu means 'having arrived' in French, and refers to people who have come from humble beginnings and made good, generally through the acquisition of wealth.

What has happened to you if you are described as *hors de combat*?
It means you are temporarily out of action. Generally, it is used if you have been disabled through illness or accident. It is the French for 'out of the fight'.

What is *sang froid*?
It is the French term for coolness or composure in moments of crisis (literally, cold blood).

What are *pince nez*?
They are a special type of spectacles in which the two lenses and frame are supported by clips on the nose. (French, pinch nose.)

What is a *cul-de-sac*?
A blind alley. If you come to a road marked cul-de-sac, you will not normally be able to get out of it at the other end.

Why would someone use the phrase *jacta alea est*, or its English equivalent, the die is cast?
It was the phrase used by Julius Caesar when he stood by the Rubicon river in north Italy, deciding to cross and go south, thereby starting what he believed to be a necessary civil war. So, it means 'I can't turn back now.'

What does *in vino veritas* mean?
It means, the truth comes out in wine, and that you are more likely to show your real feelings if you have had a lot to drink. The idea, however, is certainly open to question.

Where would you expect to see a *gendarme*?
Usually in France. *Les gendarmes* are soldiers used for police duties, but foreigners often use the word *gendarme* to mean any kind of policeman.

What is a *snorkel*?
It is a piece of simple apparatus of mouthpiece and tube, enabling one to swim for long periods under water. It probably comes from the German *snarchen* to snore.

What is *karate*?
A Japanese form of unarmed combat. It is taught and used as a form of recreation so widely now in the West that the term has come to be regarded as any kind of unarmed combat.

Would you feel honoured if you were presented with a *festschrift*?
Probably. It is a book of essays or papers specially written by scholars on the subject on which you are a leading authority, and presented to you on

retirement or on reaching a certain age. It comes from the German meaning festival writing.

What is *cologne***?**
It is short for *eau de Cologne*, (French, water from Cologne), a scented water, refreshing especially in hot weather when applied to the skin.

What is a *boutique***?**
From the French for shop, the word is now used to indicate a particular kind of small store that specializes in ready-made fashion clothes, and perhaps crafts, scents and soaps.

Why do children shout '*Cave!*' **when a master is approaching the classroom?**
Because they want to warn their friends to stop fooling about, etc. *Cave* is Latin for Beware!

What is *poste restante***?**
Part of a post office where letters are kept for collection.

What does *in toto* **mean?**
Entirely or completely.

What does *id est* **mean?**
Simply 'that is'; however, you are already likely to be familiar with its abbreviated form, ie.

Who or what is an *aegrotat***?**
Literally meaning 'he (or she) is ill', an aegrotat is one considered worthy of being awarded a degree or similar honour, despite having been unable through illness to sit the examination or test required for such an award.

Who or what is a *sabra***?**
A Jew, born in Israel, considered to have the qualities of the sabra or desert pear which is prickly on the outside and soft on the inside.

When a papal pronouncement is made *urbi et orbi*, **to whom is the pope speaking?**
To everyone! It means 'to the city (Rome) and to the world'.

What is *l'esprit de l'escalier***?**
This is 'staircase wit'. The phrase refers to the witty answer one wishes one had made in the drawing room but only thought of later on, going down the stairs on the way out!

What did the hand write on the wall of Belshazzar's banqueting hall, and what did it mean?
Mene, mene, tekel, upharsin (Daniel v: 25). These words are Aramaic and they can be translated as 'God has numbered your kingdom and brought it to an end; you are weighed in the balance, and are found wanting; your kingdom is divided'.

What is the meaning of *mens sana in corpore sano***?**
What we all strive for, doubtless. Expressed by the Roman writer Juvenal, its meaning is 'a sound mind in a sound body'.

What is *chili con carne***?**
This is basically meat cooked in a spicy sauce, a dish emanating from Mexico and neighbouring parts of the USA.

What was *suttee***?**
This was a custom abolished by the British in India, by which a Hindu widow would throw herself onto the funeral pyre of her husband.

What is *jai alai***?**
This is a handball game, native to the Basque country in Spain, which is played in a court by two or four players with long curved wicker baskets strapped to their right wrists.

How was the wireless first used at sea to help in crime detection?
The murderer, Dr Crippen was travelling to the US in a liner in disguise. A radio message was sent by the police to the ship's captain and he was discovered, arrested and brought back to Britain in 1910.

When was the BBC established?
In 1922, as the British Broadcasting Company. This was dissolved in 1927 and the British Broadcasting Corporation founded with a 10-year charter.

Which famous abdication speech was broadcast on radio in December 1936?
The speech by Edward VIII. It was broadcast from Windsor.

Who was the first director-general of the BBC?
John Reith, later Sir John and later still, Lord Reith. He retired in 1938.

When was Radio Times first published?
1923.

Who was the first commentator on the Oxford–Cambridge Boat Race?
John Snagge, who started in 1928.

Which famous West Indian cricketer became a governor of the BBC?
Learie Constantine, later Lord Constantine.

What did the initials ITMA stand for?
It's That Man Again, the name of a highly popular radio comedy show, starring Tommy Handley (who was 'that man').

When were radio waves discovered?
In 1864 by James Clerk-Maxwell, and first successfully transmitted in a laboratory by Heinrich Hertz in 1888.

Who were the most regular and most popular members of the long-running weekly radio programme, the Brains Trust?
Professor C. E. M. Joad, Professor (later Sir) Julian Huxley, and Commander Campbell.

When did a member of the Royal Family first use radio to speak to the nation?
Indirectly, in 1924, when George V gave his speech opening the British Empire Exhibition at Wembley, and was recorded.

Who succeeded in transmitting radio waves across the Atlantic?
Guglielmo Marconi, the Italian born physicist, who directed radio waves from a point at Poldhu in Cornwall to a point in Newfoundland, in 1901.

Which is Britain's longest running radio serial?
The BBC's farming family programme, *The Archers*, begun in 1948.

Which famous London musical concerts were saved by the BBC?
The Promenade Concerts, which had been founded in 1895 by Sir Henry Wood and held at the Queen's Hall (which was destroyed during World War II) and then at the Royal Albert Hall.

Who was the Radio Doctor?
Dr Charles Hill, later Lord Hill of Luton, who eventually became chairman of the BBC.

Who said, 'The Martians have landed' and frightened a whole city?
Orson Wells produced a radio drama in New York in 1938, about invasion from outer space, opening the programme with the announcement 'The Martians have landed'. Many thought the statement to be true, and panicked.

Who was Uncle Mac?
Derek McCulloch, introducer of
Children's Hour.

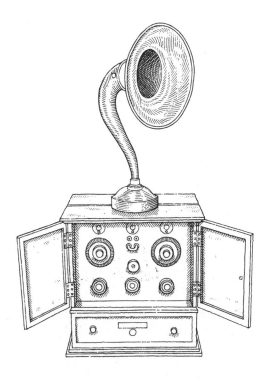

Three valve battery receiver made by
General Electric Company 1923

How many recordings on discs and tapes are there in the BBC's Sound Archives Library?
About 101,000.

How many broadcast receiving licences were issued in the first full year of broadcasting, 1927, and in the last completed year?
(1927), 2,269,644 and (1983), 18,494,235.
The latter figure, by the way, is not the
highest recorded. The 1981 figure was
18,667,211.

Who plays the part of June in the popular BBC TV series *Terry and June*?
June Whitfield, who also played the part
of Eth in the regular sketch about Ron
and Eth and Mr Glum in the weekly
radio serial *Take It From Here*, one of the
top BBC radio programmes of the 1950s
and early 1960s.

What dramatic incident took place during the famous BBC Radio programme, *The Archers*, on the same night on which commercial television opened in 1955?
During the episode of *The Archers* on
22 September, Grace Archer, wife of Phil
Archer, lost her life through rushing into
a burning stable to rescue a horse. The
incident attracted widespread publicity,
and was described by the *Daily Herald* as
a 'mean, callous stunt'. Phil Archer,
incidentally, was played by Norman
Painting, who is still playing the part, 29
years later (1984).

How long has the BBC's External Service by radio been operating?
Since 19 December 1932, when it started
as the Empire Service, broadcasting
throughout the old British Empire.

When did both king and prime minister address the nation over BBC radio on the same day?
On the day of the outbreak of World War
II, 3 September 1939. The prime
minister, Neville Chamberlain, spoke at
about 11.00 in the morning, and the
king, George VI, about 6 o'clock in the
evening.

When did the first Scottish national radio service, Radio Scotland, begin broadcasting?
On 23 November, 1978.

At which battle was a king of Sweden killed in the moment of victory?

Lutzen in 1632. King Gustavus Adolphus of Sweden, commander of the Protestant forces fighting in Germany during the Thirty Years' War, defeated the Catholic Imperial forces under Wallenstein, but was himself wounded. As evening fell after his army had triumphed, he was killed by a fleeing enemy soldier.

At which battle was a king of Ireland killed in the moment of victory?

At Clontarf in 1014. King Brian Boru had just routed the Vikings not far from Dublin, when one of the Viking leaders running from the battlefield came upon him in his tent and slew him.

What was the Battle of the Bulge?

At the end of 1944, when the German armies were being pushed back into their own territory in Europe, the German leader Hitler launched one final attempt to stave off total defeat by an assault upon the US forces in the Ardennes Forest. For a few days, the Germans managed to punch a hole in the US lines and formed a pocket of recaptured territory. This came to be called The Bulge. The attack was not sustained, and with British help, the US forces drove the Germans back into their Rhineland.

What was achieved by the Battle of Omdurman?

Lord Kitchener, in command of the Anglo-Egyptian army, defeated the fierce and bold warriors of the Dervish army in the Sudan on September 1898 and the Sudan was absorbed into the British Empire.

At which battle did Alfred the Great defeat the Vikings in 878?

At the battle of Ethandune in the west country of England. The site was either near Edington in Wiltshire, or near Slaughterford in south Gloucestershire.

At which battle was the son of Napoleon III of France killed?

At the battle of Isandlwana in Zululand in 1879, when the Zulu chief, Cetewayo, defeated a British army in which the prince imperial, eldest son of Napoleon III, was serving.

Where was the siege of Dien Bien Phu?

Dien Bien Phu was a town in French Indo-China (now Vietnam). In 1954 French and allied troops were besieged by communist forces under Ho Chi Minh, and they had to surrender. This led to the withdrawal of France from Indo-China altogether.

At which battle did Julius Caesar defeat Pompey the Great?

At the battle of Pharsalus in Greece, in 48 BC. Caesar defeated an army more than twice the size of his force, and by so doing established himself as supreme in the Roman world.

Which battle stopped the Arabs from conquering all France in the 8th century?

This was the great battle of Tours, near Poitiers, in central France, where in 732 Charles Martel, king of the Franks, crushed a huge Arab army under Abd-Er-Rahman over several days' fighting.

What was the battle of Tsushima in 1905?

It was a great naval victory for the Japanese fleet over the Russian fleet during the Russo-Japanese War of 1905–1906. The battle was fought in the strait of water beside the island of Tsushima off Korea.

At which battle did Nelson put a telescope to his blind eye?

Copenhagen in 1801. Nelson was second in command under Sir Hyde Parker, but ignoring a signal to break off action, he

sailed into the Danish fleet when it was not expecting him and destroyed or disabled the entire fleet.

Which famous siege in France was conducted and won by a cardinal?
The siege of La Rochelle, by Cardinal Richelieu, in 1627. The fortress of La Rochelle was held by Huguenots who held out for over a year, but the cardinal finally compelled them to yield after a relief force promised from England failed to arrive.

At which battle in 1571 was the Turkish fleet defeated?
Lepanto – a tremendous sea battle between the Turkish fleet and a Christian combined fleet of Spaniards, Venetians, Genoese and others under the command of Don John of Austria, illegitimate son of the emperor Charles V of the Holy Roman Empire.

Which was the decisive battle of World War I on the Western Front?
It was the battle of the Marne, fought in early September 1914, where the Allied British and French forces stemmed the advance of the German Army through France on its way towards Paris. The war went on for another four years, but the Germans lost their only chance to take Paris.

What happened at the Battle of the Falkland Islands in 1914?
This was a naval victory by the British fleet under Admiral Sir Doveton Sturdee over the German fleet under Admiral von Spee.

What battle is depicted in the famous Bayeux Tapestry?
The battle of Hastings in 1066 when Harold of England was defeated and slain. This date marked the beginning of the Norman conquest of England by William of Normandy.

At which battle was Sir Philip Sidney killed?
At the battle of Zutphen in the Netherlands, in 1586, where he led an English contingent on the Dutch side against the Spanish.

What English general named his palatial residence after his greatest victory?
John Churchill, Duke of Marlborough, named Blenheim Palace after the battle of Blenheim in the war of the Spanish Succession.

What was the result of the Battle of Cannae in 216 BC?
The Carthaginian army under Hannibal utterly defeated the Roman army in a desperate battle by the river near Cannae, in South Italy. About 50,000 Romans were killed or wounded. The victory left the way open for Hannibal to march on Rome, but he failed to do so.

How did the rain help Clive to win the Battle of Plassey, in 1757?
During the battle, the Indian forces under Suraja Dowlah, the Nawab of Bengal, neglected to cover their barrels of gunpowder. It rained, and the powder was soaked. The British supplies, on the other hand, had been well-protected. As a result, Clive completely routed the Nawab's army.

Who destroyed one part of an enemy's fleet before breakfast, breakfasted, then destroyed the remaining part?
Admiral Dewey, the US commander fighting the Spanish at the Battle of Manila Bay in 1898.

Who defeated whom at the battle of Tannenburg in 1914?
The Germans defeated the Russians, thus reversing the latters' advance into what was then Prussia.

What is the highest British decoration for bravery?
The Victoria Cross, instituted by Queen Victoria in 1856 to decorate heroes of the Crimean War.

Why have there been no new Knights of the Order of St Patrick since 1922?
Because of the creation of the Irish Free State in 1922, a first step towards the complete separation of Ireland politically from Britain.

What is the emblem indicating 'mentioned in despatches'?
An oak leaf or leaves, worn usually on the ribbon of the Victory Medal for World War I, the Victory Medal for World War II, or on other ribbons by order.

When did the orders of the Star of India and the Indian Empire stop being awarded?
In 1947, when British India was given self-government and partitioned into India and Pakistan.

When was the Order of Merit founded?
In 1902, by Edward VII. It carries no title, but it is one of the highest awards that the sovereign can bestow.

How many OMs can there be at one time?
Twenty-four. At one time it was divided into twelve military members and twelve civilian members.

When is a 'bar' awarded to the holder of a decoration?
When the person is awarded the same decoration a second time, for a similar service, such as a second act of great bravery. Bars are awarded to DSOs, MCs, DFCs, DSCs and some others. Only three bars have ever been awarded to holders of the Victoria Cross. One was a New Zealander, Second Lieutenant Charles Upham, who was first awarded the medal during the German attack on Crete in 1941, then won a bar in the Western Desert in 1942.

Why is the Order of the Bath so named?
In medieval times, the bestowal of knighthood was generally accompanied by a ritual taking of a bath. The order is generally accepted as having been established by Henry IV (1399–1413) as a mark of distinction he conferred on several knights and lords at the time of his coronation.

What is the order Pour le Mérite?
Though French in title, it was in fact a high Prussian decoration, introduced by Frederick the Great (1740–1786) as an adaptation of the earlier Order of Generosity. In the early 19th century the Pour le Mérite was limited to military services.

Who founded the Legion d'Honneur?
It was founded by Napoleon Bonaparte in 1802. He introduced it to encourage civilian and military achievement; as he said, it is easier to manage men by giving them toys.

What is the highest award of the United States?
The Medal of Honor, for military or naval services. It was instituted in 1861 and is generally known as the Congressional Medal.

What is the Purple Heart?
It is an old US decoration (which began in the 1780s) that in recent years has been awarded to any US member of the armed forces who is wounded in action, and it is also awarded posthumously.

Who was the only person to receive the Grand Cross of the Iron Cross of Nazi Germany?
Reichsmarschall Hermann Goering.

Who founded the French Order of Liberation?
This was instituted by General de Gaulle in 1940, when he came over to England after the French government surrendered to Hitler. It was to be given to military and civilian people who gave distinguished service towards the cause of liberating France. Holders of the award are *Compagnons*.

Which is the highest order awarded in Denmark?
The Order of the White Elephant, which goes back to the 15th century.

What was the origin of the English Order of the Garter?
It was founded by Edward III (1327–1377) in 1348. He intended the members to be a brotherhood of knights and lords who had distinguished themselves in battle, especially those who had helped to win the great victory over France at Crécy (1346). There were to be 25 members. It is England's highest award, after the Victoria Cross, and is no longer restricted to military personnel.

Can a medal cease to be awarded, its previous recipients then being given another decoration?
Yes. Of the total of 113 Empire Gallantry Medals awarded, all but one were later exchanged for the George Cross which was instituted in 1940.

What is the most recent British campaign medal?
The South Atlantic Medal, which was instituted after the Falklands campaign of 1982. This award is suspended from a ribbon consisting of five vertical stripes, shaded and watered in empire blue, white, sea green, white and empire blue.

What is the highest decoration awarded in the Soviet Union?
The Order of Lenin.

What was the Order of Polonia Restituta?
It was created in 1921 by the newly restored Polish state that rose out of the ashes of World War I. It was a civilian, not a military decoration, and it is still in existence.

When were Companions of Honour instituted, and are their numbers restricted?
In 1917, by King George V. The number of ordinary members is restricted to 65, while foreigners are only admitted as honorary members.

In which country was the Order of Leopold instituted in 1832?
In Belgium. Reflecting the bilingual nature of this country, the legend on the Order's medallion appears in both French and Flemish; on the other hand the title of this Order is only listed in French.

Little Quiz 6
Of which nationality were or are these people?
1. Pope John Paul II
2. Che Guevara
3. Don John of Austria
4. Hitler
5. Cleopatra
6. Caractacus (Caratacus)
7. Erasmus
8. Robert Burns
9. Count Cavour
10. Pocohontas

At what age do British field marshals retire?
Officially, field marshals never retire. They remain on what is called the active list for the rest of their lives.

What was Nelson's rank when he was killed at Trafalgar in 1805?
In spite of his unparalleled achievements as a naval commander, Nelson was still only a vice-admiral at the time of his greatest – and last sea battle.

Which is the highest rank in the United States Army?
General of the Army.

What is a non-commissioner Officer?
An officer of lower rank, such as sergeant or corporal, in the armed forces, who has not been awarded a commission.

Why did some officers in the British Army have the word Brevet before their rank?
This usually meant that the rank was honorary, and carried no extra pay. Often it was a sign that in due course the actual rank would be granted and the pay increased.

Which are the equivalent Army and Royal Navy ranks for the Royal Air Force Wing Commander?
Commander, Lieutenant-Colonel.

Who are the first five people in the Order of Precedence, after the Royal Family, in England?
The Archbishop of Canterbury, the Lord High Chancellor, the Archbishop of York, the Prime Minister, the Lord President of the Council.

Is a bishop senior to a dean in the Church of England?
Yes, but a dean is the head of the chapter of a cathedral or collegiate church.

What was the title of the commander of a Roman legion?
He was a *legatus*.

Which British field marshal was drowned at sea?
Field Marshal Earl Kitchener of Khartoum, KG. After a very distinguished military career, he became secretary of state for war in World War I, and prepared the British Army for eventual victory. On 5 June 1916, he set out in HMS *Hampshire* for a visit to Russia, but the ship struck a mine, or was torpedoed, and it sank with all but a handful of passengers.

Who was the 'Father of the RAF'?
Sir Hugh Trenchard, the first marshal of the Royal Air Force.

What was Captain Bligh's rank at the time of the famous mutiny on the *Bounty*?
Bligh was a lieutenant in the Royal Navy. He survived the mutiny to distinguish himself in many later naval actions, and ended as a vice-admiral.

How many US generals later became presidents of the USA?
Four – Ulysses S. Grant (1869–1877), Andrew Jackson (1829–1837), George Washington (1789–1797) and Dwight Eisenhower (1953–1961).

What does a quarter-master sergeant do?
He is a non-commissioned officer who provides the clothing, food, weapons, and accommodation for a body of troops.

How was it that Winston Churchill, a statesman, was allowed to wear the uniform of a British air commodore?
He was made honorary air commodore of the No 615 Fighter Squadron of the Royal Auxiliary Air Force in 1939.

Who was known as the Little Corporal?
Napoleon Bonaparte, who became emperor of the French, 1804–1815.

Who was in command of the English fleet which defeated the Spanish Armada in 1588?
It was Lord Howard of Effingham, a relative of the then Duke of Norfolk. Drake was effectively second-in-command.

Which Nigerian general and statesman afterwards became a post-graduate student at a British university?
General Yakubu Danjuma Gowon, at one time head of the Federal Military Government and commander-in-chief of the forces of the Federal Republic of Nigeria (1966–1975). He later came to Britain to study at Warwick University.

What is a sergeant-at-arms?
In Britain, he is an official who attends the speaker of the House of Commons or the lord chancellor.

Where did the rank of colonel-general appear in the Nazi German Army list?
Below field marshal and above general.

What are the functions of Black Rod?
Black Rod is an official of the House of Lords, his full title being 'Gentleman Usher of the Black Rod'. The name of the post derives from the nature of the staff the bearer carries, an ebony rod topped with a golden lion. He is the principal usher of a number of court and political ceremonials, including those concerning the Order of the Garter. He has responsibilities for maintaining order in the House of Lords and has the power to arrest offending peers. He is best known for summoning the attendance of the Commons to the House of Lords to hear the sovereign's speech from the throne.

What were the ranks of the men who were posthumously awarded the Victoria Cross for gallantry during the Falklands campaign of 1982?
Lieutenant Colonel H. Jones and Sergeant Ian McKay.

Does a rector enjoy a higher rank than a vicar in parishes of the Church of England?
Not really. The essential difference was that a rector enjoyed the greater and lesser tithes of the parish of which he had the care, while a vicar only received the lesser tithes. Such a distinction vanished with the abolition of tithes in 1936; for parishes which are still served by a single clergyman, the historical title of either rector or vicar has been retained.

What were the German army equivalents of these British army ranks in World War II: company sergeant-major; captain; major-general?
Oberfeldwebel or Hauptfeldorwebel; Hauptmann or Rittmeister; Generalleutnant.

Little Quiz 7
  What were the earlier names of these countries, once part of European empires?
  1. Ghana
  2. Zambia
  3. Malawi
  4. Tuvalu
  5. Tanzania
  6. Zaire
  7. Guyana
  8. Campuchea
  9. Sri Lanka
  10. Malagasy

What was a *civitas* capital?
The administrative town of a *civitas*, or tribal state, in Roman Britain. *Civitas* capitals were self-governing and their magistrates were elected by local electors.

What was Crambeck ware?
A type of pottery made in kilns in North Yorkshire, principally near Malton, in the 4th century.

How long was Hadrian's Wall?
It was 80 Roman miles, which is about 73 English miles or 117.53 km from Wallsend on the east to Bowness-on-Solway in the west.

Where was the Antonine Wall?
It ran between the Forth at Carriden to the Clyde at Old Kilpatrick, in Scotland. The Wall was built of turf, though some of the fort buildings along it were of stone.

What was the *Classis Britannica*?
It was the Roman fleet operating in British waters.

Which were the Roman forts of the Saxon Shore?
There were nine, from north-east to south, namely: Brancaster (Norfolk), Burgh Castle (Norfolk), Walton (Suffolk), Bradwell on Sea (Essex), Reculver (Kent), Richborough (Kent), Lympne (Kent), Pevensey (Sussex) and Portchester (Hampshire). The fort at Dover is sometimes included as a tenth.

Briefly, how did the Romans build their roads?
They built them straight where possible, changed direction on hill-tops, and skirted round major obstructions if the need for the road was urgent. The foundations were slabs of stone or small stone blocks. On top of these were spread layers of rammed down gravel or cinders.

Occasionally roads were paved with blocks. Most roads were built on raised banks to allow drainage.

What was the *annona militaris*?
It was a tax raised from the provinces of the Roman Empire which was directed towards paying for the upkeep of the military forces in the provinces. It was paid in cash or in kind (notably farm produce, grain, etc.).

What was a winged corridor villa?
It was a villa building with a central range of rooms having a wing of rooms at one end, or both ends, and with a corridor or verandah at front or back, or both, along the central range. The style began to appear in Britain in the 2nd century.

What was a *mansio*?
It was a large inn or hotel, built round a courtyard, often with an associated bath-house. *Mansiones* were official resting-places, and were erected in *civitas* capitals, towns or occasionally beside main roads in the countryside.

Who was Cartimandua?
She was queen of the Brigantes tribes from about the 50s to the 70s. While she reigned, her tribes maintained relatively peaceful relations with the occupying Roman forces. Towards the end of her reign, her husband Venutius left her and formed an opposition movement, and even rebelled against the Romans, and the queen had to ask them for help.

Did the Romans actually win the battle of Mons Graupius in AD 86?
The historian Tacitus says that they did, but he was prejudiced because the Roman army commander, Agricola, who was governor of Britain at the time, was his father-in-law. The Romans are said to have killed and wounded about 10,000 Caledonians at the battle in North East Scotland, but another 20,000 got away.

And after the battle, the Romans pulled back many miles to the south.

Where were the principal gold mines in Roman Britain?
At Dolaucothi, near Pumpsaint, in Carmarthenshire, Wales.

Why are inscriptions so important to archaeologists?
Because they can often establish the date or the period of the sites at which they are found, or by relating them to other inscriptions with some of the same information on them, they can enlarge knowledge about a particular person, or event, or building.

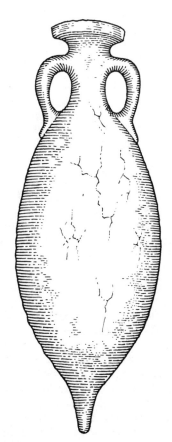

Wine amphora

What was an amphora?
It was a large, two-handled container for transporting wine, oil or other liquid.

What was an aisled building?
It was a long timber building with one or two rows of posts down the length, to support the roof, like a church nave. It was used for residential quarters for workers on a villa, or for storage or as workshops.

Which Roman emperors died in Britain?
Severus in 211 and Constantius I in 306.

What was the top rank in the magistracy in the Roman Republic?
Normally, it was that of consul, of which two were elected to serve for one year. In certain instances, notably of supreme danger to the state, a dictator might be appointed to govern as long as the emergency lasted. That office was normally held for a very short time, until the time of Julius Caesar who was appointed dictator for life.

What is the Pharos at Dover?
The Pharos, or lighthouse, is one of the most remarkable survivals from Romano-British times. It is in the grounds of the great medieval castle there. It is a stonework tower of octagonal plan, of the 2nd century, which today reaches to about 19m (61ft). The top 5¾m (19ft) of stonework are a medieval rebuilding, but the lower 13m (43ft) are of Roman flint-rubble construction which was faced with smooth stone blocks (which have now mostly disappeared). It is thought the tower originally rose to about 24m (80ft), and would have supported a contrivance for a beacon of fire that could be seen by ships in the Straits of Dover.

When was the first sustained flight by man and vehicle through the air?
On 21 November 1783, when Jean Pilatre de Rozier and the Marquise d'Arlandes piloted a balloon over Paris.

Who first took a balloon across the English Channel?
John Jeffries and Jean-Pierre Blanchard, who crossed from Dover to Calais on 7 January 1785.

When was the first man-carrying airship tested?
In France by Henri Giffard in 1852. His vehicle was powered by a 3 hp engine and managed about 9 kmh (6 mph).

When was the first flight by man in a powered heavier-than-air craft?
This was the famous flight by Orville Wright on 17 December 1903 at the sands at Kitty Hawk, North Carolina. The craft was built by him and his brother Wilbur. Orville sustained the flight for a distance of over 259.25 m (850 ft).

Which is the first recorded air raid during wartime?
In the Italo-Turkish war of 1910–11 in North Africa, a Lieutenant Cavotti flew over the Turkish lines in Libya, on 1 November 1911 and dropped four bombs weighing about 2.042 kg (4½ lb) each.

Who said 'Aviation is good sport, but for the army it is useless.'?
This was said by General (later Marshal) Ferdinand Foch of France. He was to become commander-in-chief of the Allied Armies on the Western Front in the last months of World War I, in which aeroplanes did in fact play a small but useful role.

Who first flew an aeroplane across the English Channel?
Louis Blériot, of France, on 25 July 1909.

Photographs were taken of M. Blériot in flight.

When was the first Zeppelin airship flight?
On 2 July 1900. Zeppelin airships were invented by Count von Zeppelin.

How many Zeppelin airships were built between 1900 and the outbreak of World War I?
At least 25. The most celebrated was the Viktoria Luise, built in 1912, which made more than 400 flights, carried over 8500 passengers and flew for more than 47.334 km (29,400 miles).

How many passengers were killed in Zeppelins during the years 1900–14?
Miraculously, none. Although several accidents happened to Zeppelins, there were no fatalities.

When was the first Zeppelin air raid on Britain in World War I?
A Zeppelin dropped several bombs on East Anglia on 19 January 1915, and 4 people were killed, 17 injured.

Who produced the first British official paper on ways of dealing with enemy airships in time of war?
Winston Churchill, when he was first lord of the Admiralty. He wrote a paper about it in 1913.

When was the Royal Flying Corps founded?
In April 1912, with two wings, one for the navy and one for the army.

What armament did the Sopwith Camel fighter plane carry?
This was built in 1917, and it carried two Vickers synchronized machine guns and also four 11.3 kg (25 lb) bombs. It flew at about 193.2 kmh (120 mph) maximum speed.

Which nation first produced anti-aircraft guns?
The Germans. The Krupps armament factories introduced at least three types of A.A.gun in the last years before the outbreak of World War I, a 65 mm, a 75 mm and a larger 105 mm gun which fired a shell weighing 18.16 kg (40 lb). It is believed that about 35 of these guns were ready by the outbreak of the war. The United Kingdom had none.

Who were the first commanders of the R.F.C.?
Captain, later Admiral Sir Godfrey Paine, and Major, later Marshal of the Royal Air Force Viscount Trenchard.

What was Baron von Richthofen's favourite aircraft for aerial combat?
In the last year or two of his life the German airman favoured the Fokker Dr.I (dreidecker), a triplane. Richthofen was killed in combat 21 April 1918.

Which German air ace of World War I was an air force general in World War II?
Ernst Udet. In the middle of the war, however, Udet grew increasingly unhappy about the way Hitler and the Nazis managed the war and treated the people they had conquered, and he committed suicide.

Which was the first aircraft carrier in the Royal Navy?
HMS *Furious*, a battle-cruiser which was converted in 1918 and provided with a long, flat upper deck for take-off and landing. The *Furious* also served in World War II.

Who was the first British pilot killed in an aeroplane crash?
Charles S. Rolls, of the Rolls-Royce partnership. His plane crashed at Bournemouth during Aviation Week, 12 July 1910.

When was the first commercial airline between England and France opened?
In August 1919, when Air Travel and Transport Company Ltd organized flights from London to Paris, using converted de Havilland DH9 bombers. These craft were open to the elements and passengers had to wear flying helmets.

How many Supermarine Spitfire fighters were produced in World War II?
22,759.

Which was the last biplane heavy bomber to serve with the Royal Air Force?
The Handley Page Heyford, which was withdrawn in 1939. It had two engines, carried a ton of bombs and could fly at about 225.4 kmh (140 mph).

When was the retractable undercarriage first used on a monoplane in the RAF?
In March 1935, with the Avro Anson general reconnaissance plane.

Who was Lord Brabazon of Tara?
J. T. C. Moore-Brabazon (1884–1964), a pioneer of British aviation, who made the first three flights by any British aviator (1909) and won a £1000 prize for flying over one mile in a Short–Wright biplane. He received the first flying certificate, No. 1 in 1910. Later, he became a politician and was minister of transport, 1940–41.

PATRICIA

The Liberator
Daniel O'Connell (1775–1847), the Irish national leader who championed the cause of Catholic Emancipation in the 1820s in England.

Lord Haw-Haw
William Joyce (1906–1946), the American-born (of Irish parents) political agitator who became a fascist and went to Germany at the beginning of World War II, where he broadcast anti-British speeches over German radio. He was tried and executed after the war. The name came from the pretentious voice he used.

The Ladies of Llangollen
Lady Eleanor Butler and Miss Sarah Ponsonby, two Irish women who were close friends and lived together at Plas Newydd in Llangollen, Wales, from 1774 to the 1820s. They were visited by many famous people.

The Wolf of Badenoch
Alexander Stewart, Earl of Buchan (c.1343–1405), a son of Robert II of Scotland, who was lord of Badenoch and spent much of his life in violent quarrels with neighbours, particularly the bishop of Moray. He burned Elgin Cathedral and did much other damage.

The Sage of Chelsea
Thomas Carlyle (1795–1881), Scottish-born writer and historian who settled in Chelsea and through his writings and speeches exerted a major influence upon British literature and historical writing. His works included histories of the time of Frederick the Great and of the French Revolution.

Bell-the-Cat
Archibald Douglas, 5th earl of Angus (c.1449–1514), who seized and put to death Robert Cochrane, the unpopular adviser of James III of Scotland.

Satchmo
Louis Armstrong (1900–1971), the American Negro trumpeter and jazz composer.

Vinegar Joe
General Joseph Stilwell (1883–1946), commander-in-chief of the US forces in China, Burma and India in World War I.

Philippe Égalité
Louis Philippe Joseph, duke of Orléans (1747–93), cousin of Louis XVI of France (1774–1793) who supported the French Revolution and hoped he would succeed as king when Louis XVI was deposed.

Bloody Mary
Mary I of England (1553–1558), who as a devout Catholic attempted to reverse the Protestant settlement in England arranged during the reign of her half-brother Edward VI (1547–1553) by persecuting and sending to the stake hundreds of Protestants.

The Young Pretender
Prince Charles Edward Stuart, Bonnie Prince Charlie, 1720–1788, son of Prince James Edward Stuart who was the heir of James II of England and Scotland. Prince Charles came to Scotland to try to win the throne for his father in 1745, but his cause collapsed after defeat at Culloden in 1746.

Toom Tabard
John Baliol (1249–1315), chosen king of Scotland in 1292 but forced to abdicate in 1296. Toom Tabard means Empty Jacket.

General Tom Thumb
Thomas Sherwood Stratton (1838–1883), an American dwarf who was never taller than 1.01 m (3 ft 4 in).

Ike
General of the US Army Dwight David Eisenhower (1890–1969), who was also 34th president of the USA.

Q
Sir Arthur Quiller-Couch (1863–1944), Cornish-born author and poet.

Steenie
George Villiers, 1st duke of Buckingham (1592–1628), favourite of James I (1603–1625) who heaped honours and estates upon him.

Che
Ernesto 'Che' Guevara (1928–1967), the Argentine-born revolutionary leader who became a hero among the young all over the world. (See also p 144.)

K of K
The affectionate abbreviation of Field Marshal Earl Kitchener of Khartoum (1850–1916), a great military figure who as secretary for war became the organizer of the army in World War I.

Prinny
George, prince of Wales, eldest son of George III who became prince regent and ruled in place of his incapacitated father, 1811–1820.

Capability Brown
Lancelot Brown (1715–1783), famous landscape gardener who was employed by many rich and famous people to lay out their gardens and estates, notably Blenheim and Kew.

Bird
Charlie Parker (1920–1955), the American jazz composer and virtuoso of the alto saxophone.

The Pelvis
Elvis Presley (1935–1978), the American rock singer, was given this nickname which conveniently rhymed with his first name in the early part of his career. It is supposed to have derived from his gyrating hips.

Rakehell
John Wilmot, 2nd Earl of Rochester (1647–1680) was a member of the licentious set of courtiers who attended Charles II. Despite his profligacy, which earned him his nickname, he was a poet of some note and a patron of the arts.

Caligula
This is an example of a nickname that has been passed down as if it were the real name of its bearer, the Roman emperor Gaius Caesar who ruled from 37–41. Caligula derives from the Latin word for soldiers' boots. He had worn a diminutive pair as a child in the company of the legions on the Rhine, who accorded him that nickname.

Scarface
The derivation of the nickname of Al Capone (1899–1947) hardly need be stated here. Head of a bootleg and vice syndicate in Chicago in the 1920s and early 1930s, he was also known as Public Enemy Number One.

The Red Dean
The Very Reverend Hewlett Johnson, (1874–1966), dean of Canterbury from 1931 to 1963, who was famous for his support of the Communist cause.

Little Quiz 8
Re-arrange the following into the correct pairs:
1. Clive   Gaul
2. Wolfe   Mexico
3. William of Normandy   Peru
4. Cortes   Alamein
5. Pizarro   India
6. Caesar   Hastings
7. Montgomery   Quebec
8. Marlborough   Crécy
9. Edward III   Bannockburn
10. Robert Bruce   Blenheim

What were the real names of these people?

Anthony Hope, novelist
Sir Anthony Hope Hawkins (1863–1933), author of *The Prisoner of Zenda* and *Rupert of Hentzau.*

Ouida, novelist
Marie Louise de la Ramée (1839–1908). English-born woman novelist who died in poverty in Italy is best known for *Under Two Flags.*

AE
The pseudonym under which George William Russell (1867–1935), the Irish writer, nationalist and poet wrote his verse. He was also editor of *The Irish Statesman* newspaper, 1923–30.

Sapper, novelist
Lt Colonel Cyril McNeile (1888–1937); after a career as regular soldier in the Royal Engineers, he wrote the 'Bulldog Drummond' stories.

Tito, Yugoslav general and statesman
Josip Broz (1892–1981) organized guerrilla opposition to the Nazi occupation of Yugoslavia in World War II and afterwards became premier of post-war Yugoslavia. He called himself Tito, and was created a marshal.

Voltaire
François-Marie Arouet (1694–1778), one of the most celebrated of all French philosophers and writers, whose ideas helped significantly to shape the course of the French Revolution.

Marilyn Monroe, American film star
Norma Jean Baker (1928–1962).

Stalin
Joseph Vissarionovich Dzhgashvili (1879–1953), Russian revolutionary leader and dictator of the USSR from the early 1930s to his death.

Currer Bell
Charlotte Brontë (1816–1855), who is best known as the author of *Jane Eyre.*

Ian Hay, Scottish novelist
Major General John Hay Beith (1876–1952), who was both professional soldier and novelist/playwright.

Lenin
Vladimir Ilyich Ulyanov (1870–1924), leader of the communist revolution in Russia, 1917–18 and founder of the Soviet Union.

Trotsky
Lev Davidovich Bronstein (1879–1940), Russian revolutionary leader, second to Lenin, but driven out of Russia after Lenin's death by Stalin, and eventually assassinated in Mexico.

O. Henry, American writer
William Sidney Porter (1862–1910), American short-story writer, who spent some of his early years in prison on fraud charges.

Molière
Jean Baptiste Poquelin (1622–1673), French playwright and satirist, author of *Tartuffe, Le Misanthrope, Le Bourgeois Gentilhomme* and many others. He revolutionized the theatre in France.

Hugh MacDiarmid
Christopher M. Grieve (1892–1978), Scottish poet and nationalist.

Kemal Ataturk
Mustafa Kemal (1881–1938), Turkish general and statesman who founded modern Turkey after the fall of the Ottoman Empire.

Alcuin
Ealhwine (735–804) English-born scholar and abbot, who became adviser and tutor to Charlemagne.

Tintoretto
Jacopo Robusti (1518–1594), Venetian painter. Among many works he completed the largest canvas by any great master, *The Paradise*.

Donatello
Donato di Betto Bardi (1386–1466), Florentine sculptor, generally regarded as the founder of modern sculpture.

Baron Corvo
Frederick Rolfe (1860–1913), British writer. His best work was *Hadrian VII*.

Malcolm X
Malcolm Little (1925–1965), the American radical black politician and activist, adopted the name Malcolm X. He took the view that X reflected his true yet unknown African family name, whereas 'Little' had come from the slave-owner who had been master of his forebears. For similar reasons, the British black power activist Michael Abdul Malik (1933–1975) renamed himself Michael X.

Twiggy
Lesley Hornby, born 1950, the English fashion model, actress and singer, adopted this pseudonym in the late 1960s at the beginning of her career. Derived from her slim build, it might in other circumstances have been used as a nickname.

John Paul II
Born Karol Wojtyla in Poland in 1920, the then cardinal adopted the above name upon becoming pope in 1978. Throughout the history of the papacy, popes have always relinquished their lay names.

J J Marric
Or 23 others! For John Creasey (1908–1973), the English crime novelist and thriller writer, used his own name and 24 pseudonyms throughout his career as an author.

Spy?
This was the pseudonym of Sir Leslie Ward (1851–1922), the English caricaturist, who became famous for his caricatures of prominent people in the journal, *Vanity Fair*, between 1873 and 1909. Ward was the son of a well-known Victorian painter, Edward Matthew Ward.

Harry Houdini
This Jewish-American magician and escapologist was born Erich Weiss in Appleton, Wisconsin in 1874. He adopted his stage name in 1891.

Rock Hudson
Born 1925 as Roy Scherer, at the age of eight he adopted his stepfather's surname of Fitzgerald. The talent scout who discovered him in 1946 named him Rock after the Rock of Gibraltar and Hudson after the Hudson River. Hudson is on record as disliking his stage name, although it has certainly not inhibited his career. In any case the forename Rock was perhaps preferable to Crash or Brick, alternatives considered by his 'discoverer'.

Little Quiz 9
  Where are these British monuments?
  1. The Wallace monument
  2. Cabot's Tower
  3. King Alfred's statue
  4. Martyrs' Memorial
  5. Mayflower Stone
  6. King Richard's Well
  7. Marquess' Column
  8. Locomotion I
  9. Prince Charles Edward Monument
  10. HMS Victory

What is jet?
It is very hard coal, and was used for jewellery in Celtic Britain and parts of Celtic Europe. There was a revival in popularity of jet as jewellery in Victorian Britain, pioneered by makers in Whitby in Yorkshire.

Which is the largest diamond ever found?
The Cullinan Diamond, which weighed 3106 carats. It was named after Sir Thomas Cullinan, chairman of a mining company in the Transvaal (South Africa). It was given to Edward VII as a birthday present.

What is *repoussé* work?
It is a decorative technique in which the design is hammered out from the back side of thin sheeting of gold or silver.

What is *cloisonné* decoration?
A form of decorative treatment for jewellery produced by separating stones or enamels with wire or thin metal strips.

What is a scarab?
It is one or other of a number of types of beetle, of Mediterranean habitat. The Ancient Egyptians mounted dead scarabs as pendants or on rings. Imitations of this technique are known as scarabs.

How is a cameo produced?
The art of cameo-making began in Roman times. The design is carved in relief on a shell or on a stone such as malachite.

What is a *cabochon* in jewellery terms?
A gemstone cut in domed shape, round or pear-drop shape, then polished but not given any facets.

Why is a paste diamond so called?
Paste is the name for a hard substance made from glass and lead, which sparkles brilliantly like a diamond, and which has often been used to imitate the real diamond.

What is a bloodstone?
A dark green jasper stone which has red spots.

Who was René Lalique?
One of the leading Art Nouveau jewellers, who worked with exceptional skill and daring in a variety of materials, especially glass. He lived from 1860 to 1945.

Egyptian scarabs

What is lapis lazuli?
An opaque, hard, deep blue rock, the best of which is found in the Near East.

What is a kap-kap?
This is a jewel from the Pacific Islands made in disc form from sea shells, decorated with tortoiseshell.

Why is a fighting bracelet so called?
These are bracelets worn by some African tribes to lend weight to the arm when they strike their enemies. The Masai wore metal bracelets with spikes for warlike purposes.

What was a Sévigné brooch?
A brooch made up in the form of a decorative bow with pendant drops, as originally worn by Madame de Sévigné (1626-1696), the French writer and lady of fashion.

What is electrum?
It is an alloy of gold and silver (about half silver to three-quarters gold) found in a natural state and used in the ancient world.

What is a torc?
A neck ring, generally of gold, worn among the Celtic peoples of Britain and west Europe.

What is Alfred's Jewel?
A piece of Anglo-Saxon jewellery which has inscribed round its edge the phrase (in Anglo Saxon) 'Alfred had me made'. It is of gold, bears a portrait in enamel and is covered on both sides with crystal. It is now in the Ashmolean Museum in Oxford.

Where did turquoises come from?
These pretty stones came originally from Khorasan in Persia, but they were called turquoise because they were generally exported through Turkey.

What is a nef?
A pendant consisting of a jewelled ship, particularly popular in Venice in the 15th to 17th centuries.

What is a sardonyx?
A form of onyx which has two or more layers of orange to red stone backed by, or interspersed with, a layer of whitish chalcedony. This stone lends itself well to deep carving.

What form of jewellery was Nicholas Hilliard noted for?
Hilliard was both a painter and a jeweller who served Elizabeth I, James I and their courts. He was noted for his miniatures, exquisitely painted portraits which were set in jewelled frames, often in the form of lockets.

Little Quiz 10
   What instruments do or did these people play?
1. James Galway
2. Harry James
3. Franz Liszt
4. Sarasate
5. Reginald Dixon
6. Madame Suggia
7. Sidonie Goossens
8. Leon Goossens
9. George Thalben-Ball
10. Acker Bilk
   Who composed?
11. The Walk to the Paradise Garden
12. Country Gardens
13. Clair de Lune
14. The Pastoral Symphony
15. The Harmonious Blacksmith
16. The Tristesse Étude
17. Jesu, Joy of Man's Desiring
18. Sonata Facile
19. God save the Queen (King)
20. The Enigma Variations.

What is a cruciform plan church?
A plan in the shape of a cross, with – generally but not always – a tower over the centre where the arms of the cross meet.

Where are the transepts of a church?
They are the north and south arms of the cross plan, and where they meet is called the crossing.

What is a chapter house?
This is the room, square or polygonal, where the dean and canons of a cathedral meet to conduct their business. The room is usually a separate part of the cathedral.

Where in the church is the baptistery, or baptistry?
Usually, the baptistery is at the west end and it contains the font. In some cathedrals, notably some of the magnificent Italian ones, the baptistery is a building separate from the main cathedral.

What is a baldachino?
It is a canopied structure, of marble or stone but sometimes of wood, placed over an altar. It may be suspended, or supported on columns.

Where is the clerestory?
It is in the nave, transept and choir walls, or in one or two of these parts. It is at the upper level below the roof and is pierced by windows to let in more light. Not all churches and cathedrals have clerestories.

Is the pulpitum the same as the pulpit?
No, the pulpitum is a solid screen, generally of stone but occasionally of wood, which shuts off the choir from the nave. In many instances it has a gallery above.

Why is a flying buttress so called?
It is a stone buttress in the form of an arch that acts as a prop against an outer wall of a church (or cathedral). The upper part rests against the wall (of the nave, transept or choir) and the lower part rests against a pier, to absorb the outward thrust of the wall.

Where would you expect to find misericords?
They are part of the choir stalls. A misericord is a carved wooden bracket or ledge underneath a hinged seat in the stalls, which when the seat is tipped up provides support if you have to stand for long periods. Many misericords were most beautifully carved.

Lancet windows

Has the tympanum anything to do with a drum?

No, it is the space above the lintel and beneath the arch of a doorway, and this space is usually decorated.

What is an apse?

A round, polygonal or rectangular recess or projection, usually though not only, at the east end of a church. An apse usually has a vaulted roof. In some Gothic cathedrals, the east end was a cluster of rounded apses set symmetrically, with a chapel in each of the apses.

Where is the reredos?

It is the screen at the back of an altar, and is generally elaborately decorated.

What is a triforium?

It is an arcaded wall passage below the clerestory and above the nave arcades (and continuing round the transepts and choir in some cathedrals).

What is the difference between the undercroft and the crypt of a church?

None, really, for they mean the same thing, that is, a vaulted chamber under a church.

What is a retable?

The retable is a shelf behind and above an altar. It carried the cross and other ornaments.

Where is the presbytery?

This is part of the eastern end of the church between the choir and the high altar. In some cases, the word is used to describe the whole of the east end, but chancel is a better word for this.

Why are the entrances to some churchyards covered with a roof?

When they are, they are known as lych-gates, and this is where coffins rested before being admitted into the church by the priest.

What is the name of the building that contains the church or cathedral's principal bell?

This is the campanile, and it is usually a bell tower that is separate from the church building. There are several famous campaniles in Italy, most famous of all being the Leaning Tower of Pisa.

What is a lancet?

It is a tall, narrow window with a pointed top.

What are voussoirs?

Wedge-shaped stones which form an arch.

Little Quiz 11

To which countries do these civil aircraft markings refer?

1. CCCP
2. OY
3. YR
4. YU
5. TF
6. GB
7. HB
8. N
9. OO
10. PP

And these international car registration letters?

11. CH
12. RA
13. V
14. SF
15. T
16. FL
17. SK
18. GBG
19. PL
20. U

Who was the first Russian aviator to fly successfully?
Van den Schrouff, in a Voisin biplane at Odessa, 25 July 1909.

When did women begin to fly aeroplanes?
Probably the first woman pilot was Miss Spencer Kavanagh, whose real name was Edith Maud Cook, who made several flights in the Pyrenees in 1910.

Which nation built and flew the first four-engine aeroplane?
Russia. The Bolshoi biplane with four engines flew at St Petersburg on 13 May 1913. The pilot was Igor Sikorsky, the inventor of the single-rotor helicopter. Sikorsky also designed the first 4-engine air bomber.

Which was the first aircraft carrier specially built for the purpose?
The Japanese carrier, Hosho, launched in 1922.

Which was the largest flying-boat built for military uses in Britain?
The Short Shetland, but only two were constructed. It was tested in December 1944. Its wing span was 47.75 m (150 ft) and it could fly at up to 421.82 kmh (262 mph).

What was a *kamikaze* attack?
This is the name of a special air attack by Japanese pilots who volunteered to crash their planes on their targets in 1944–5.

What was the Hughes H2 Hercules aeroplane?
It was an enormous 180 ton flying boat with eight engines, a wing span of 97.6 m (320 ft), which could carry up to 700 passengers. Only one was built, by the eccentric billionaire, Howard Hughes of the USA, and it flew only once, for about 1.61 km (one mile) in 1947.

Who was Amy Johnson?
A woman pilot who flew a De Havilland DH 60 Gipsy Moth monoplane from England to Australia, 5 to 14 May 1930. It was the first such flight.

What was the 'Comet'?
This was the famous De Havilland DH 106 Comet I jet-propelled airliner, which had four engines. It was the first jet airliner to fly regular commercial air services anywhere.

What was the R 101 disaster?
The R 101 was a commercial airship which crashed at Beauvais in France on its flight from Cardington in Bedfordshire en route for Egypt and India in 1930. On board were 54 people, 48 of whom were killed, including Lord Thomson, secretary of state for air.

What is the Harrier jump jet?
It is a jet-propelled military aircraft which can take off vertically, without the need of a runway, and land again, also without runway. It is ideal for aircraft carriers, difficult terrain and for use on airfields perhaps rendered useless to other aircraft in an enemy raid in war time.

What was the Schneider Trophy?
It was a seaplane contest with a trophy for the winner. It was first competed for in 1913, and it was won three times in succession by Britain, 1927, 1929 and 1931. The last competition produced a world speed record of 544 kmh (340 mph).

Which British bomber pilot accompanied the US air crew which dropped the second atomic bomb on Japan?
Group Captain Leonard Cheshire, VC, OM, DSO, DFC, who was so appalled by the destruction the bomb caused that he decided to devote his life thereafter to helping disabled people, founding since

1945 numerous Cheshire Homes all over the world.

What machine first flew on 28 March 1910?

This was the date of the first flight of a seaplane which was made at La Mède near Marseilles. The machine, constructed and flown by the French pioneer, Henri Fabre, bore some resemblance to a flying fence!

Which leading fighter ace of World War II had no legs?

Group Captain Douglas Bader of the RAF had lost both his legs in a flying accident in 1931. Undeterred, he not only learned to walk again using artificial legs, but also resumed his flying career. He was shot down over France in 1941 and spent the remainder of the war as a prisoner of the Germans. He was awarded the DSO with bar, the DFC with bar, the Croix de Guerre and the Legion of Honour and later was knighted.

Who were the Blue Eagles?

This was a helicopter display team, part of the British School of Army Aviation, which was formed in 1968 and which flew until 1977.

What is the significance of Leonardo da Vinci in aviation history?

In about 1500, Leonardo drew design sketches for a helicopter with a rotating helical wing which demonstrated the possibility of vertical lift-off.

Who is regarded as one of the most successful German fighter pilots of World War II?

Major Erich Hartmann of the Luftwaffe, who achieved a total of 352 confirmed aerial victories during service on the Russian Front in World War II. His decorations included the Knight's Cross with Oak Leaves, Swords and Diamonds.

What was the most disastrous day in terms of losses ever experienced by a single air force?

Contrary to what might have been expected, the losses suffered by the Luftwaffe when Germany was on the crest of a wave on 10 May 1940 make that the most disastrous day. The Luftwaffe then lost 304 aircraft with another 51 damaged; casualties amongst their aircrew and other personnel (killed, wounded and missing) amounted to 1066. Those figures, for the day in which Germany invaded the Netherlands and Belgium, exceeded their cumulative losses from the start of World War II.

What was the first jet aeroplane to make a successful flight?

This was the German Heinkel He 178, which flew for the first time on 27 August 1939. The Luftwaffe were not, however, able to use a jet-propelled aircraft in operational service until 1944.

What was the great achievement of the American woman aviator, Amelia Earhart?

She was the first woman to fly across the Atlantic. This feat was undertaken on 17 June 1928 in a Lockheed Vega aircraft, between Newfoundland and Burry Point in Wales. She was lost on a flight over the Pacific in 1937.

For what unusual purpose did Canadair develop the CL-215 twin-engined amphibious flying boat?

This aircraft was specifically developed to fight forest fires, a major threat to the economy of the country. The first flight was made on 23 October 1967. The aircraft picks up water by means of two probes and has been able to drop 545,520 litres (120,000 gallons) in one day.

Who was Cardinal Mazarin?

Jules Mazarin (1602–1661) was a Sicilian by birth, and entered the service of the papacy as a diplomat. He was appointed papal nuncio to France in 1634, and there made a great impression on Cardinal Richelieu, virtual prime minister under Louis XIII. Richelieu offered Mazarin a high post and he became a naturalized Frenchman. When Richelieu died in 1642, Mazarin was chosen to follow as chief minister, and for the next nineteen years he guided the destinies of France, already fast becoming the top nation of Europe. There was much opposition to Mazarin between about 1648 and 1653, but he skilfully crushed it by intrigue and negotiation as well as with force, and continued in office unmolested until his death in 1661.

Who was Agrippa?

Marcus Vipsanius Agrippa (63–12 BC) was one of the most remarkable men of ancient, indeed of all history. In his time he was the leading general, admiral and statesman in the Roman Empire of Augustus. You can see his name across the portico of the famous Pantheon building in Rome, which was begun by Agrippa, and completed by Emperor Hadrian.

Who was Aurungzebe?

Aurungzebe (1618–1707) was the last – and some consider the greatest – of the Mogul emperors of India. He was the third son of Shah-Jehan, the emperor who built the Taj Mahal, and he took over the empire in the declining years of his father. His long reign of fifty years was marked by prosperity, but there was much trouble over religious issues, and Aurungzebe, who had in the first years proved a tough and skilful commander, became suspicious and cruel, and alienated many of those at first pleased to support him.

Who was St Thomas Aquinas?

St Thomas Aquinas (1225–1274) was an Italian scholar, philosopher and theologian who studied in Paris for several years and earned a great reputation for clear thinking and swift reasoning. The pope invited him to teach in several places in Italy and elsewhere. Aquinas founded a college at Cologne. He was canonized in 1323.

Who was Petrarch?

Francesco Petracco (1304–1374) was one of the leading Italian poets of the early Renaissance. As a young man he fell hopelessly in love with a happily married woman (who did not return his love), and he wrote her a stream of the most beautiful love poems which won him fame throughout Italy.

Who was Machiavelli?

Niccolo Machiavelli (1469–1527) was a Florentine diplomat and writer who worked for a time as right hand man to Cesare Borgia, the swashbuckling military commander who aimed to make some sort of union out of the central Italian states in the early years of the 16th century. Machiavelli survived Cesare's downfall, and produced *Il Principe,* a work on how a leader should run a government. It was to become a kind of handbook for dictators.

Who was Adam of Bremen?

This German historian, who died in about 1080, wrote a long and useful work about the political and military history of Germany between about 700 and 1050, with details of the religious issues and the activities of the church throughout the period. It was called *Gesta Hammaburgensis Ecclesiae Pontificum,* and it also contained much about the Vikings, their homeland of Scandanavia, and their explorations westwards, including their voyages to the north American continent.

What was the Schlieffen Plan?

A military strategic plan for advancing from Germany on two fronts across France, north and south of Paris and encircling the capital. It was conceived by Count Albrecht von Schlieffen (1833–1913), general and military thinker, who was chief of the German general staff, 1891–1905. When World War I broke out the plan was watered down and failed.

Which famous 17th century English statesman and philosopher was accused of taking bribes and fined £40,000?

Viscount St Albans, much better known as Francis Bacon (1561–1626), one of the greatest figures of early 17th century England, was scientist, inventor, philosopher, lawyer, essayist and statesman. Solicitor-general in 1607, attorney-general in 1613 and lord chancellor in 1618, he succumbed to temptation and accepted bribes while carrying out his judicial duties. He was detected and dismissed, tried and fined £40,000 and thereafter disgraced. But he left behind him some of the most profound scientific and philosophical works that have had a major influence upon the generations that followed. He is regarded as the father of experimental research.

Who was Prince Eugène?

Prince Eugène of Savoy (1663–1736) a brilliant Austrian soldier, was French-born but because his mother had been banished from France by Louis XIV he espoused the cause of Austria in its struggles with the great king. He joined the Imperial army, fought against the Turks in the 1680s, and led armies against Louis XIV in the 1689–97 War of the Grand Alliance, and again in the War of the Spanish Succession (1701–1714). He also fought alongside Marlborough at Blenheim and at Oudenarde.

Who was Bolingbroke?

Henry St John Viscount Bolingbroke (1678–1751), was an amazing English statesman and orator. Some thought him the greatest man of his time: his father thought he ought to be hanged. He was foreign secretary from 1710 to 1714 and helped to end the costly War of the Spanish Succession. Then he took the side of the Elder Pretender (James Edward Stuart) in the 1715 Jacobite rising against the succession of George I to the throne of England and Scotland. Later, he made his peace with George. In George II's time, his activities earned him a period of exile which he spent in France.

Who was *Pam*?

Henry John Temple, Viscount Palmerston (1784–1865), was a British statesman and prime minister, and for nearly a quarter of a century, with a few breaks, he was foreign secretary. He championed small states in Europe in their struggles for independence, and he upheld British prestige, rattling the sword when needed. Few would dispute that 'Pam' was one of the greatest foreign secretaries Britain ever had.

Who was the Redeemer?

Kwame Nkrumah (1909–1972) was a lawyer in the former British colony of the Gold Coast (now Ghana). He joined the national movement for independence early on, and was a leading light in the Convention People's Party which clamoured for self-government. He endured punishment, including jail, for his activities, but eventually became the first prime minister of the new independent Ghana in 1957 and later on, president. Nkrumah championed independence movements in other black countries of Africa, but in 1966, having become increasingly dictatorial at home he was overthrown and took refuge abroad.

Which is the largest planet in our Solar System?
Jupiter. It is about ten times the diameter of the earth, and rotates on its axis in about ten hours, which is faster than Earth.

What are the rings round the planet Saturn made of?
Probably lumps of rock and ice. The three rings visible from Earth have been shown by space probes to be made up of hundreds of separate ringlets. The rings appear to be less than 1 km thick.

Why is Mars called the Red Planet?
Because it appears orange-red to the naked eye and through a telescope. When the United States Vikings probes of 1976 landed on Mars, they sent back photographs that confirmed the reddish colour of the surface.

What is a light year?
It is the distance that light travels in a year, which is about 10 million million kilometres (6 million million miles).

Which is the nearest star to Earth?
Proxima Centauri, which is 4.3 light years away.

How many stars are there in our Galaxy?
Probably about 100,000,000,000 (one hundred thousand million).

Where did the Moon come from?
Although it is not known for certain, the Moon probably was formed at the same time as the Earth. It was once thought that it might have come from the Earth.

What is a comet?
It is a member of the Solar System made up of dust, gas and ice. It becomes visible when it approaches the sun, developing a shining 'head' and a 'tail' that streams away from the Sun.

What is the average temperature on the surface of the planet Venus?
Over 450°C. which is four and a half times the temperature of boiling water.

Who discovered the planet Uranus?
Sir William Herschel (1738–1822) on 13 March 1781.

How long did it take to discover the last planet of our Solar System, Pluto?
The search began in 1906 at an Arizona observatory, later called Lowell Observatory, named after Percival Lowell who started the search. Pluto was found in 1930 by Clyde Tombaugh, at the same observatory.

Is the Sun a planet?
No. It is a star.

What is a sunspot?
It is an area on the Sun's surface where the temperature is somewhat colder than its surroundings, producing a dark effect in contrast.

What are the equinoxes?
There are two, the vernal (spring) and autumnal equinox, and they are the dates (about 21 March and 23 September) when the position of the Sun in relation to Earth is such that day and night are of almost equal length everywhere.

How hot is the Sun's surface?
It is estimated to be about 5,800°C.

What is the Milky Way?
It is the name given to our Galaxy, which is shaped like a disc with a central bump. It is also the name for the dense band of stars that spans the sky.

How far is the Sun from Earth?
About 150,000,000 km (93,000,000 miles).

What is the Sun's corona?
It is the 'halo' of gas that surrounds the Sun. The corona can only be seen from Earth during a total eclipse of the Sun, or by means of a special apparatus called a colonograph in an observatory.

What is a lunar eclipse?
This is when the Moon passes into the shadow of Earth, which cuts out the sunlight. The Moon appears dim rather than bright and remains so until it comes out of the shadow. The eclipse may be partial or total, and one occurs fairly frequently, occasionally at the rate of two or three a year, or only once in two years.

What is the Big Bang theory?
It is the theory that the Universe began in a cataclysmic explosion. A tiny, very dense and very hot mass blasted apart about 15–20,000 million years ago to create the universe, which has been expanding ever since.

Has it been established that the changes in the dark areas on Mars are not due to growing vegetation?
The American astronomer Carl Sagan suggested that the seasonal changes in the dark areas on Mars were caused by wind-blown dust; this suggestion was subsequently confirmed by photographs from the Mariner 9 probe.

In simple terms, what is a black hole?
A black hole cannot be observed directly, although this theoretical object may be implied through the effects that it has on other matter. It is assumed that beyond a certain point, a star that has been shrinking is impelled by its massive surface gravity to disappear within a single mathematical point within which is trapped both space and time themselves. Beyond this 'black hole', the density of the star would then rise to infinity – but outside the space-time continuum that is our Universe.

Saturn's rings

What is a Red Letter Day?
Originally a day marked in red in a calendar to indicate the day of a saint or festival, the phrase also means a particularly happy or successful day.

Why is the Red Sea so called?
Because, quite simply, that is its colour, which comes from the mineral rocks on the sea bed.

What is red tape?
Documents in the British Civil Service used to be tied up with red tape (in some cases, they still are). The words 'red tape' have come to be a derogatory term for civil service methods which cause irritation due to delays or over-fussiness.

What is 'The Red Flag'?
'The Red Flag' is a song written in the 1880s for the newly formed Labour Movement, and it has become the party's anthem.

Where is the Red River?
It is at and near Winnipeg in Canada. A settlement of Scottish emigrants was founded there in the early 19th century.

How did the Red Cross come to be founded?
The inception of this international organization for the relief of suffering is owed to Jean Henri Dunant (1828–1910), a Swiss banker who was moved by the suffering of those who were wounded at the battle of Solferino in 1859. Five years later, Dunant's promptings led to a diplomatic conference which signed the first Geneva Convention. As a symbol of neutrality, the colours of the Swiss flag were reversed to provide a red cross on a white ground. Moslem countries generally use an analogous red crescent, while the equivalent symbol in Iran is the Red Lion and Sun.

What is the Red Duster?
It is a slang term for the Red Ensign, the official flag of the British merchant navy.

What is the white of an egg?
In nature, the egg-white or albumen's purpose is to protect the yolk within the shell. For culinary purposes, egg-whites may be separated from yolks and used for specific recipes, such as in the preparation of meringues.

What is a white sauce?
This is sauce made with a roux (flour, fat, liquid such as milk or chicken, veal or fish stock) together with any desired flavouring. It is normally served to complement a white or light-fleshed dish.

What is a whitebeam?
This is a Eurasian tree, in Britain most commonly found in a natural state in woods with chalk or limestone soil in Southern England. It is a species of Rosaceae which grows to a height of 6–8m (20–40ft). Its wood is used in turning, and a kind of beer is produced by fermenting its fruit.

What is a white lie?
It is a lie which you may claim some justification for telling.

What are whitebait?
Small fish, about 2½ to 7½ cms (1 to 3 inches) long, which are usually fried and served dryish and on their own as an hors d'oeuvre.

Where is White Russia?
It is the part of Russia that borders with Poland. It is one of the republics in the USSR (Union of Socialist Soviet Republics). Its capital city is Minsk.

Has Whit Sunday anything to do with the colour white?
Yes, it is the festival when the spirit of

Jesus came down to the disciples, after the Crucifixion and Resurrection. On this festival, people are baptized, generally wearing white clothing, a tradition that is thought to go back to the earliest days of Christianity.

Where is the Vale of White Horse in England?
Several claim this title, but the one usually recognized as the Vale of White Horse is the valley near Abingdon, in Berkshire, on one side of which is cut a huge white horse, nearly 131 m (400 ft) long. This is at Uffington, and was possibly cut after the defeat of the Danes by Ethelred and Alfred in 871.

Why was the White Tower at the Tower of London so called?
Because in the Middle Ages it was sometimes whitewashed with a lime-based paint.

Who were the Bluecoat Boys?
They were boys at Christ's Hospital School which was founded in London and later moved to Horsham in Sussex (where it still is). The original boys wore blue gowns, and they still wear similar clothing today.

What is the Blue Riband of the Atlantic?
It is a title held by the ship which made the fastest crossing of the Atlantic Ocean in both directions. It was held by the SS *Queen Mary* between 1938 and 1952.

What was the Blue Division?
It was a division of Spanish troops which were sent by General Franco to fight with the Nazi German armies in Russia in World War II.

What is an Oxford blue?
A sporting honour given to undergraduates for high performance in some sport or athletic activity. The award is signified by a dark blue ribbon. At Cambridge, there is a similar award, which is a light blue ribbon.

What are Blue Bonnets?
The Scottish Highlanders or Scotsmen generally, so called because of the blue woollen caps which were once worn.

Who is Bluemantle Pursuivant?
He is one of the four pursuivants of the College of Heralds.

What is the proper name for the 'Blues' regiment?
These are the Royal Horse Guards of the Household Cavalry.

What is a bluethroat?
This is a Eurasian songbird, closely related to the nightingale. There are two species, a red-spotted and a white-spotted, which are passage migrants or vagrants in respect of the British Isles.

What were 'Blue Meanies'?
Villains in the Beatles cartoon film *Yellow Submarine*.

What is a blue cheese?
No, it is not entirely blue, it merely has blue veins as, for example, Gorgonzola.

Little Quiz 12
  What were the dates of these peace treaties?
  1. Bretigny
  2. Ghent (Britain & US)
  3. Luneville
  4. Paris (Spain & US)
  5. Vereeniging
  6. San Stefano
  7. Belgrade
  8. Antananarivo
  9. Paris (Britain & US)
  10. Brest-Litovsk

Which are the two main species of oak tree native to Britain?
The common oak and the durmast oak.

What is the main difference between the two?
The common oak has its leaves on short stalks or no stalks at all, and its acorns singly or in bunches of several on stalks generally no more than 127 mm (5 in) long. The durmast oak has its leaves on stalks at least 25.4 mm (1 in) long, but the acorns have no stalks or are clustered close to the twigs.

Why is the locust tree so called?
The locust tree, otherwise the false acacia tree, came from North America. It was brought to Europe, especially to France, by missionaries in North America who thought it was the acacia tree from which John the Baptist obtained locusts in the wilderness.

Why is the hickory tree good for making axe and other tool handles?
Because it is very tough, light in weight and springy. Hickory trees are common in the United States.

What is an arboretum?
It is a collection of trees of different kinds, generally of the rare kinds, that are grown for display. Many stately homes have an arboretum in their grounds, in some cases planted more than a century ago.

Many trees are called hybrids: what does this mean?
A hybrid is an 'offspring' produced by cross-breeding of two different kinds of trees.

What is a monkey puzzle tree?
It is a pine tree native to Chile, which is also grown in the US and Britain, and is notable for its whorled branches and stiff leaves arranged in spirals.

What is a Leyland cypress?
This is a well known example of a hybrid that is very popular in Britain. It is a conifer bred from a Nootka cypress from North America and a Monterey cypress. The Leyland grows very fast, up to over a metre (4 ft) a year if the conditions are good, and should reach about 12 m (40 ft).

Which tree grows and flourishes in salt water?
The mangrove tree throws its roots out above water level and the root tips droop into the water and mud. Mangroves grow in swamps as a rule, in central America, along the Florida and Atlantic coasts, and also in Africa and the Philippines.

What is a deciduous tree?
It is a tree which sheds all its leaves once a year.

What is a Judas tree?
This is a most attractive broadleaf tree that has small, pretty pink flowers that flow out of the trunks of the branches as well as from the branch ends. It is called the Judas tree because it is thought to be the tree from which Judas hanged himself.

What is the General Sherman Tree in Sequoia National Park?
This is an example of the sequoias dendrosa giganteum species of tree which is said to be nearly 4000 years old. It is over 82 m (270 ft) tall.

Why are mulberry trees associated with silk manufacture?
The leaves of some species of mulberry provide food for silkworms.

Why do you so often find a yew tree in an English churchyard?
The yew tree has a very long life, sometimes of several hundreds of years. It was a symbol of eternal life in pagan times, and this was adopted by the

Christians. But it is also probable that the tree proved useful as a shelter for congregations on sites of churches before the buildings were completed.

What is Dutch elm disease?
A particularly virulent disease attacking elm trees by means of a fungus Ceratostomella Ulmi, which is carried by bark beetles. The leaves turn yellow and drop off, and the tree dies. Elm trees in Britain were hit by the disease in the late 1970s and over 10,000,000 were affected.

What are other names for the linden tree, the mountain ash and the great maple?
The lime, the rowan, the plane.

What is Robin Hood's larder?
It is a hollow oak tree in Sherwood Forest in which Robin Hood is said to have hidden deer he had killed.

When were the first fig trees grown in Britain?
It is possible that fig trees were introduced by the Romans during their occupation (1st to 5th centuries), but the first known fig trees were planted in Lambeth in the reign of Henry VIII.

What were the original cedars of Lebanon?
They were tall conifers which reached as high as 30.5 m (100 ft) and which grew in the Lebanon and the Taurus Mountains in Turkey, which Solomon used for the construction of his famous temple in Jerusalem. The trees in this instance were given to him by Hiram, king of Tyre.

What is the cricket bat willow tree?
A species of willow (salix coerulea), also called the blue willow, which can be as tall as 30.5 m (100 ft). In England, the wood is used for cricket bats, and the trees grown for this purpose are cut down usually when the trunks have reached a width of 457–482 mm (18 to 19 in).

What is the rarest native British tree?
The whitty pear *Sorbus domestica*, of which only one example is known. It grew in the middle of the Wyre Forest in Worcestershire, but after being damaged in 1862 was only kept alive in cultivation. Happily, this tree, which was first recorded in 1678, was successfully replaced on its old site. Elsewhere, the nearest whitty pears are found in Brittany.

Why is it considered unlucky to bring hawthorn into a house?
Because of the tradition that its thorns were fashioned into a crown for Christ at his Passion.

Mangrove tree

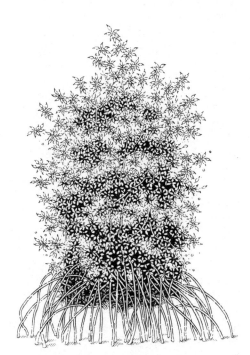

How old is Skara Brae village, in Orkney?
This prehistoric village of stone-built houses is at least 5000 years old. The settlement appears to have flourished for several generations, and depended upon sea food and cattle. It was overwhelmed by some natural disaster but when it was excavated it was found to be in a remarkable state of preservation.

What is a passage grave?
An artificial burial mound of stone construction. At the centre of the inside there is a vaulted chamber that is connected to the outside by a straight passage.

What was so remarkable about Maes Howe passage grave, in Orkney?
Its state of preservation after 5500 years of existence. The stone blocks appear to have been cut and shaped with astonishing skill, so accurately that it is almost impossible to slide a knife into the joins.

What was a causewayed camp?
An enclosure of two or more concentric rings of ditches and banks, the banks being levelled at one or two points and the earth tipped into the adjacent ditching, to provide causeways in and out of the camp.

How many periods of building were there at Stonehenge?
At least three, the first being about 2600 BC. The huge, tall sarsens (sandstone blocks) are probably from the third phase, which was at least 4000 years ago.

What is a henge monument?
It is a round or oval enclosure of raised bank outside an inner ditch, used for religious or ceremonial purposes. There were entrances in the bank. Most henges were built during the 2nd millennium BC, a few earlier.

What is the age of the famous passage grave at Newgrange in Ireland?
At least 5000 years old. At the entrance is a fine stone slab which is decorated with carved whorls and lozenges.

What is a dun?
It is an Iron Age fortlet built from stone blocks resting on each other, without mortar, which is called dry stone construction.

When were hill forts first built in Britain?
It used to be said they were a Celtic invention of about the 9th century onwards up to Roman times, but it is now clear that they were built by pre-Celtic Iron Age people, probably as far back as about 1000 BC.

What does megalithic mean?
It refers to structures built from huge stone blocks weighing several tons each.

What was an *oppidum*?
It is the Latin for town (often in a loose sense), and was used by the Romans in their first contacts with the Gauls and Britons, to indicate their settlement areas, often on hill tops.

What is a vitrified fort?
More generally found in Scotland than anywhere else in Britain, a vitrified fort was an enclosure of dry stone wall construction interlaced with timber posts. When the timber was set alight and burned, the heat melted the surface of the stonework, creating a glassy, slippery surface on the wall. It is not known if the burning was deliberate as a defensive technique or if it was the result of fire-raising by enemy assault.

What was a barrow?
A mound of earth covering a grave. Barrows were round or rectangular, the latter usually called long barrows.

What is a wheelhouse?

An Iron Age round house of dry stone and wattle walling in which the rooms were arranged by partitions set in radiating lines, like the spokes of a wheel.

What was a cist?

This was a grave or burial pit, sometimes lined with stone, with a cap stone as a lid. There were many shapes and sizes of cist.

What do we mean by crouched burial?

A custom of burying the dead by folding the body with the knees drawn up to the jaw, and lying on its side.

What is a trilith or trilithon?

It is a construction using three very large stones, two upright with a third across the top. Stonehenge has a ring of trilithons.

What marked the end of the Stone Age?

It did not end at the same time everywhere, but it was when Stone Age people gave up using stone tools and started to work in copper and bronze.

Where and what are Grime's Graves?

They are near Brandon on the Norfolk–Suffolk border and are an interesting series of over 360 flint mining shafts which began to be worked as far back as about 3000 BC. They appear to have been worked for hundreds of years. When one shaft was worked out, the craftsmen dug another shaft and began to work that.

Who was the first British tribal chief to be mentioned by Caesar in connection with his invasion of Britain?

Cassivelaunus, chief of the Catuvellauni tribe who occupied Hertfordshire, parts of Buckinghamshire, Bedfordshire, Cambridgeshire and Essex. He was defeated in battle by Caesar at Ravensburgh in south Bedfordshire.

Where is the Icknield Way?

This prehistoric trackway runs from the North Norfolk coast near Wells-next-the-Sea to Goring in Oxfordshire. It passes through Swaffham, Newmarket, Royston and Luton – towns which did not, of course, exist when this route came to be formed. For much of its length the Icknield Way has become incorporated into the modern road network; beyond Goring it continues as The Ridgeway along the Berkshire Downs, eventually reaching Salisbury Plain.

How long have Celtic languages been spoken in Britain?

A wave of newcomers, perhaps already in the Bronze Age, brought the first Celtic tongues to Britain about 1000 BC; they were reinforced in the Iron Age about 500 years later by a second wave. The former, or Goidelic, groups gave us the languages which developed into Scottish and Irish Gaelic, and Manx; the latter, or Brythonic, groups likewise Welsh and Cornish (and the Breton tongue of Brittany).

Little Quiz 13

What is the French for:

1. eight
2. thirty
3. ninety

The German for

4. three
5. twenty
6. thousand

Italian for

7. forty
8. five hundred
9. eight

and the Spanish for

10. five

What is a dressoir?
Introduced in the late Middle Ages in Europe, it was a tall item consisting of a chest with doors, or a small cupboard, supported on a stand on a plinth. Some dressoirs had a drawer underneath the upper chest or cupboard.

How is lacquer work done?
Briefly, by applying several layers of paint and special varnish to produce a decorated surface on a piece of furniture. Lacquer work was usually done in black, red or green.

Where did the *vargueno* originate?
A *vargueno* is a cabinet of drawers of different sizes on a stand, with a flap across the cabinet front, which is lowered to form a writing surface. It was peculiar to Spain and Portugal, and first appeared in the late Middle Ages.

Why are Gobelins tapestries so valuable?
In 1667, Louis XIV of France founded the Manufacture Royale des Gobelins, an organization centred in workshops in the Gobelins district of Paris, specifically to produce furniture, decorative materials, tapestries and so on, for the royal palaces and apartments. He engaged the leading craftsmen not only of France but of many other European countries to work there. Tapestries woven by Gobelins workers are among the finest ever produced anywhere.

What is a *cwpwrdd tridarn*?
It is a special three-tier cupboard, with the top part an open shelf, and the middle and lower parts cupboards with doors, and is usually made of oak. It is peculiar to Wales, though imitations have been made elsewhere. Most of these *cwpwrddau* were made in the 17th and 18th centuries, rather fewer in the 19th.

Who was the first furniture-maker to produce a book of his own furniture designs?
Thomas Chippendale (1718–1779), who was born at Otley in Yorkshire and who settled in St Martin's Lane in London in about 1750. In 1754 he published *The Gentleman and Cabinet-Maker's Director*, which was filled with his designs for all kinds of house furniture. The book was an instant success and was reprinted the following year and again in 1759.

What is a bachelor chest?
This was a small chest of drawers, with two short top drawers and three long drawers under them, and having on the top a fold-over lid which could be opened 180° to produce a writing flap, converting it into a desk.

What is *pietre dure*?
It is the Italian phrase for those stones which are classified in English as semi-precious, namely, the hard stones such as jasper and agate, used for inlaid work.

What is Tunbridge ware?
It is an exclusively English form of wood mosaic, first made in and around Tunbridge Wells by local craftsmen in the 17th century. The method used minute strips of wood in numerous natural and contrived colours to form geometric patterns, floral decorations, even landscapes, and this was applied to the tops (and occasionally sides) of boxes, desks, tea caddies, etc.

What was an armoire?
It was the French word for wardrobe (still in use), and was a much used piece in the 17th and 18th centuries, lending itself to the most elaborate decoration.

What was a love-seat?
This was an upholstered couch specially designed for two people, known in French as *causeuse*.

What was an encoignure?
A French introduction, it was a corner cupboard, usually made in pairs, first manufactured towards the end of the 17th century. Most encoignures were surmounted by a shaped marble top.

What is oyster veneer?
An innovation of 17th century Dutch craftsmen, it is a decorative veneer made by cutting slices of small branches and laying them together to create a pattern that looks like a number of oysters beside each other.

What is a farthingale chair?
An upright chair introduced in the 17th century, with a high seat, tallish back and no arms, designed to accommodate the farthingale, or hooped dress worn by women.

Farthingale chair

What is a bureau-plat?
A French innovation of the 18th century, it was a desk with long legs and flat top, with three drawers in line under the top (occasionally two drawers), lending itself to adornment on the corners by bronze or gilt bronze mounts, edging round the top with bronze or brass rail, and with a tooled leather top to the desk.

What is the carcase of a piece of furniture?
It is the body of the piece, such as a chest of drawers, desk, cupboard, on which the finishing and decorative veneers and inlays are applied.

What is a console table?
It is a type of side table with a single leg, or at most two legs, that stands against the wall which provides support. Console tables were often made in pairs and decorated in gilt, and usually had marble tops.

What is a dumb waiter?
An 18th century invention consisting of a tall pillar supporting three or occasionally four, round trays, one below another increasing in diameter towards the bottom. The pillar ends in a tripod stand. These were used for foods, wine bottles and so forth, and were put in the corner of the dining room to provide what we would today describe as a buffet meal.

Why is Shaker furniture so called?
It is a range of household furniture items made by the early 19th century American religious sect, the Shakers, and it is characterized by its simplicity, its excellent proportions and its sound construction. It was generally made in pinewood, maple, walnut or fruitwood. Typical pieces were chairs, tables, benches and chests of drawers. Shaker furniture is in demand today among collectors. Some pieces can be seen in the American Museum at Bath.

What is the origin of the game of tennis?

The game seems to have been played in some form in the 15th century in England and France, and it was played in a covered court. Real tennis (or Royal, or Court Tennis) is still played indoors. Henry VIII of England was one of the best players of his time.

When did tennis begin to be played outside and on grass?

In the 1870s, in England. It came to be called Lawn Tennis, but the game can be played on surfaces other than grass.

How did Wimbledon become the centre for the world's greatest Lawn Tennis Championships?

Because the meeting which founded the Championships took place at the offices of the All England Croquet and Lawn Tennis Club in Worple Road, Wimbledon, at the beginning of June 1877. The first tournament was held on 9 July.

What does 'seeding' mean?

This is the process of putting selected players in a tournament in certain places in the draw so as to prevent them meeting until the later stages of the tournament. It was first used at Wimbledon in 1924.

What is the origin of the scoring method in tennis?

The beginnings of scoring 15, 30, 40 and Game are not known, but it is generally agreed that they go back to the earliest years of the game in the late Middle Ages, and they may relate to the four quarters of the clock. A game was finished at the end of an hour. The intervals may have been marked by rest periods at the quarters.

What is the Grand Slam in tennis?

The achievement by an individual of winning the Singles Championship of Britain, the US, France and Australia all in one year. Several people have won it. The first was Donald Budge for the US in 1938.

Who was Little Mo?

Maureen Connolly, who won the Women's Singles Championships at Wimbledon in 1952, when she was only 17, and at her first attempt. She won again in 1953 and 1954, and in 1953 was also the first woman to win the Grand Slam.

What rules govern the size of a tennis racket for championships?

It has to be not more than 812.8 mm (32 in) long including the handle, and not more than 317.5 mm ($12\frac{1}{2}$ in) wide. The string surface must not exceed 393.7 × 292.1 mm ($15\frac{1}{2}$ in × $11\frac{1}{2}$ in).

Who was Suzanne Lenglen?

One of the greatest of all tennis stars. Born in 1899, she was a French player of exceptional skill, who won six Wimbledon Singles' Championships (1919, 1920, 1921, 1922, 1923 and 1925). She died in 1938.

Which international tennis star was Czechoslovakian born, played for his country, for Egypt and for Britain?

Jaroslav Drobny (born 1921) left Czechoslovakia when the country was absorbed into the Eastern bloc and was offered refuge in Egypt. In 1954 he became Men's Singles Champion in 1954 representing Egypt. Later on, he became a naturalized Briton and played for the UK.

What is the make-up of the tennis ball?

Basically, it is a rubber sphere covered with a 'furry' cloth or 'nylon' substitute. Its diameter should be 63.5 mm to 66.7 mm ($2\frac{1}{2}$ in to $2\frac{5}{8}$ in) and it should weigh between 275 g and 284 g (2 oz and $2\frac{1}{16}$ oz).

Who was Gorgeous Gussie Moran?
She was an American women's singles player in the 1950s who startled Wimbledon spectators with the frilly lace edges of her tennis skirt and underskirt.

What is the height from the ground to the top of the centre of the tennis net?
It should be 0.914 m (3 ft), a regulation introduced in 1882.

Has a left-handed player ever won a Wimbledon Championship?
Yes, several times. The first was Norman Brookes, in 1907. Other famous left-handers are Drobny, Rod Laver, Jimmy Connors and John McEnroe.

What is the greatest number of Men's Singles Championships at Wimbledon won by the same player since 1922.
Five, by the Swedish player Bjorn Borg, who won five years running, 1976 to 1980. Rod Laver has won four, but not all in a row.

How many times has Billie Jean King won a Wimbledon Championship?
Twenty, including six Women's Singles.

What was Sphairistiké?
This name was given by Major Walter Clopton Wingfield to the form of lawn tennis which he developed and marketed over the years from 1869 to 1875. The name was derived from an ancient Greek ball game known as *Sphairisis*. Wingfield's game was played on an hourglass-shaped court, with service being delivered from one side only; it rapidly lost popularity once an official code for lawn tennis was drafted in 1875, to which Wingfield graciously agreed.

What traditional English summer sport did lawn tennis begin to replace in the late 19th century?
Croquet. It must, however, be recorded that this ancient game did not vanish completely from the lawns of England. It is still played widely, and its rules are governed by the Croquet Association of the Hurlingham Club, London.

Which member of the royal family played in the Wimbledon Championships?
The Duke of York, later George VI, played in the men's doubles of the Fiftieth Anniversary Jubilee Championship of 1926. He and his partner, Wing Commander Louis Greig, were defeated in the first round.

Which former men's doubles champion wore a leg iron?
Sydney Howard Smith (1872–1947), was a doubles champion in 1902 and 1906. He was particularly noted for his fierce forehand drive. Apart from his successes at lawn tennis, he also played badminton and was the All England singles champion in that sport in 1900.

What are the most northerly and most southerly lawn tennis clubs in the world?
The most northerly is at Hammerfest in Norway, where the sun in fact never sets from 19 May to 29 July each year; the most southerly is at Punta Arenas, Chile.

When was a tennis court first floodlit?
At Cheltenham in 1881.

Has lawn tennis been played as part of the modern Olympic Games?
Yes, in all the Olympics from 1896 to 1924 inclusive – except in 1916 during World War I when the Games did not take place. Bad weather and controversy surrounding control of the sport at Paris in 1924 led to its being withdrawn. The game was once again included as a 'demonstration' sport in Mexico City in 1968.

What is a dinghy?
It is a small, open boat for sailing, which can also be rowed. The word comes from the Hindi for little boat, *dingi*.

What does clinker built mean?
It means that the hull of the boat is built with the outer planks overlapping, downwards and fastened with clinched nails.

Where is the bilge of a boat?
The part of the hull where the sides meet the bottom, usually from the keel to the point where the sides start to rise.

What is the difference between a round bilge vessel and a hard chine vessel?
A round bilge vessel has a curved bilge where the bottom meets the sides, whereas a hard chine vessel has the sides meeting the bottom at an angle.

What is a sailing boat's rig?
It is the term that covers the boat's masts, yards and sails.

Is rig the same as rigging?
Rigging describes the lines (of rope) and chains aboard a boat used for controlling the sails and for supporting masts and spars.

What is a Bermudan sail?
A triangular sail, the shortest of the three sides being the lower edge (or foot).

What are sails made of?
They are made from sail cloths sewn together. These cloths are manufactured in different weights, measured as a rule in ounces per square yard of cloth (or grams per square metre). Heavier cloths are for larger boats and stronger winds.

What is a taffrail?
It is the rail across or around the stern of a boat.

How are glass-fibre boat hulls manufactured?
Layers of glass-fibre matting are laid in a hull mould, each being soaked in resin. When the resin cures, the hull is taken out of the mould and is ready.

What is a sloop?
It is a fore-and-aft rigged vessel, generally having two sails (mainsail and headsail).

What is a ketch?
A two-masted sailing boat, rigged fore and aft, with the smaller mizzen mast stepped forward of the rudder post.

What does it mean to 'heave to'?
It means to stop. This is generally done by backing the headsail and lashing the helm to leeward.

Trimaran

What is a spinnaker?
A large, light, generally triangular sail carried on a long, light pole, on the side opposite the mainsail.

What is close-hauled?
This means having the sails trimmed for sailing as close to the wind as possible.

What do windward and leeward mean?
Windward means towards the wind, leeward means downwind or away from the wind.

What are the scuppers on a boat?
They are small holes that let water taken on board run off the deck.

How long is a nautical mile?
About 1,854 m (6,080 ft) that is, the distance equal to one minute of longitude at the Equator.

What is the Beaufort Scale?
A scale for measuring the force of the wind according to a set of numbers devised by Admiral Sir Francis Beaufort in 1806.

What is the world's largest yacht?
HMS *Britannia*, the British royal yacht launched in 1953. Her displacement is 4715 tons.

What is a trimaran?
This is an unballasted single-hull boat constructed with twin floats port and starboard which provide excellent stability.

What was the first fully crewed Round the World race?
This was organized by the Royal Naval Sailing Association and started on 8 September 1973. The winner was the 19.5m (64ft) ketch *Sayula II* owned and sailed by the Mexican, Ramon Carlin.

What is a sheerstrake?
The topmost plank of the topsides of a vessel.

Who made the first single-handed ocean crossing?
The Danish-American, Alfred Johnson, who sailed his 6m (20ft) dory *Centennial* across the Atlantic from Nova Scotia to Wales in 46 days in 1876. As the name of the craft might suggest, this was a celebration of the centenary of the American Declaration of Independence.

What is the national authority for yacht racing in the United Kingdom?
The Royal Yachting Association, which was originally founded in London in 1875.

When did yachting become popular in England?
Yachts were widely used in Holland in the early 17th century. Charles II of England spent part of his exile in Holland and it was there that he became familiar with these craft. Upon his Restoration in 1660, the Dutch presented the monarch with a 15m (52ft) armed yacht called *Mary*. English boatbuilders then tried to improve on the Dutch design, and yachts and yachting thus gradually grew in popularity.

Little Quiz 14
   In which countries are these mountains?
1. Snowdon
2. K2 (Godwin-Austen)
3. Nanda Devi
4. Elborus
5. Great Ararat
6. Mount Logan
7. Watkins
8. Mount Massive
9. Cotopaxi
10. Fujiyama

What is a Hiram Codd's bottle?
A fizzy mineral water or fruit juice bottle that is sealed by means of a glass ball held against a rubber ring by the pressure from the gas. They are now collectors' items.

What is treen?
It is an old word meaning wooden, and is used as a collective term for small antique articles of wood, such as pepper mills, napkin rings, platters, salad servers, spice boxes, back-scratchers and so on.

What is a Staffordshire flatback?
An item from a considerable range of coloured glazed earthenware figures produced in the later 19th century by the Staffordshire pottery firms. They are known as flatbacks because only the front view is properly shaped and coloured, the remainder being glazed white. Models included Queen Victoria, Prince Albert and other famous people.

What is pressed glass?
A process invented in the United States in the 1820s whereby molten glass is forced into patterned moulds by mechanical means to produce objects in glass that look as if they were of better quality mould-blown glass.

Is amber a rare stone?
No, it is a fossilized resin which occurs in some quantity in Scandinavia and on the east Baltic coast, and has also been found in Britain.

Why is an Apostle jug so called?
It is a straight-sided jug with relief modelled figures of the apostles on its sides, surmounted by Gothic arcading, looking like a heavily decorated pulpit. The style was introduced in the 1840s by Charles Meigh of the Staffordshire potteries during the great Gothic revival of the early Victorian period.

What is the difference between pewter and Britannia metal?
Pewter is an alloy of tin, lead, copper and antimony (or bismuth) which has been used for plates, cups, tankards and vessels for at least 2000 years. Britannia metal is a cheap copy of the same, first produced in the 18th century but more popular in the 19th century. Britannia metal is an alloy of tin, copper and antimony, produced by a spinning process, and is generally much shinier than pewter.

What is a what-not?
A light, portable stand of three or four wooden shelves graded downwards small to large, supported on uprights at the corners, used for ornaments or books.

What is a pouncepot?
A vase-shaped bottle for sprinkling powdered pumice (or pounce) upon writing paper, used before the days of blotting paper.

What is soapstone?
A brown-green mottled stone which can be carved and shaped for a variety of decorative objects or utensils. Among the best known figures popular since the 19th century are the famous Three Monkeys – see no evil, hear no evil, speak no evil.

What was a Meerschaum pipe?
A smoker's pipe whose bowl and part of the stem were carved, often intricately and with skill. Meerschaum pipes were usually made of a soft white claylike mineral from the Near East, called meerschaum, which became stained through usage and often in the end looked like amber.

What is a bygone?
An increasingly popular term for any object no longer in use, such as an old farm implement, a pair of bellows etc.

What is a trivet?
A three-legged stand on which utensils rested in front of a fire, though there were many varieties, some of which had no legs but instead had hooks which gripped the bars of the fire.

What is a chain mail purse?
A purse with a clip at the top two edges, the sides made of thin steel links, like medieval chain mail armour only much thinner. This type of purse was popular in the late Victorian age.

What was a moustache cup?
A special cup with an arrangement across an arc at the top which allowed a moustache wearer to drink a cup of tea or coffee down to the dregs without wetting his moustache.

What is a fairing?
It is the word applied to a great variety of objects made of glass or china in the later 19th century, and sold at stalls at travelling fairs as souvenirs. They were made in Germany and France and imported into Britain in great quantities. Later it meant any present bought at a fair.

What were lazy tongs?
These were a contrivance enabling women, when dressed in fashionable billowing crinolines, to pick up objects off the floor. They were a strip of trellis (wood, metal or ivory) with finger holes at one end and 'grippers' at the other. When you squeezed the finger holes together (like scissors) the trellis extended and reached beyond the dress to clasp the object.

What is bentwood?
Introduced in central Europe in the mid-19th century, it was a type of furniture made of beechwood stick, steamed and bent into shapes. The curving lines, uninterrupted by joints, allowed for an interesting range of flowing furniture styles, especially rocking chairs.

What is a stereoscope card?
This is a long, rectangular card consisting of two identical photographs of the same size placed side by side and set at a very slight angle to each other. The card was placed in a stereoscope, a 19th century invention which was a gadget consisting of a strip of wood with an eye-piece at one end and at the other end a slot for the card. The eye-piece could be adjusted forwards or backwards for the right distance from the card, so that when you looked through the lenses you obtained a three-dimensional view of the picture.

How did the 19th century polyphon work?
The polyphon was our Victorian ancestors' juke-box. The mechanism was in a glass-fronted cabinet, often fixed to the wall in a place of public entertainment, such as a public house or café, and it was coin-operated. For one penny, a steel disc dotted with perforations would rotate, causing small pieces of metal to drop down and strike a series of metal keys in an order that produced a popular tune, say, a favourite music hall song or an air from a Gilbert and Sullivan comic opera.

Little Quiz 15
Who were the husbands of?
1. Messalina
2. Roxana
3. Boudicca
4. Cartimandua
5. Empress Matilda
6. Madame de Maintenon
7. Hatshepsut
8. Mary II of England, Scotland and Ireland
9. Philippa of Hainault
10. Berengaria of Navarre

What is hepatitis?
It is a serious disorder of the liver, generally caused by a virus infection. It can be cured, but this takes time and much care has to be taken with diet.

What is lumbago?
It is a term for backache in the lumbar region of the backbone.

How does a disc slip?
Each of the vertebral bones in the spine is separated from the next by a thick pad of fibrous tissue. The pad is roughly disc-shaped and has a soft centre. If the tissue is damaged, the soft centre can bulge out to squeeze a nerve and so cause pain.

What does hardening of the arteries mean?
The arteries are normally quite elastic, and they allow the passage of blood at speed as it moves round the body. But some people's arteries become less elastic when the artery walls get too thick, which may be caused by a variety of problems such as high blood pressure or too much smoking or by too much eating of rich food. The condition is technically called arteriosclerosis.

What is a coronary?
This is short for coronary thrombosis, which is the medical term for heart attack, and it occurs when a branch of a coronary artery gets blocked, which stops oxygenated blood reaching the heart muscles, so affecting the operation of the heart.

What is laryngitis?
The larynx is the proper name for the vocal chords. If this organ becomes inflamed, the condition is called laryngitis.

What is catarrh?
This is an inflammation of the membranes of the nose and throat with a thick mucous discharge. Catarrh sometimes accompanies a heavy cold, or may occur without a cold, and sometimes may be of nervous origin.

What is heartburn?
This is an uncomfortable, sometimes painful, condition in which a burning sensation occurs behind the ribs and in the pit of the stomach. It has nothing to do with the heart, normally, but is a digestive complaint caused by a spasm at the bottom end of the oesophagus (windpipe) aggravated by acid bubbling back from the stomach.

What are chilblains?
These affect the fingers and toes (and occasionally the ears) when they get very cold in winter. An inflammation sets in and produces red swellings that can hurt and/or itch once the coldness wears off.

What is diphtheria?
It is an acute and dangerous bacterial infection affecting the mucous membrane in the throat. It is highly contagious and can, if not treated swiftly, be fatal. Children can now avoid diphtheria altogether by having an injection when only a few months old, and a 'booster' injection when they are about five.

How do you get malaria?
Usually, if you are in the tropics, or hot countries, and are bitten by the *anopheles* mosquito.

What is tetanus?
It is the medical name for lockjaw, and is caused by the tetanus bacillus that can get into a simple wound, such as a cut, and which produces a poison that makes the muscles move in spasms. Tetanus can be treated, and it is usually dealt with by having an anti-tetanus injection.

What is gingivitis?
A disease of the gums which starts round

the arcs where the gums meet the teeth. The gums swell and become tender. It can be treated.

Is gingivitis the same as a gumboil?
It may feel like it, but it isn't. A gumboil is an abscess on the gum caused by a decaying tooth.

What is Parkinson's disease?
It is a term to describe a range of nervous diseases in which the main symptoms are trembling and weakness of the muscles. It develops very slowly as a rule, often starting with a slight tremor in the hands, and progresses to a more widespread muscular debility.

What are kidney stones?
These are stones, usually very small, that can be formed from excessive salts and uric acid. They can obstruct the proper functions of the kidney and cause much pain. The condition can be treated.

What makes you faint?
Fainting occurs when there is a sudden drop in blood pressure which reduces the blood supply to the brain, and so produces temporary loss of consciousness.

What is arterial grafting?
This is a technique whereby a diseased or damaged section of artery is replaced with tubing prepared either from synthetic materials, or with a section of healthy artery from the patient or from another person.

What is a boil?
This is a subcutaneous infection which derives from bacteria invading a hair follicle or sweat gland. The body responds to such an attack by sending millions of white cells to the area, and many boils are thus resolved without need of medical assistance.

What is pleurisy?

This is inflammation of the pleura, the membrane enveloping the lungs and which lines the inner wall of the chest cavity. It can be caused by a number of factors, especially by bacterial, viral or fungoid infections of the lungs, by tumours, or by such general disorders as rheumatic fever or rheumatoid arthritis. Treatment includes pain-relieving drugs and the draining of excessive fluid accumulations, as well as measures directed at the underlying condition which has triggered off this illness.

What is scarlet fever?
This is an infectious disease most prevalent among children but which is relatively uncommon nowadays. There is a rash on the face and body, accompanied by fever. The rash flakes off after a few days. The principal treatment is penicillin. As with many infectious diseases, once a patient has recovered from scarlet fever he or she is normally immune from a further attack.

What is stuttering or stammering?
This is a disorder of speech in which some sounds are difficult to produce. It may bear some relationship to tensions experienced by a growing child. Treatment is usually through psychotherapy or speech therapy to which it responds well, and the earlier the better.

Little Quiz 16
Where are?
1. Dallas
2. Meerut
3. Bretton Woods
4. Biarritz
5. Quimper
6. Grenada
7. Geneva
8. Kiel
9. Beirut
10. Quatre Bras

Who said?

The Holy Roman Empire was neither holy, nor Roman nor an Empire.
Voltaire.

The English country gentleman galloping after a fox – the unspeakable in full pursuit of the uneatable.
Oscar Wilde.

Do not do unto others as you would they should do unto you. Their tastes may not be the same.
George Bernard Shaw.

He has occasional flashes of silence that make his conversation perfectly delightful.
Sydney Smith.

War is much too important a matter to be left to the generals.
Georges Clemenceau.

Mad dogs and Englishmen go out in the midday sun.
Noel Coward.

Russia is a riddle wrapped in a mystery inside an enigma.
Winston Churchill.

There are three kinds of lies: lies, damned lies, and statistics.
Benjamin Disraeli.

Genius is one percent inspiration and ninety-nine percent perspiration.
Thomas Alva Edison.

They say kings are made in the image of God. I feel sorry for God if that is what He looks like.
Frederick the Great.

All Gaul is divided into three parts.
Julius Caesar.

No man but a blockhead ever wrote except for money.
Samuel Johnson.

I don't know who my grandfather was: I am much more concerned to know what his grandson will be.
Abraham Lincoln.

Soldiers win battles and generals get the credit.
Napoleon Bonaparte.

Well, if I called the wrong number, why did you answer the phone?
James Thurber.

A radical is a man with both feet firmly planted in the air.
Franklin Delano Roosevelt.

History is the essence of innumerable biographies.
Thomas Carlyle.

A man's a man for a' that.
Robert Burns.

A week in politics is a long time.
Harold Wilson.

Cauliflower is nothing but cabbage with a College education.
Mark Twain.

I would never read a book if it were possible to talk half an hour with the man who wrote it.
Woodrow Wilson, later US president.

Those in the cheaper seats clap. The rest of you rattle your jewellery.
John Lennon.

The physician can bury his mistakes, but the architect can only advise his client to grow vines.
Frank Lloyd Wright.

What is a centrifuge?
A machine that rotates at high speed a container holding mixtures in order to separate them, such as mixtures of solids and liquids or liquids of different densities.

What is a cyclotron?
A particle accelerator, which accelerates atomic particles to a very high speed. The particles move in spiral paths in a magnetic field.

What is a dynamo?
A kind of electricity generator which produces direct current. A simple dynamo has a powerful magnet between the poles of which an armature is rotated to produce the electrical energy.

What is an electron microscope?
A kind of microscope that uses beams of electrons to form an enlarged image of a very small object on a fluorescent screen or photographic plate.

What is a geiger counter?
A special instrument for detecting and counting nuclear radiations and particles. It is named after Hans Geiger (1882–1945), a German professor of physics who along with others developed it.

What is a solenoid?
A cylindrical coil of wire that creates a magnetic field within itself when fed with electric current, thus drawing a core of iron or steel into its body.

What is a rheostat?
A piece of apparatus that varies the resistance to electric current.

What is a thermostat?
A piece of apparatus that is sensitive to temperature changes, which keeps the temperature of something, such as a water boiler, within a narrow range.

What is a cloud chamber?
A device for observing the movement of fundamental particles by means of the tracks they leave. The best known kind is the Wilson Cloud Chamber invented by Sir C. T. R. Wilson (1869–1959).

What is a radio telescope?
A special instrument that collects radio waves from space.

What is a Pitot tube?
This instrument is used for the measurement of speed or velocity of a fluid, either in gas or liquid form. It works on the principle that an open-ended tube facing the flow of a liquid will experience a pressure build-up which will increase according to the velocity of flow; a pressure gauge placed at the outlet of the tube can be contrived to indicate this velocity.

What is a Bunsen burner?
A laboratory tool giving a hot, non-luminous flame, which does not leave sooty deposits on the articles it heats. Gas is injected under pressure through a narrow jet into a vertical tube. As it enters this tube, it causes air to be drawn in through holes level with the jet, the amount of air which can be drawn in being regulated by a rotating collar.

Little Quiz 17
  What were the dates of the reigns of?
  1. Alfred the Great
  2. Joanna the Mad (Spain)
  3. Frederick the Great
  4. St Louis IX of France
  5. Edmund Ironside
  6. Casimir III of Poland
  7. Suleiman the Magnificent
  8. Catherine the Great
  9. Macbeth
  10. Llywelyn Fawr (the Great)

What is ballet?
In simple terms, it is a form of theatrical art using specially devised dancing, music and scenery to tell a story or convey an atmosphere. The performers always act in mime.

How long has ballet been performed?
Certainly since ancient Greek times, but modern ballet began in France in the later 17th century.

What is a prima ballerina?
She is a female ballet dancer who has performed a range of leading rôles in classical ballets. One of the first ballerinas was the French dancer Marie-Anne Camargo, who in the 1720s introduced the shorter skirt, allowing freer movement.

When did ballet first come to Britain?
Apparently, foreign dancers performed ballet as early as the mid-18th century, but most audiences in Britain regarded these as music-hall turns. Towards the end of the 19th century, Adeline Genée, a Danish-born ballerina (1878–1970) came to London and made regular appearances as a prima ballerina in ballets at London's Empire Theatre.

What is a *pirouette*?
It is a ballet movement in which the dancer makes a rapid spin or whirl of the body on one toe, with the other foot touching the knee-cap. There are several varieties of *pirouette*.

What is choreography?
It is the art of arranging a ballet performance and the notation representing the steps of the dances.

What is a *divertissement*?
It is a collection of unrelated dances performed in interludes during classical ballets.

Who is the *maître* or *maîtresse de ballet*?
The ballet master or mistress. The job is to supervise the classes and rehearsals of a ballet company. At one time ballet masters were also expected to compose ballet.

What is so special about the Romantic Ballet?
It was an age of ballet, lasting roughly from the late 1820s to the early 1850s, when ballets consisted chiefly of fairy tale, make-believe themes, in which the characters were as a rule immortal or fantastic, like wood-nymphs, swan-maidens, goblins, beautiful young demi-gods and so on.

Which are the seven principal dancing movements in ballet?
tourner (to turn), *glisser* (to glide), *sauter* (to jump), *élancer* (to dart), *plier* (to bend), *étendre* (to stretch), *rélever* (to rise).

Prima Ballerina

When were ballet 'tights' introduced?
By a Paris costumier, Maillot, in the
1820s. Another tight-fitting costume, the
leotard, was introduced in the mid-19th
century by Jules Leotard, a trapeze
artist.

**What was the achievement of Dame
Marie Rambert?**
Dame Marie Rambert was born in 1888
in Poland, danced with the Diaghilev
ballet, and in 1926 founded the Ballet
Rambert which she directed for over 50
years.

Who was Nijinsky?
Vaslav Nijinsky (1890–1950), a Russian
born ballet dancer, made his debut in
1908, then joined Diaghilev in Paris, and
for about ten years was one of the
greatest of the Diaghilev dancers.
Nijinsky also choreographed many
ballets.

**How did the Moscow audience react
to the first performance of** *Swan Lake*
in 1877?
The performance was a disaster and the
audience booed and stamped their feet.
This was for a variety of reasons – the
interference of the choreographer with
Tchaikovsky's lovely music, the
drabness of the costumes and sets and
the poor performances of individuals.

**What were Dame Ninette de Valois'
origins?**
She was born Edris Stannus in Wicklow,
Eire, in 1898, of French Huguenot
descent. She became a dancer with
Diaghilev, then prima ballerina at
Covent Garden in 1919. Dame Ninette
has dominated British ballet since the
1920s. She was made DBE in 1951.

Whose music is the basis of the ballet
Les Sylphides?
Frederic Chopin, and it was orchestrated
in the early part of the 20th century by

Glazunov. It was first performed at St
Petersburg (now Leningrad) in 1908.

Who was Diaghilev?
Sergei Pavlovich Diaghilev (1872–1929)
was a Russian ballet producer who
introduced a whole scheme of new ideas
into ballet centred on the coordination of
dancing, mime, music, costume, stage set
and lighting. He adapted ballet to famous
orchestral compositions, such as Rimsky-
Korsakov's *Scheherazade* and Debussy's
L'après-midi d'un faune. He founded Le
Ballet Russe in France in 1909 which he
ran for twenty years, employing the
greatest names of the day, such as
Pavlova, Nijinsky, composers like
Stravinsky and Prokofiev, and artists
such as Picasso and Braque.

What is a tutu?
This is the ballet skirt which became
standard for female dancers in 1832. It
has three forms, which, from longest to
shortest, are the romantic, the classic,
and the horizontal.

What is the *corps de ballet*?
It is the term to describe all those
members of a ballet who are not principal
or solo performers.

Who was Pavlova?
Anna Pavlovna Pavlova was born in
St Petersburg in 1881 and entered the
Imperial Ballet Academy there when she
was ten. Upon graduating in 1899 she
joined the Maryinsky Theatre where she
became prima ballerina in 1906. In 1907
she created the *Dying Swan* which
became her most famous solo dance.
Subsequently, she embarked upon
numerous foreign tours. She was
motivated by conservative aesthetic
principles, and had little sympathy with
the new ideas promoted by Diaghilev
with whom she worked for a few years
before World War I. She died at The
Hague in 1931.

When and where was the Chavin de Huantar civilization?

In Peru, South America, and it lasted from about 1300 BC to about 400 BC. It was one of the first civilizations in South America, and remains of several important buildings of the period have been found.

Who defeated the armies of the cities of ancient Sumer in the 24th century BC?

Sargon I, king of the Akkadians, who captured the cities of Ur, Lagash and others, and built a new city called Agade.

Who was Murshili the Hittite?

He was king of the Hittite people who occupied what is now Turkey, during the 2nd millennium BC. In the 1590s he captured the city of Babylon, far away in the land between the Euphrates and the Tigris rivers.

Where was the city of An-Yang?

It was in China, north of the Huang-ho or Yellow river. Here, the Shang dynasty which ruled in China from about 1600 to about 1025 BC, built its last capital city. It has been excavated and many remains of large buildings found.

What was the result of the great volcano eruption on the Aegean island of Thera?

The shock waves destroyed several of the towns of the Minoans on Crete and led to the decline of Minoan civilization in the 15th century BC.

Who were the Mycenaeans?

They were wandering peoples who settled in southern Greece in the middle of the 2nd millennium BC, about 1600–1500. They built several fine cities, notably a capital at Mycenae. They took advantage of the decline of the Minoan civilization in Crete, and overran the island in the 15th century BC.

Who were the Chou rulers?

They were Chinese kings who followed the Shang dynasty. They ruled China for nearly eight centuries, in two distinct periods and from two different capitals, one following the other. The first was near Sian, in what is now Shensi province and this has been excavated. The Chou were warlike rulers and appear to have spent much of their time fighting.

Who were the Dorians?

They were a warlike race from Eastern Europe who descended upon Greece in the early 1st millennium BC, overturned the ruling Achaeans and founded new cities such as Corinth, Megara and Sparta.

How did the ancient Indus civilization come to an end?

The Indus civilization began to decline in the period 1700 to 1600 BC, and by the middle of the millennium it had given way to hordes of invaders from Asia Minor, notably the Kassites who had been ravaging Babylonia.

Why was the old Hebrew State of Saul, David and Solomon divided?

Largely because, although these great rulers had managed to unite the Hebrew peoples under one government, it was not really the wish of the Hebrews to be one people. When Solomon died in about 930 BC, his kingdom was broken up into two, Israel and Judah.

What is the origin of the Celts?

They were a group of peoples speaking two basic languages, who came to central Europe, probably from the Near East (and also perhaps from central Russia) in the last years of the 2nd millennium BC. They were skilled metal workers, they bred horses, and they held deep religious beliefs.

What happened at the battle of Karkar?

The Israelite king, Ahab, led a combined army of Hebrews, Phoenicians and other Levantine peoples against the all-powerful Assyrians and crushed the Assyrian army in a splendid victory, in about 853 BC.

What was the Hallstatt period of Celtic civilization?

Hallstatt was a site of big salt deposits in Austria which Celtic people worked and used for trading with Mediterranean people, chiefly in the period 750 to 500 BC. These people were iron users, skilled artists and craftsmen, and also warriors.

Who were the Olmecs?

One of the earliest civilized peoples in Mexico and central America, who built cities at La Venta, Santorenzo, and Tres Zapotes, and other sites, in the 1st millennium BC.

What happened to the kingdom of Judah in 586 BC?

Nebuchadnezzar II, king of Babylonia, invaded Judah and captured Jerusalem, destroying the principal buildings. The people of Judah were taken into captivity, many of them being transported to Babylon.

What were the Vedas?

They were hymns written in ancient Sanskrit in India during the 2nd millennium BC.

What were the Upanishads?

They were sacred teachings of the Hindu faith, going back to the 1st millennium BC, and were compiled in more than 100 volumes.

What is an Ashoka pillar?

A column of sandstone, finely polished and bearing a symbol on the top, and sometimes with an inscription carved into the main trunk. Many of these pillars were set up in ancient India by the Mauryan king, Ashoka (3rd c BC), generally at holy Buddhist sites.

What was a *quipu*?

A string and knot device for calculations, employed by the Incas, probably as far back as about AD 1100. The *quipu* consisted of strings of different colours which, with the knottings, could be permutated to represent a range of calculations, statistics and other information.

Where did the La Tène Celtic culture begin?

At and around the village of La Tène near Lake Neuchatel in Switzerland, in the 6th century BC.

Where is Leptis Magna?

It is a now ruined city in Libya, about 120km (75 miles) east of Tripoli. It was originally founded by the Phoenicians, later occupied by the Carthaginians, and became a Roman colony in the 1st century BC, possibly in Caesar's time. It was the birthplace of the Roman emperor, Septimius Severus (AD 193–211). The ruins have been excavated, and among them are fine remains of a theatre, a forum, a senate house, and some baths built in the time of Emperor Hadrian (117–138). Severus also erected major buildings there.

Who were the Kassites?

They were a people from Persia who moved from Mesopotamia in the 1800s BC. They may have come from the Caucasus, originally. In the 1500s they established a ruling dynasty in Babylon and gradually absorbed Mesopotamian culture. The Kassites survived until the 12th century BC when they were overthrown by Elamites from what is now south-west Iran and the border district with Iraq, near the Persian Gulf.

What is the Commonwealth?
It is a free association of sovereign states which at one time had been part of the old British Empire. The term Commonwealth of nations was suggested as long ago as 1917 by Field Marshal J. C. Smuts of South Africa.

Why are the British known as 'Pommies' in Australia?
It is the slang word for British emigrants to Australia. Their fresh complexions remind Australians of the colour of the flesh of a pomegranate.

What happened at the Treaty of Waitangi?
The Maori inhabitants of New Zealand accepted British sovereignty by this treaty in 1840.

Who was the Father of Modern Kenya?
Jomo Kenyatta (1893–1978), who led the nationalist opposition to British rule in the 1950s and, after several years' imprisonment, became the first president of the new independent state of Kenya in 1964, three years after the formal granting of independence.

Where is Belize?
This used to be known as British Honduras, a small British colonial territory in central America adjacent to the republic of Guatemala.

What was the condominium of the New Hebrides?
An archipelago of islands in the western Pacific until 1978 administered jointly by Britain and France as an Anglo-French condominium.

Where is Tristan da Cunha?
It is a group of islands in the South Atlantic, between South America and South Africa, which is a British dependency.

Where is the 'outback'?
It is a word to describe areas in Australia that are far away from principal urban and populated rural areas.

Why was South Africa 'dropped' from the Commonwealth in 1961?
Technically, the Union of South Africa withdrew from the Commonwealth following a referendum in 1960, but the other Commonwealth members did not want South Africa to remain within, because of its national policy of *apartheid*, which discriminates against coloured people.

What was the Partition of India?
When, after World War II, the British government withdrew from India to give the sub-continent independence, it was decided that, because India was partly Hindu dominated and partly Moslem dominated, the country should be divided into two parts, India (Hindu) and a new state of Pakistan (Moslem). This arrangement was put into effect in 1947.

Why is Singapore a separate state from Malaysia?
In 1963, a federation was formed of the old British colonies of Sarawak, North Borneo, the Federation of Malaya and Singapore. The Federation of Malaya became known as Malaysia, and Sarawak, Sabah (formerly North Borneo) and Singapore joined. But in 1966, Singapore decided to drop out and remain an entirely independent state.

What is Malaysia's principal export?
Rubber.

Who brought Jamaica into the British Empire?
A Spanish possession from 1509 to 1655, it was taken from Spain by Admiral Penn during the Protectorate of Oliver Cromwell. Jamaica became an independent state in 1962.

Where do the Gurkhas come from?
They are, in military terms, soldiers
recruited in the kingdom of Nepal in the
Himalayas, who serve with the British
Army. They have a very well deserved
reputation for bravery, and many
individual Gurkha soldiers have won the
Victoria Cross.

**Who was the first prime minister of
the old Union of South Africa?**
Louis Botha (1862–1919), one of the
leaders of the Boer army in the Second
South African War (1899–1902), who
after the surrender to Lord Kitchener in
1902, became a firm friend of Britain. He
was appointed first prime minister of
South Africa in 1910, and brought his
country into World War I in 1914, on the
British side.

**When was the Sudan brought into the
British Empire?**
In 1898, after Lord Kitchener defeated
the army of the Khalifa at the battle of
Omdurman. The Sudan became an
Anglo-Egyptian condominium in 1899
and this arrangement lasted until 1956
when it was given full independence.

**What Commonwealth country in
Africa was once known as
Bechuanaland?**
Upon achieving full independence in
1966, the former British protectorate
of Bechuanaland in Southern Africa
adopted the name of Botswana. The
capital of the republic is Gaborone
(Gaberones).

**Where is Heard Island, and what
physical feature is it noted for?**
Heard Island is situated in the sub-
Antarctic zone of the Indian Ocean and
belongs to Australia. It has an active
volcano called Big Ben, 2745m (90,000ft)
covered with a mantle of snow.

Where is Pitcairn Island?

Pitcairn Island is a remote island in the
South Pacific Ocean. It is a British
dependent territory, subject to the
authority of the governor who is the
British high commissioner in New
Zealand. It does, however, have an Island
Council, made up of representatives of its
inhabitants – only 61 in number in 1980.

**What Commonwealth country in East
Africa was once a German colony?**
Tanzania, or rather the mainland part of
this country, once known as Tanganyika,
which was mandated to Britain at the
end of World War I. Offshore, Zanzibar,
too, once belonged to Germany; it passed
into British control in 1895.

**What parts of the former Indian
Empire have not remained within the
Commonwealth?**
Burma became an independent republic
outwith the Commonwealth on
4 January 1948; Pakistan left the
Commonwealth in January 1972
following the recognition of its former
Eastern Province as the independent
republic of Bangladesh by British and
other member states.

**When was the Isle of Man granted
self-government?**
In 1866.

Little Quiz 18
   Who was the winning commander at?
   1. Naval battle of the Falklands (1914)
   2. Austerlitz
   3. Omdurman
   4. Teutoburg Forest (AD 9)
   5. Oudenarde
   6. Tel-el-Kebir
   7. Qarqar
   8. Pharsalus
   9. Brunanburh
   10. Naval battle of Camperdown

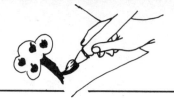

Why was Impressionism so called?
Impressionism was a derisive term originating from the title of Monet's *Impression, Sunrise* painted in 1872.

Which famous English painter was the son of a barber from Maiden Lane in London?
Joseph Mallord William Turner, who was born there on 23 April 1775.

What was perhaps the most important influence on late 19th century painting?
Photography. It opened up completely new angles and vistas, as may be seen in Monet's *Rue St Denis on the National Holiday*, 1878.

Who was known as the 'Father of Impressionism'?
Camille Pissarro (1830–1903).

What was the group of painters known as the 'Wild Beasts' or 'Fauves' and when did they flourish?
They were a group of Post-Impressionist painters who exhibited in the early years of this century. They included Matisse, Vlaminck, Derain, Bonnard and Rouault, and they were described by one critic of an exhibition of their works, as 'Fauves', the French for wild beasts.

Which was the first well-known painting of a railway train and who painted it?
Rain, Steam and Speed painted by J. M. W. Turner.

What inspired Picasso to paint *Guernica*?
The sufferings of the Spanish people during the Civil War (1936–39). The Nationalists invited the German and Italian air forces to take part on their side, and these forces bombed several towns, including Guernica, and killed many citizens.

What famous painter had a blue period, a pink period and a brown period?
Pablo Picasso.

Why did painters in water colours form a society in the 18th century?
If an artist wished to become a full member of the Royal Academy, he had to be a painter in both water colours and oils. Water colourists were discriminated against because they were thought to be of much lesser stature than oil painters, and their paintings were hung very badly in the Gallery as a consequence.

What was the *camera obscura*?
This was a box, developed in the 16th century from an idea known to the ancient world, which contained an arrangement of lenses and mirrors. The view was reflected onto a sheet of paper so that it could be traced round by a draughtsman. The apparatus was particularly useful for topographical artists.

How many paintings did Van Gogh sell during his lifetime?
None.

What is Dadaism?
Dada is the French for a hobby horse, and Dadaism is the name of an 'anti-art' movement that began in 1916 among some artists who were tired of World War I. Examples are a bicycle wheel signed by Marcel Duchamp, and the *Mona Lisa* with a moustache and a rude caption.

What is the difference between water colour and gouache?
Water colour is mixed only with water to create transparent washes that are applied over each other on rough white paper. Gouache is water colour mixed with white to make it opaque. This was considered 'frenchified' and anathema to the purists.

What did George Stubbs and Sir Alfred Munnings have in common?
They both excelled in painting horses.

Goya painted two portraits that are thought to have been of the Duchess of Alba. What were they called?
La Maja Vestida and *La Maja Desnuda*. ('The Clothed Maja' and 'The Unclothed Maja'.)

What is 'genre' painting?
It is a style of painting depicting the objects of and scenes from everyday life.

For what branch of art apart from painting is Rembrandt well known?
Etching.

Who was Hieronymus Bosch?
Bosch flourished in the Dutch city of s'Hertogenbosch in the late 15th century. His best known paintings appear somewhat surreal, visions of strange landscapes with demons, monsters and bizarre machines, reflecting the concern of the times with themes of sin, judgement and potential damnation. Two of his most famous pictures are *Gardens of Delight* and *Temptation of St Anthony*. In addition, Bosch painted many works dealing with more conventional religious themes.

What is a pietà?
This is an Italian word meaning pity. In works of art, it is a subject which shows the dead Christ supported by the Virgin immediately after being taken down from the Cross.

Who was Henri, Comte de Toulouse-Lautrec?
This French painter (1864–1901) was also noted for his poster designs. He turned to painting after suffering crippling injuries to both of his thighs in childhood. His work reflects much of the visual excitement of late 19th century Paris with its bars, cabarets and circuses; he also associated with many of the literary-artistic figures of the time, such as Oscar Wilde and Aubrey Beardsley.

What famous picture was sold on 5 July 1984 for a record price of £7,300,000?
Seascape: Folkestone, which was painted by J. M. W. Turner (1775–1851), one of the greatest of all British artists. The picture had belonged to Lord Clark, the famous art historian, whose sons had to sell it to pay death duties on their father's estate.

Who painted *The Laughing Cavalier*?
This is the best known work of Frans Hals (1581–1666), perhaps the greatest Dutch portrait painter after Rembrandt.

What English city lent its name to a school of landscape artists?
The Norwich Society of Artists organized by John Crome the elder, or 'Old Crome', in 1803, is better known now as the Norwich School. His son John Bernay Crome, John Sell Cotman, James Stark and Joseph Stannard were also members of the Society. A large proportion of their works may still be seen in the galleries of the Norwich Castle museum.

Little Quiz 19
  Of which countries were these the rulers?
  1. Pedro the Cruel
  2. Charles the Bold
  3. Canute the Great
  4. Philip Augustus
  5. Ethelred the Unready
  6. Rhodri Mawr
  7. Henri Christophe
  8. Ch'ien Lung
  9. Tutankhamen
  10. Cetewayo

What is magma?
It is very hot molten matter underneath solid rock.

What is lava?
It is magma that is shot out onto the surface when the Earth's crust is ruptured by volcanic action.

What is the Earth's crust?
It is the outer 'skin' of the Earth, and is anything from about 6 km to 70 km (3 to 43 miles) deep.

What are metamorphic rocks?
They are hard, solid rocks whose composition or texture have been altered by heat or pressure in the Earth.

What are sedimentary rocks?
They are rocks formed out of layers of sediment bonded together.

What is loess?
It is a fine yellowish dust or silt spread and deposited by the winds in the interior of central Asia, in parts of Europe and in North America (especially the United States). This material is very fertile.

What is alluvium?
It is a mixture of silt, sand and gravel deposited by flowing water, such as rivers and streams.

Where is the Continental Shelf?
It is a shelf or ledge round the Earth's continents, that continues descending very gradually under the water edging the continents. When it reaches 182.8 m (100 fathoms) or so, the ledge drops sharply to deep ocean.

What were Continental drifts?
It is believed that the Earth's present continents were formed when two huge continents broke up into smaller parts by a very slow drifting process.

Where is the Great Rift Valley?
It is a long valley in the Near East and East Africa, created by the landmass having sunk between two geological faults, or breaks in the Earth's crust. The Rift runs from Syria down to Zimbabwe.

What is an estuary?
It is the part of a river near the coast into which the sea flows.

Where are the pampas?
They are huge areas of grassland totally without trees in South America, especially around the estuary of the River Plate.

Where is the Great Barrier Reef?
It is a huge coral reef off the north-east coast of Australia.

What are Zones of Latitude?
The Frigid Zones, within the Arctic and the Antarctic circles, the Torrid Zone in the region north and south of the Equator and including the Equator, and the Temperate Zones, those areas between.

What is savanna?
It is tropical grassland which has tree clumps scattered about it.

What is a flood plain?
It is the floor of a valley that is regularly flooded by a river and which receives a layer of alluvium each time.

Where are the Roaring Forties?
They are areas of ocean, south of about latitude 40° South, in which the prevailing winds come from the north-west to west, and blow fiercely more or less all the time.

What is tundra?
Tundra is the name given to areas of land in the higher latitudes where short, cool summers do not permit trees to grow.

The frost which grips the tundra for much of the year does melt sufficiently to allow carpets of bright flowers, mosses and lichens to grow, and the whole area attracts a wealth of insect, bird and animal life. Much of Siberia and Canada are covered by tundra, as is the coast of Greenland and parts of Iceland; in the southern hemisphere tundra is restricted to the extreme south of South America and a few isolated islands.

What are moraines?
Moraines consist of material borne along by, beneath or within glaciers. This debris has been worn away from the Earth's surface by the action of the ice, or has merely fallen onto it. If the glacier becomes stationary, this material is left as a 'terminal' moraine. When a particular glacier has terminated at a number of positions throughout its long history, such spots are marked by 'recessional' moraines – each one having once been a 'terminal' moraine.

What is seismology?
The study of earthquakes and the waves of energy generated by them. It is an aim of seismologists to work towards accurate predictions of earthquakes, thus avoiding loss of life and material damage.

What is a mesa?
This is a flat-topped hill or mountain left isolated by the erosion of softer rocks all round it. Mesas are common in the south-western United States and can often be seen in 'Western' films. Masada in Israel is a mesa made famous by its defence by Jews against the Romans in the 70s.

What is a nunatak?
A hill or peak sticking through an ice cap, mostly found in Greenland or Antarctica. It is an Eskimo word.

What is a fumarole?
A vent in the Earth's surface which emits steam and gases, essentially associated with volcanic regions. The best known fumaroles are situated in California, Alaska and Iceland.

What is an oxbow lake?
Currents of a slow moving river meandering across a flood plain dictate that eventually the channel will cut through the neck of each meander. When this occurs, the ends of the abandoned loop silt up to leave a crescent-shaped, oxbow lake. In time, it too silts up and becomes a marsh.

Volcano erupting

2, 5, 7...

Who were the Twelve Apostles?
They were the twelve disciples of Jesus, namely, Simon Peter, Andrew, James, John, Philip, Bartholomew, Matthew, Thomas, James son of Alphaeus, Simon Zelotes, Judas (brother of James) and Judas Iscariot (who later betrayed Jesus).

Who were the Gang of Four in politics?
They were former Cabinet ministers in the Labour Party who in 1981 founded the Social Democratic Party, and were Roy Jenkins, Shirley Williams, David Owen and William Rodgers.

How long did the Hundred Years' War really last?
Of course the fighting did not last all the time, but the war began in 1337 and only ended in 1453. It was the struggle between England and France for the throne of France.

When was the Six Day War?
It was a lightning strike by Israeli forces against Egypt early in June 1967, in an attempt to prevent Egypt and other Arab countries attacking them. The Israelis caught the Egyptian army and air force unprepared and within six days had reached and taken the east bank of the Suez Canal.

What happened at 11.00 am on the 11th day of the 11th month of 1918?
World War I officially came to an end by an armistice which was ordered to start from that moment.

Who was the Third Man in British fiction?
It was Harry Lime, an unscrupulous racketeer who made money out of the distress of the defeated German and Austrian people after World War II. He was the 'hero' of a story by Graham Greene, which was made into a most successful film in 1949.

In what sports does the cry 'Seconds Out' occur?
In boxing or wrestling. Contestants are attended by seconds, or helpers, who assist them in the intervals between fighting bouts. Seconds are told to get out of the ring before a fresh round starts.

When was the Six Weeks' War?
1866, a short war between Prussia and the Austria-Hungarian Empire, which Prussia won as a result of the victory at the battle of Sadowa.

Why did people in England in 1752 say 'Give us back our eleven days'?
In September 1752, it was decided to correct the calendar in Britain which had already been corrected everywhere else in Europe in 1582, and which had slipped by about eleven days. September 3rd was changed to September 14th, the next day September 15th and so on. But many people felt they had been cheated.

Who were The Few?
They were the pilots of RAF fighter planes, who in the days of the Battle of Britain, 1940, shot down hundreds of German fighters and bombers, thus denying the German air force the air supremacy it needed to ensure that Hitler's projected invasion of Britain could be successful. The term comes from Winston Churchill's tribute to the pilots – 'Never in the field of human conflict was so much owed by so many to so few.'

What is a baker's dozen?
13.

What does being at sixes and sevens mean?
It means being in a state of considerable confusion.

What was a four-in-hand?
A carriage drawn by four horses and driven by one person.

What is the 64,000 Dollar Question?
Originally, it was the top prize on an American TV quiz game in which a contestant could win up to that sum of money in stages, by answering correctly questions put to him. The phrase has come to mean 'the important question'.

What is a nine-days' wonder?
Something that creates sensational interest for a short time and then is forgotten.

What is talking nineteen to the dozen?
A phrase meaning to talk incessantly.

How many eyes did the Cyclops have?
One, in the middle of his forehead.

Who were the Three Musketeers?
Athos, Porthos and Aramis in the novel by Alexandre Dumas.

What was 'the Fifteen'?
An unsuccessful attempt by James Edward Stuart, the Old Pretender, to gain with the help of the Jacobites, the throne of England in 1715.

Who were the Five Members?
They were five members of Parliament whom, in 1642, the king, Charles I, attempted to arrest in the House of Commons for opposing him. They were John Pym, John Hampden, Arthur Haselrig, Denzil Holles and William Strode.

What was the Five Mile Act of 1665?
Because the established church priests abandoned their churches during the Great Plague, non-conformist ministers took them over. This angered the established churchmen so much they persuaded Parliament to pass this act ordering these ministers not to go within five miles of their churches or of any town where they might have preached.

What was the Seven Years' War about?
Fought between 1756 and 1763, with Britain and Prussia on one side against France, Austria and Russia on the other, it was a conflict over Prussian aggression in Europe and rivalry between Britain and France in India and North America.

What were the Six Acts?
These were tough, repressive laws introduced in 1819 to prevent rioting among the working classes. There was much distress among the workers in the newly industrialized parts of the country, about which the government did nothing. The acts enabled the authorities to search houses for arms, to ban printed propaganda and protests etc.

Where is the 38th Parallel?
It is the border between North and South Korea as determined at the Potsdam Conference between the victorious allies at the end of World War II in 1945.

When is Twelfth Night?
It is the evening of the twelfth day after Christmas Day, and in the Christian calendar is the Feast of the Epiphany. On that day it is usual to take down Christmas decorations and cards.

What was the Third Estate in France?
A term describing the various classes in pre-Revolutionary France below the nobility and the clergy. The third estate paid almost all taxes.

What were Luther's 95 Theses?
These were the complaints Luther had against the practices of the orthodox church in Europe, and in 1517, he listed them in some detail and nailed the sheets of paper to the doors of Wittenburg Cathedral. This is often taken to be the starting point of the Reformation.

What is the origin of boxing?
The ancient Greeks used to box with bare hands, though it is not known for certain if they staged special bouts in their Olympic or other games.

When did boxing become organized in Britain?
In 1719 James Figg opened a stadium in Oxford Street in London where among other things boxing bouts were put on. Incidentally, Figg also gave coaching in the sport.

When were gloves first used for boxing?
In the mid-18th century, John Broughton, once champion prize fighter of England, began to use bandaging to protect his hands for practice purposes. Gloves began to be worn in contests on a wide scale after the introduction of the Queensberry Rules in 1867, which included regulations on gloves.

What were the Queensberry Rules?
In the 19th century boxing had become a most brutal sport, with fighters hammering each other for hours on end, often encouraged by heavy betting on the outcome. In 1866 the 8th Marquis of Queensberry and some associates drew up a set of rules. These eliminated fouls, introduced points scoring and limited rounds to three minutes and made glove-wearing obligatory. These rules, with few amendments, have governed the sport ever since.

What was the particular winning punch of Britain's Henry Cooper?
His left hook, known as 'Enery's 'ammer', with which he floored many opponents. He once put the world's greatest boxer of the day, Muhammad Ali, on the floor with such a punch. Cooper was British heavyweight champion for ten years (1959–69) and again 1970–71.

Who was Jack Dempsey?
One of the most popular world heavyweight champions, he was born in Colorado, USA in 1895. He won the world heavyweight championship in 1919 and held it until 1926 when he was knocked out by the challenger Gene Tunney.

What is the maximum weight allowed for a boxer to be admitted to the featherweight class?
Nine stone.

Who was the only British-born boxer to win the world heavyweight title?
Bob Fitzsimmons.

What are the correct dimensions of a boxing ring?
Boxing rings are not exactly the same size everywhere, but the rules state they should be between 1.3 and 1.86 m square (14 and 20 ft square), must have three horizontal ropes on the four sides and properly padded corner posts.

Which body governs the sport of professional boxing throughout the world?
The World Boxing Council, founded in 1963.

How many rounds should be boxed for a world title fight?
Unless one contestant is knocked out or the referee stops the contest, the fight should go for 15 rounds of 3 minutes each.

Who was Freddie Mills?
He was a British light heavyweight champion who won the World Championship in 1948. He was challenged in 1950 and beaten by Joey Maxim, and then retired to run a restaurant in London. Freddie Mills was murdered in a gangland quarrel in London in 1965.

How many challenges to his world heavyweight title did Joe Louis defeat?

Joe Louis became world heavyweight champion in 1937 when he was twenty-three, and he held it for twelve years against twenty-five challengers. In the end he retired undefeated, but made a come-back a few years later, himself to challenge another world champion, Rocky Marciano, but he was knocked out.

What happened to Rocky Marciano?

He was a most remarkable heavyweight boxer who became world champion in 1952, held it against six challengers and then retired. He was killed in an aeroplane crash in 1969.

Who taught the poet Byron to box?

John Jackson (1769–1845), who had been British Boxing Champion from 1795 to 1803.

Why was Muhammad Ali stripped of his World Heavyweight title?

Because he was called up and refused to serve in the US Army in Vietnam. He had been boxing as Cassius Clay, but he adopted the Muslim faith and changed his name to Muhammad Ali. This did not absolve him from military service.

Who defeated the American world champion Sugar Ray Robinson?

Randolph Turpin, British middleweight, in London in 1951, by beating Robinson on points. Just two months later, Turpin had to meet a return challenge by Robinson and lost when the referee stopped the fight towards the end.

Who was the oldest man to win a world championship?

Bob Fitzsimmons, the English-born New Zealander, won the light-heavyweight title in 1903 aged 40 years and six months. He outpointed George Gardner over 20 rounds.

Who was the heaviest heavyweight world champion?

Italy's Primo Carnera, who weighed just over 19 stone.

When was the last prize ring world title bout fought?

On 8 July 1889 at Richberg, Mississippi, when John L. Sullivan beat Jake Kilrain over 75 rounds.

Which British monarch first showed an interest in boxing?

George I, who set up a 'Ring' for the populace in Hyde Park in 1723.

When was Muhammed Ali's first professional defeat?

On 8 March 1971, when Joe Frazier beat him on points at Madison Square Gardens, New York. Ali did, however, win two subsequent fights with Frazier.

What championships has John Conteh held and when did he retire from the ring?

From 1973 to 1978, Conteh gained the British, Commonwealth, European and World light-heavyweight titles (World Boxing Council). After losing the latter body's recognition as champion, he tried to regain a title but won no more fights. He retired from boxing in 1980.

Little Quiz 20

What are the manufacturing nations of these motor cars?

1. Citroën
2. Lada
3. Buick
4. Ferrari
5. Datsun
6. Skoda
7. DAF
8. BMW
9. AC
10. Saab

When was the first photograph printed?
In 1826, by Nicéphore Niepce (1765–1833), a French amateur scientist. He began to make copies of drawings by contact printing in about 1822, and four years later produced the first photograph from nature on a bitumen covered plate.

What was the Daguerreotype process?
It was the earliest practical method of photography whereby a positive image could be produced upon a silvered plate. It needed between 15 and 30 minutes' exposure for brightly lit views. The process was introduced by Louis Daguerre (1787–1851), also French, who had been in partnership with Niepce to develop the latter's process.

What is a fish-eye lens?
It is a very wide-angle lens capable of covering at least 100° of viewing, but it produces pictures which are distorted at the edges.

What is hypo?
It is sodium thiosulphate (once called sodium hyposulphite), a chemical in solution which is used for fixing photographs after developing. The chemical was introduced in 1839.

What is the origin of the word Kodak?
It was a word invented as a trade mark by George Eastman (1854–1932), the American amateur photographer who introduced the first simple camera for the amateur in 1888. The name was thought to be easily remembered or pronounced in any language.

What other process did Eastman introduce with his Kodak popular camera?
Developing & Printing (D & P) service, which was offered to customers buying his films.

What is the aperture of a camera lens?
It is the hole that regulates the amount of light coming in through a lens, affecting the brightness of the image and it can be varied in size.

What does it mean to retouch a negative or print?
It means to improve it by removing blemishes, creases and scratches by using a fine brush or pencil.

What is photogravure?
A process for printing in ink by mechanical means from an etched plate.

What is the origin of the word photography?
From the two Greek words, *photos* (light) and *grapho* (I write), which when combined were to mean 'writing by means of light'. The term was coined by Sir John Herschel in discussions with William Fox Talbot, the British photography pioneer, probably in 1839.

What was Fox Talbot's contribution to photography?
He made many, but perhaps the most significant was producing the first permanent photographic negative on photographic paper, which he patented in 1841 as the Calotype process.

Who was Julia Margaret Cameron?
She was an eccentric, wealthy amateur photographer of the mid-Victorian period who lived for a time in the Isle of Wight, near the poet Tennyson. She took numerous photographs of celebrities which were striking in the way they caught the sitter's personality.

What is a telephoto lens?
It is a long-focus lens which provides a large image of a distant object or individual, rather like the image produced in a telescope.

Why do you have to wash photographs during the printing process?

To remove all unwanted chemicals and reduce the risk of unexpected chemical reactions taking place.

When did the twin-lens reflex Rolleiflex camera first appear?

In 1928, as a German invention.

Early Rolleiflex camera

How does an exposure meter work?

It converts light into electric current, by means of an electric cell. The apparatus measures the intensity of light in the area in which the picture is to be taken, to allow the photographer to adjust the aperture.

What is panchromatic film?

It is black-and-white film whose photographic emulsions (that is, light-sensitive salts in gelatin) are equally sensitive to every colour, thus producing the differences in correct tones of darkness and light.

When was the first flash-bulb produced?

In 1929, and it was devised for newspaper photographers.

Why do people still talk about black and white prints as bromides?

Because the process of using photographic paper covered with silver bromide in a gelatinous base for printing black and white pictures is still being used, nearly 120 years after its invention.

What was Peter Henry Emerson's major contribution to photography?

Emerson (1856–1936) led a revival of nature photography. He is particularly noted for his studies of the life and landscape of the Norfolk Broads, where he worked over a ten-year period in the late 19th century.

Little Quiz 21

What do the following abbreviations stand for?

1. DNA	21. pp
2. HMSO	22. lbw
3. CIA	23. oz
4. SS	24. cc
5. UCH	25. ie
6. Bart or (Bt)	26. inst.
7. OUDS	27. etc.
8. CUP	28. mph
9. NUS	29. rpm
10. Litt. D	30. bhp
11. LJ	31. ca.
12. ICBM	32. cwt
13. JFK	33. aux
14. SJ	34. non seq
15. RAM	35. pub
16. NSPCC	36. pa
17. MFH	37. del
18. IOW	38. v
19. TT	39. CID
20. op. cit	40. Ky

Who founded the Cistercian Order of monks?
The abbot of Molesmes, Robert of Champagne, who established a monastery at Cîteaux in 1098. He aimed to bring his community back to the disciplines of the Benedictine Order. Cistercian monasteries were famous for their interest and skill in agriculture.

Who was Bernard of Clairvaux?
A Cistercian monk who was at Cîteaux from 1112 to 1115. Then he left to found a new monastery at Clairvaux, of which he became abbot. Bernard (1090–1153) promoted the Cistercian order throughout France and other parts of west Europe, wrote numerous letters, sermons and tracts, introduced the Cistercians to England, and was regarded as the most influential theologian of his day in Europe.

Why was Fountains Abbey so called?
The Cistercian abbey was called Fountains because the site lies in a part of the Skell valley in North Yorkshire which contains springs of good water as well as the river itself. The abbey was dedicated to St Mary by the Springs, in Latin, *Sancta Maria de Fontibus*.

Who was Charles Martel?
Charles Martel (c.688–741), a royal duke of the Franks governed part of the Frankish kingdom from about 717 to about 731, in which year he became king of all the Franks. In 732 Charles defeated a huge Arab army near Poitiers in a great victory which effectively stopped the advance of Islam into West Europe. Martel was a nickname meaning Hammer.

Which is the first identifiable stone castle in France?
The castle of Doué la Fontaine. It was built by Theobald, Count of Blois, about 950.

What was the Great Schism?
It is the title given to the period in European history when there were two rival parties in the Christian Church supporting their own candidates for the office of pope (from 1378 to 1417). Urban VI had been chosen in 1378 and recognized by most of western Europe, but France and some German states refused to accept him. The French chose another man, who became Clement VII and he reigned at Avignon in southern France. The split lasted until 1417 when both sides accepted the election of Martin V at Rome.

What was the objective of the First Crusade?
To recover the Holy Land (Palestine) from the Seljuk Turks. The Crusade was announced in 1095 by Pope Urban II and a multi-national European army set out for the Near East. The Crusaders set up several small states in Syria and Palestine and captured Jerusalem in 1099.

Where did the Seljuk Turks come from?
They were a warlike group of tribes from central Russia who in the 1040s, under their leader Tughril Beg, began to invade Moslem lands in the Near East. They overran all Persia by about 1060, and moved into Asia Minor.

Who were the Toltecs?
They were people who established a powerful state in the southern narrowing neck of Mexico in the 10th to 12th centuries. They were great builders, and left behind among their splendid monuments the Temple of the Warriors at Chichen Itza.

What was the Battle of Manzikert?
It was a great battle between the Byzantine army led by the Byzantine emperor Romanus IV and the Seljuks

under their leader Arslan, nephew of Tughril Beg, in 1071. The Seljuks were triumphant, and captured Romanus, whom they later released. Manzikert is in Armenia, near Lake Van.

When was Greenland discovered and colonized?
In the 980s, by Eric the Red, a Viking warrior from Iceland who was on the run for murder. He spent several years founding a settlement.

What was the Swiss Confederation of 1291?
An alliance between three of the largest cantons south of Lake Lucerne formed to resist dominion over them by the Habsburgs. This was perhaps the first move towards the eventual creation of the independent Swiss grouping of cantons which has become Switzerland.

When did the Inca civilization in Peru begin to flourish?
It is not easy to be precise, but in the 13th century, Andean people organized themselves into a coherent state, with a capital at Cuzco, 3400 m (11,160 ft) high up in the Andes mountains. Their ruler was called the Inca and to him they accorded absolute power.

What happened at the battle of Largs in 1263?
Largs is in Strathclyde in Scotland. Here in 1263 Alexander III (1249–1286) roundly defeated the Viking chief Haakon in a battle at sea and on land. The result was that the Hebrides, hitherto held by the Vikings, passed into Scottish hands. It was also the beginning of the end of Viking power in the other remoter parts of Scotland.

What was Edward I's Model Parliament?
This was a parliament called by Edward I in 1295 chiefly to grant funds to carry on his wars, especially in France. Out of it emerged the doctrine 'what touches all should be approved by all', a phrase perhaps uttered by the king himself.

What was Tenochtitlan?
It was a splendid city built in the early 14th century on an island in Lake Texcoco by the Aztecs of central Mexico. The city was eventually destroyed by Hernan Cortés in the Spanish invasion of Mexico, 1519–21.

When was there a previous civilization of Zimbabwe?
From about 800 to about 1500, when a Bantu-dominated state flourished in south-east Africa, erected splendid buildings including an acropolis and several temples, and kept its enemies at bay.

What was the Statute of Labourers?
The first assault of the Black Death upon England, 1348–9, severely depleted the national labour force. After it, the survivors found they could press for higher wages because of the increased need for their services. The statute was intended to compel them to accept payment at the rate they had had before the plague. It contributed to the general revolt of the peasants in 1381.

What was the Statute of Kilkenny, of 1366?
It was an attempt by the English government to prevent the English colony round Dublin in Ireland, an area known as The Pale, from becoming too friendly with the native Irish. The statute aimed to keep the two races apart by stopping inter-marriage, by making it compulsory to use English in the colony and by imposing English law. The statute, however, proved very difficult to enforce, and in the later years of the 14th century and the 15th century, more forceful measures were necessary.

What two works are attributed to Homer?

The *Iliad* and the *Odyssey*. The *Iliad* tells the story of the Trojan War and the *Odyssey* describes the adventures of Odysseus, King of Ithaca, one of the Greek commanders at the war, who took ten years to get home after the war was over.

What kind of play did Aristophanes write?

Aristophanes (c. 450–c. 380 BC), the Athenian playwright, mostly wrote comedies, many of a strongly satirical nature. His output was over 40 plays, among the best known being *The Birds*, *The Frogs*, and *Lysistrata*.

Who is considered Germany's greatest poet and dramatist?

Johann Wolfgang von Goethe (1749–1832) who started his career as a lawyer. Goethe's most famous works were *Faust*, *Götz von Berlichingen*, and *Iphigenie*.

What is the main theme of the novel *War and Peace*?

War and Peace, by Count Leo Tolstoy (1828–1910), is about the Napoleonic invasion of Russia, 1812–13.

Which great British writer refused a peerage and the OM?

George Bernard Shaw (1856–1950), Irish-born playwright, political writer, philosopher and essayist, who claimed to have invented Communism (along with Sidney and Beatrice Webb and others) and who disliked titles and honours. He accepted the Nobel Prize for literature in 1925.

Which Dickens character said 'Please, Sir, I want some more'.

Oliver Twist, in the novel of that name, first published in 1837–9. The young boy Oliver Twist, who was at an orphanage, was asking for a second helping of gruel.

Who was Rabindranath Tagore?

Sir Rabindranath Tagore (1861–1941) was an Indian poet and philosopher who founded an international university to bridge the divide between Eastern and Western thought and education. He wrote poetry, plays and novels, political and philosophical treatises, and was also a fervent supporter of Indian nationalism. He was awarded the Nobel Prize for literature in 1913.

What did William McGonagall write?

He was the son of an Irish weaver, who lived in Scotland in the later 19th century. His very bad verse was in what is called doggerel, that is, in irregular verse measure, and was composed in great quantity, often to celebrate events of the times. He used to publish it in broadsheets, read it out in public houses and on stage and it never failed to entertain.

What was Molière's main contribution to literature?

Jean Baptiste Poquelin (1622–1673), known as Molière, founded his own theatrical company in Paris and wrote plays for it to perform. These plays were in the main comedies, but they were also attacks upon the worst aspects of high society. Molière discarded formal Greek style comedy plots and constructed situations which were relevant to his own times, which he highlighted through sharp exposure of hypocrisy.

Which was Oscar Wilde's most successful comedy?

The Importance of Being Earnest. This was written in 1894 and produced in 1895. The play is one of the finest comedies in the English language.

Who was Pirandello?

Luigi Pirandello (1867–1936) was a remarkable Italian playwright and novelist, who won the Nobel Prize for literature in 1934. Among his many plays was *Six Characters in Search of an Author*, considered one of the best plays of the 1920s.

What was the theme of Ernest Hemingway's novel *For Whom the Bell Tolls*?
The story is set during the Spanish Civil War (1936–1939), and the principal characters are on the side of the Republicans who were eventually defeated by General Franco.

What was *Murder in the Cathedral*?
This is the title of a play in verse by Thomas Stearns Eliot (1888–1965), American-born poet and playwright who was naturalized British in 1927. The play is about the murder of Thomas Becket, archbishop of Canterbury, at the cathedral in December 1170.

What was a 'miracle' play?
A religious play put on in medieval times. The plot was centred on the life of a saint or a story from the Scriptures. Miracle plays were put on at festivals such as Easter. As a dramatic form, these plays developed into cycles of plays on a series of themes.

What is the theme of the principal novels of P. C. Wren?
Percival Christopher Wren (1885–1941) produced a number of novels about life in the Foreign Legion.

Who wrote *Pride and Prejudice*?
Jane Austen (1775–1817).

Who wrote the *Forsyte Saga* and what are its components?
John Galsworthy (1867–1933). The saga essentially consists of the novels *A Man of Property* (1906), *In Chancery* (1920) and *To Let* (1921). These together with two short pieces entitled *The Indian Summer of a Forsyte* and *The*

Awakening, were brought together, appearing as the *Forsyte Saga* in 1922. Two further Forsyte stories, *A Modern Comedy* and *End of the Chapter*, appeared in 1929 and 1933, respectively.

Who was Joseph Sheridan Le Fanu?
Le Fanu (1814–1873), a great-grand-nephew of Richard Brinsley Sheridan wrote mystery novels and short stories which often had a strong macabre element. His best known work was *Uncle Silas*.

Little Quiz 22
  What is the word for the person who – ?
1. joins steel plates together by melting with a blow-torch
2. sells newspapers, magazines, writing equipment, etc.
3. specializes in bird life studies
4. rings bells in church
5. works on steeples and chimneys to carry out repairs etc.
6. makes ironwork objects in a forge
7. fits shoes on horses
8. sells supplies for boats, ships, etc.
9. rides horses in flat races and steeplechases
10. pilots or travels in a spaceship
11. looks after the passengers and money on board ship
12. sells ribbons, buttons, hooks, tape etc.
13. repairs boots and shoes
14. draws maps
15. fabricates or mends locks
16. treats patients with mental or emotional troubles
17. grinds wheat, barley and other cereals
18. cuts or blasts rock or stone out of the ground
19. studies elections and voting patterns
20. loads and unloads ships

Where can Rodin's *Le Baiser* (The Kiss) be seen?
In the Tate Gallery, London.

Donatello was a sculptor of the 15th century to whom Michelangelo was indebted. They both did sculptures of a famous Biblical character. Who was it?
David, king of Israel.

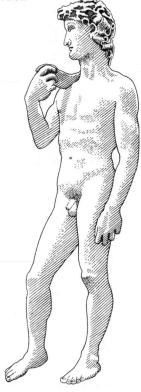

Statue of David by Michelangelo

Why did Degas turn to wax and bronze figure sculpture?
The great Impressionist painter began to lose his eyesight in his later years.

Early sculpture was done from wood and stone. What other materials are commonly used today?
Bronze and lead.

What famous Florentine goldsmith and sculptor wrote an autobiography which is still read today?
Benvenuto Cellini (1500–1571).

What is the word for the structure on which a sculptor puts his clay?
An armature.

Picasso's early painting was influenced by examples of primitive sculpture. From which country in particular?
Negro sculpture from the Ivory Coast.

What is the difference between relief sculpture and intaglio?
In the first the image is raised from the material used, and in the second it is carved out of it.

Who made the bronze doors to the baptistery at Florence Cathedral?
Lorenzo Ghiberti (1378–1455). The doors took nearly half a century to complete and Michelangelo described them as 'the gates of Paradise'.

When does a sculptor make a plaster cast?
When a piece of sculpture has not been directly carved and is to be cast in metal.

Where are these three famous sculptures executed by the artist Jacob Epstein (1880–1959); *The Rima; Christ in Majesty; St Michael and the Devil*?
Hyde Park, London; Llandaff Cathedral, Wales; Coventry Cathedral.

What other art form most resembles sculpture?
Collage, because it is done by the application of many varied materials to make a picture.

What is the 'Laocoon'?
A Hellenistic statue of the agonies of

Laocoon and his sons being crushed to death by serpents. It was discovered in 1506.

What happened to the *Unknown Political Prisoner*?
This was an almost abstract sculpture executed by Reg Butler representing an unknown political prisoner. It was exhibited in 1953 and won a major competition prize. But it gave offence to many former victims of persecution in Europe under the communist group of powers, and one refugee smashed the sculpture in a moment of anger.

Who is regarded as the greatest modern British sculptor?
Henry Moore (b 1898) OM, CH.

Who executed the recumbent statue of Lord Kitchener in St Paul's Cathedral in London?
Sir William Reid Dick.

What is a mobile?
It is a form of sculpture whose component parts are suspended from a ceiling or pole and which move more or less continuously in the varying air currents around it.

What was Eric Gill's major contribution to sculpture?
Gill (1882–1940) was most famous for his bas-reliefs, often in the form of friezes. Such work can be seen on many buildings throughout the world.

What woman has made the greatest contribution to sculpture in the 20th century?
Without doubt, Barbara Hepworth (1903–1975), D.B.E. A near contemporary of Henry Moore, Barbara Hepworth has concentrated far less on purely figurative themes. In 1939 she moved to St Ives, Cornwall, a much favoured resort of artists working in a wide range of media, spending the rest of her life there. Equally skilled with stone and with wood, her forms in the latter medium were often threaded with string or painted.

Who was Moholy-Nagy?
Laszlo Moholy-Nagy (1895–1946) had been a Hungarian law student who took up painting and drawing while convalescing from wounds received in World War I. Later moving to Berlin, he turned his attention to solids, and after an exhibition of his work there in 1922 he was invited to teach at the famous Bauhaus Academy. He became particularly concerned with the relationship between the artist and the space surrounding his work, which ideas he expressed in his book, *From Materials to Architecture*. After moving to the United States in 1937 to found a New Bauhaus in Chicago, he became fascinated with the properties of a type of plastic called *Plexiglass*.

What is a maquette?
It is a preliminary wax or clay sketch for a sculpture.

Little Quiz 23
   What are the homes of these animals?
   1. hares
   2. foxes
   3. wasps
   4. bees
   5. badgers
   6. squirrels
   7. wolves
   8. eagles
   9. spiders
   10. rabbits

What is the Gold Standard?
A monetary standard in which the basic unit of currency is defined by a quantity of gold of agreed fineness, usually marked by coinage of gold and free conversion of other moneys into gold.

When did pound notes first come into circulation?
In 1914. Previously, people used gold sovereigns.

What is dollar diplomacy?
A diplomatic policy centred on furthering a nation's financial and commercial interests abroad.

Which were the main monetary units of the Roman Empire?
The gold *aureus*, the silver *denarius*, the bronze or brass *sestertius* and the copper *as*.

What does 'catchpenny' mean?
Worthless.

When did the *franc* become the French monetary unit?
In the mid-14th century. Francorum Rex (king of the Franks) began to be inscribed on coinage.

How many groats were there to a pound?
A groat was about 4 old pence, so there were 60 groats to £1.

What do we mean when we get something 'buckshee'?
We can have it free. It comes from the Arabic *baksheesh*.

What is a debenture?
It is a document stating that a company has borrowed money from an individual in return for interest on the money. Interest on debentures has to be paid out before any shareholders are paid their dividends.

What was a doubloon?
An old Spanish gold coin, worth variously between £1 and £1.50 in the money of the time.

How does a cheque 'bounce'?
If you write a cheque on your current account at the bank when you have no money in the account, and no arrangement with the bank manager for borrowing, the cheque is liable to be marked in red when it comes to your bank for passing, with the words 'Refer to Drawer', and the money entered on the cheque will not be paid. Refer to Drawer means ask the drawer to pay by some other means!

What is the Exchange Rate?
The value of one country's currency in relation to that of another.

What is an annuity?
It is a payment of a sum of money every year to a person as a result of an investment or as a kind of special pension.

What happens if a company goes into liquidation?
Briefly, the company is wound up (that is, operations are stopped) and the assets are sold to help pay the debts. If there should be any surplus after all debts are paid, the company owners receive it.

What is inflation?
It is a situation where prices rise at a rate that reduces the buying power of money sharply, often leading employed people to press for higher wages to meet the growing cost of living.

In what year did inflation reach a post-war peak of 26%?
1975.

What is the National Debt?
It is the amount of money owed by a

government, generally in the form of bonds paying interest which are issued to raise cash to balance, or attempt to balance, a budget, or to provide money for emergencies such as war, famine, drought, flood, civil commotion and so forth.

When did England first introduce its National Debt?
In 1693, during the reign of William III and Mary II, when stock was issued to raise £1,000,000 to continue the war with France.

What does GNP mean?
Gross National Product. It is a figure that represents the total market value of all goods and services produced by a country over a period, usually calculated over a year.

What does it mean to devalue a currency?
It means lowering the currency value of a country against those currency values of other countries.

What is the origin of the three gold balls that are usually suspended over the shop front of a pawnbroker's business?
They were the symbol used by the famous Lombard bankers of the medieval period, who lent money (usually at high interest rates) to kings, princes, counts and other rulers for various purposes, notably for waging wars.

What is a 'pony' and what is a 'monkey'?
Slang words, mostly current amongst the betting fraternity, for £25 and £500 respectively.

What was a 'tanner'?
A silver coin, representing 6 old pence but used after the decimalization of British coinage on 15 February 1971 to

represent the precise equivalent of $2\frac{1}{2}$ new pence. It has now been withdrawn from circulation.

What coins minted prior to decimalization are still legal tender in Britain?
One shilling and two shilling pieces, which have precise decimal coinage equivalents of 5p and 10p.

Ind Imp used to appear on British coins. What did it mean?
This was an abbreviation for *Indiae Imperatrix* or *Imperator*: British monarchs had the title Empress or Emperor of India from 1876 until 1948.

When were coins specifically minted for a British territory overseas?
Four denominations of coins, 2d, 3d, 6d and 1s, were struck for circulation in the Somers Islands about 1616. They were collectively known as 'Hog Money', their obverse sides all bearing a representation of a hog – an animal which had earlier been beached upon these islands in small numbers, and had since greatly multiplied. The Somers Islands were later renamed the Bermudas, after the Spanish explorer Juan Bermudez who had discovered them in the 16th century.

Little Quiz 24
  Shapes
  How many sides has a – ?
1. pentagon
2. decagon
3. triangle
4. rhombus
5. isosceles triangle
6. dodecahedron
7. prism
8. cuboid
9. pyramid

What are the main recognition features of mayflies?

They have two or three long tails, one or two pairs of wings, the hind wings if present being much smaller than the front ones. They also have short antennae.

What is a stick insect?

A long thin insect with long legs, looking like a tiny stick (or in some non-European species, like a leaf). Stick insects are green or brown in varying shades. Stick insects are not common in Europe, and the European kinds usually have no wings.

Why are earwigs so called?

They are longish brown insects with short wings, as a rule easily identified. It used to be thought they crawled into the ears of sleeping human beings and chewed their way through the ear-drums.

Why are cockroaches unpopular?

Cockroaches tend to seek out warm areas, usually travelling at night time, and rest during the day, hidden under floorboards or behind dados or in air ducts. They tend to stay there and multiply, coming out from time to time to look for scraps. They create an unpleasant smell which is associated with rotting food, and so they can probably spread germs.

What sort of material do termites eat?

Termites have biting mouths, and are very destructive. They go for the wood of trees, shrubs, and houses where there are old timbers.

Why are book lice so called?

They are wingless insects which like to live among materials like old paper, where they feed upon moulds that grow there.

What are the antennae of an insect used for?

They are two sensory organs projecting from the head, which act as feelers.

How many species of insect are there in the United Kingdom?

Over 20,000.

What is a larva?

It is a baby insect, distinguishable from its parents because it is different in shape. A good example is the caterpillar, which is the larva of a moth or butterfly.

Which is the biggest flea you are likely to meet in Britain?

The mole flea, which is more than $\frac{1}{2}$ cm ($\frac{1}{4}$ in) long.

What is the human flea?

This is a species of flea called *Pulex irritans*. It is well known for being able to hop as far as 0.305 m (1 ft).

What is the largest order of insects?

The beetle order, of which there are said to be more than $\frac{1}{4}$ million species, 4000 of which are distinguishable in the UK.

What are the distinguishing features of a dragonfly?

It is a long-bodied insect, with two pairs of wings whose network of veins is readily visible, and which has two very big compound eyes (that have thousands of facets). The colouring of a dragonfly is most striking and often extremely beautiful.

What is the chief characteristic of bumble bees?

They make a loud humming noise when in flight.

What do the springtail, bristletail and silverfish have in common?

They are all primitive insects without wings.

What are the whirligig beetles?

They are beetles of the Gyrinidae family which spend their lives skimming around on the surface of still or gently moving water. They are small, shiny, black, and they dive into the water when disturbed or when in search of food.

What sort of food do grasshoppers eat?

They depend chiefly on grass, and on some other plant life.

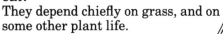
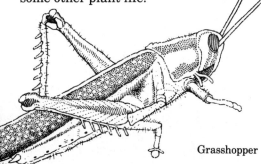

Grasshopper

How does a mole cricket sing?

By rubbing its legs against its wings. Not all species of mole cricket have wings.

What do ants, bees and termites have in common?

They are in the main social insects, that is, they live in colonies, each with their own job to do to help the colony survive.

Why do some insects shine?

Some insects, such as the fire-fly and the glow-worm, produce a chemical light to attract a mate. Other types use the light to frighten creatures which would otherwise try to eat them. The headlamp click beetle, which dwells in the South American jungles, has two spots of light behind its head. To any creature coming upon it at night, the spots look like huge shining eyes.

How do you tell moths from butterflies?

Moths and butterflies make up the order of insects called *Lepidoptera*. There are many differences. Butterflies come out during the day, rest with their wings pointing upwards and have a blob on each antenna. Moths are nocturnal insects, are not as brightly coloured, and when they rest they fold their wings across their bodies. They have no blobs on their antennae.

What do butterflies live on?

They feed on nectar, the sugary substance found at the bottom of a flower. They suck up the nectar with a long, thin tube which, when it is not in use, they keep rolled up under the head.

What is a bed-bug?

It is a brown, flattened insect without wings, which gives out an unpleasant smell. Bed bugs are found as a rule in old, deteriorating houses and they come out at night time to suck the blood of people when they are sleeping.

Who was the first statesman to try to create a united west Europe?

Julius Caesar, who by his conquest of Gaul (France and part of Belgium) between 59 and 50 BC transformed the Roman Empire from a Mediterranean to a European empire.

What other rulers attempted to create a united Europe?

Charlemagne, king of the Franks and first emperor of the Holy Roman Empire, and Napoleon Bonaparte, emperor of the French.

What was the origin of the European Economic Community?

World War II (1939–45) had devastated Europe and over 50 million people had been killed. Winston Churchill saw that the future peace of Europe could best be guaranteed by the formation of a United States of Europe.

What was the first step taken towards creating this union?

The Organization for European Economic Cooperation was created in 1947, and in 1949 the Council of Europe was formed, holding its first meeting as the Consultative Assembly, at Strasbourg, in August 1949.

Who were the member states of the new Council?

Britain, France, Belgium, the Netherlands, Italy, Sweden, Denmark, Norway, Ireland, Luxembourg, Greece, Turkey. Other states including West Germany joined later.

What was the ECSC?

The European Coal and Steel Community, which was founded in 1952, basically to pool the coal and steel resources of western Europe under one authority, and to create a single market. It was the first practical step towards a United States of Europe.

What is the Common Market?

It is the popular term for the European Economic Community (EEC), founded in 1957 as a development of the Coal and Steel Community. There were six member states, France, West Germany, Italy, the Netherlands, Belgium and Luxembourg. They reached agreement at the Treaty of Rome to form an economic union. A Council of Ministers was set up.

What is the make-up of the Council of Ministers?

It is a council with one member from each member state, according to the subject to be discussed, such as agriculture, finance, foreign affairs, etc. The headquarters are in Brussels.

What is the European Commission?

It is a body which initiates policy in the EEC and advises the Council of Ministers. It has at least one member from each member state and two from each of the larger nations. Its president is chosen from its members, and he or she is in office for two years.

Who was the first British president of the European Commission?

Roy Jenkins, PC, who had been both chancellor of the exchequer and home secretary in the government of Harold Wilson (1964–70). He entered his presidency in 1977.

What is the European Parliament?

This is a representative assembly having members directly elected from each member country. It sits at Strasbourg and has to be consulted on all major issues affecting the EEC. It has the power of veto over the European Commission, and also has control over the EEC's budget.

What is the role of the European Court of Justice?

It exists to safeguard the interpretation of the various treaties making up the EEC and its constituent bodies, and to decide if necessary on the legality of decisions of the Council of Ministers or the Commission. Member states can bring cases to the Court, as indeed individual people in the member countries may also do.

When did the United Kingdom join the EEC?
The UK applied to join in 1961, and was refused. It applied again in 1967 and was refused again. But in 1970, negotiations began once more, and on 1 January 1973 the UK became a full member, along with both Denmark and Ireland.

What was the difficulty regarding United Kingdom memberhip?
Largely, it was because of the opposition of General de Gaulle, president of France and a leading influence in the EEC. He objected to the special relationship between the UK and the United States of America, notably over defence policies. De Gaulle ceased to be president in France in 1968 and died in 1970. His departure from the sphere of power removed most of the obstacles to British entry.

Which country refused to join the EEC in 1973?
Norway, which had originally applied to join, along with the UK, Denmark and Ireland. A national referendum produced a majority against membership and the application was dropped.

What is the Common Agricultural Policy?
It is the issue that has caused the greatest difficulties among the member states. Basically, it is a system that guarantees the incomes of the farmers in the member states by fixing prices that are charged to consumers for agricultural products, including cereals, milk, beef, pigs, eggs and poultry, fruit and vegetables, wine, and sugar.

Who was the European statesman generally regarded as the architect of the Coal and Steel Community?
The French statesman Jean Monnet (1888–1981). He was its first president (1952–55).

Which other European states are considering application to join the EEC?
Spain, Portugal and Turkey.

Has any other state joined since 1973?
Yes, Greece.

What was the result of the referendum held in the United Kingdom in 1975 to confirm or change the decision to join the EEC?
Two thirds of the electorate approved the decision to join. It is said today that if the same question were asked now, the proportions would be very different.

Which is the only EEC country with which the United Kingdom shares a land frontier?
The Irish Republic.

With which potential EEC member has the United Kingdom been involved in a territorial dispute?
Spain, in respect of Gibraltar.

What overseas territory of a member state voted to leave the EEC on 1 January 1984?
Greenland, which has home rule but remains a Danish possession.

In what EEC country might you hear a language called Frisian?
In the Netherlands. Frisian is spoken in the islands which bear that name, and very locally on the northern mainland.

What were the names of the ships that Columbus took on his first voyage across the Atlantic in 1492?
The *Santa Maria* (his flagship), the *Niña* and the *Pinta*. The *Santa Maria* was wrecked off Haiti after his first discoveries, and the remains of it were discovered in 1968.

What was the name of Drake's flagship on his voyage round the world?
He set out in the *Pelican* in 1577 with four other ships. The four became detached in the Cape Horn area, and he went on alone, changing the name of the *Pelican* to *Golden Hind*.

Who were the travellers in the *Mayflower* in 1620?
They were the Pilgrim Fathers, political and religious victims of persecution who set out for the Americas. They left Plymouth and set up the first colony in New England.

Which ship was the flagship of the British Grand Fleet at the battle of Jutland?
HMS *Iron Duke*, a battleship, flying the flag of Admiral Sir John Jellicoe (later, Admiral of the Fleet Earl Jellicoe), commander-in-chief of the British Grand Fleet. The battle was fought at the end of May, 1916.

Which famous warship was sunk by the German battleship *Bismarck* in the Atlantic in 1941?
HMS *Hood*, a 42,000 ton battle-cruiser. The magazine is thought to have been hit by shells from the *Bismarck*, for the ship blew up and all but a handful of the crew were drowned.

What happened to the *Lusitania*?
This Cunard trans-Atlantic liner was

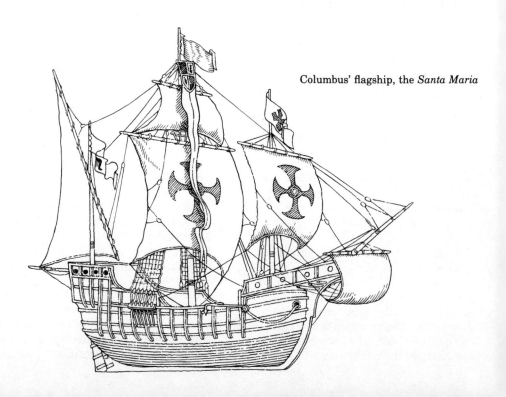

Columbus' flagship, the *Santa Maria*

sunk off the Irish coast by a German submarine on 7 May 1915, and over 1200 people were drowned, some of them women and children.

How old was HMS *Victory*, Nelson's flagship at Trafalgar in 1805?

It had been launched in 1765 and it weighed over 2160 tons. The *Victory* survived the battle, though Nelson lost his life, and the ship is still in dry dock at Portsmouth Harbour.

What happened to the *Marie Celeste*?

This small ship left the United States in 1872 with a captain and crew, and was later found abandoned in the Atlantic, with no sign of anyone aboard or any evidence as to where the ship's complement had gone.

What happened to the liner *Titanic* on its maiden voyage in April 1912?

It struck an ice-berg in the north Atlantic and sank within about two hours, with the loss of over 1500 lives, largely because there were too few lifeboats on board.

What was a monitor in the Royal Navy?

An unusual warship of shallow draught and of cruiser size, but which mounted very heavy guns. Two of the best known British monitors of this century were HMS *Erebus* and HMS *Terror*, both of which mounted 15 in guns.

What was a dreadnought?

It was a type of battleship built in the early years of the present century for the Royal Navy, named after the first of the series, HMS *Dreadnought*. The *Dreadnought* displaced about 18,000 tons, carried ten 12 in guns and was protected by 11 in armour. It could travel at 21 knots. Dreadnoughts were the idea of Admiral of the Fleet Sir John (later Lord) Fisher, first sea lord.

Who was aboard the cruiser HMS *Hampshire* when she was sunk off Orkney on 5 June 1916?

Field Marshal Earl Kitchener of Khartoum, secretary of state for war, who was travelling to Russia to help bolster up the Russian war effort against the Germans in World War I. Kitchener was drowned.

What was the *Great Michael*?

It was a splendid battleship built for James IV of Scotland at the beginning of the 16th century. At 72 m (236.16 ft) long and 11 m (36.08 ft) wide, and carrying a crew of 300, it was the largest battleship anywhere in Europe at the time. It took most of the oak trees of the kingdom of Fife to build it.

What was the *Charlotte Dundas*?

It was the first steamship to operate successfully. It plied the Forth-Clyde Canal in Scotland, starting in 1802.

What principal armament did the battleships HMS *Nelson* and HMS *Rodney* carry?

They carried three turrets of three 16 in guns, mounted in line, one higher than the next, in the fore part of the ship.

What are the characteristics of battle cruisers?

Basically, they were warships that displaced a similar tonnage to that of the battleship and carried similar armament, but at the same time had less protective armour and could travel considerably faster.

Which is the largest aircraft carrier in the world today?

There are two: the USS *Nimitz* and the USS *Dwight D Eisenhower*, both of them displacing 91,400 tons, over 332 m (1090 ft) long, nuclear-powered, and capable of carrying over 90 planes.

Where are?

The Champs-Elysées
A long, wide boulevard in Paris, stretching from the Place de la Concorde up to L'Arc de Triomphe.

The Kremlin
A huge, walled citadel, with eighteen towers, in the middle of Moscow, begun in the 12th century and containing, among other buildings, three cathedrals, the Ivan Veluki tower over 90 m (300 ft) tall, several palaces and museums.

The Grande Place
The main central square in Brussels, Belgium, containing many fine buildings including La Maison du Roi.

Princes Street
The main street of Edinburgh, and one of the finest streets in Europe.

The Four Courts
A splendid composite building of the late 1790s in Dublin, Eire, rebuilt after damage in the civil war, 1922. It used to house four separate courts, the Court of Exchequer, the Court of Common Pleas, the Court of King's Bench, and the Court of Chancery.

Cathays Park
A park in the centre of Cardiff, Wales, containing several public buildings including the law courts and the City Hall.

Table Mountain
A remarkable rocky prominence, some 1067.5 m (3500 ft) high, which lies on the edge of, and dominates the city of Cape Town in South Africa.

The Hradcany
A fortified palace and castle in Prague, Czechoslovakia, now containing the president's palace and various government headquarters.

The Prado Museum
One of the best museums and art galleries of Europe, it is in Madrid, Spain. It houses a fine collection of one of Spain's most celebrated painters, Velasquez.

Kenwood House
In Hampstead, London, this 18th century mansion standing in beautiful grounds, houses a fine collection of paintings, notably the famous self portrait by Rembrandt and Romney's portrait of Lady Hamilton.

The Wedding Cake
It is the *Vittoriano*, or Monument to Victor Emanuel II in Rome.

Fifth Avenue
The smartest and perhaps most famous street in New York, USA.

The Deichstrasse
A street in Hamburg, West Germany, which has several late medieval houses that, miraculously, survived the devastation of the city during World War II.

The Horse Guards
A splendid building by William Kent, in Whitehall, London, which backs onto a huge parade ground used for Trooping the Colour and other ceremonies.

The Doge's Palace
An amazing structure beside St Mark's Cathedral in Venice, Italy, it was begun in the 9th century. Its principal external feature is the superb Gothic front of the 14th century.

Trogir Cathedral
A splendid Romanesque cathedral of the 13th century, with some fine Gothic additions, situated on an island along the Dalmatian coast in Yugoslavia, connected to the mainland by causeway.

The Red Fort
Once the imperial palace of the great Mogul emperors of India, this is in Delhi.

Berchtesgaten
The village in south-east Bavaria, Germany, near which Adolf Hitler lived in a fortified country house called the Berghof on the top of the Obersalzburg.

Grace Cathedral
An imitation Gothic cathedral, built of structural steel and concrete, in San Francisco. It is a very fine building, and has some stained glass in the rose window at the east end specially made for it at Chartres in France.

The oldest surviving timber building in England?
The church of St Andrew at Greensted, about 12 miles west of Chelmsford, in Essex. The nave is constructed of tree trunks split in half and stood on end, and the timberwork is mid-9th century.

The Balearic Islands?
In the Mediterranean, they include some of the world's most popular holiday destinations: Majorca, Minorca and Ibiza.

Bouvet Island?
This has the distinction of being the most isolated place on earth, situated in the South Atlantic Ocean 1600km (1000 miles) from any other land. This bleak, icy island bears the name of the French explorer who discovered it in 1739, but it actually belongs to Norway.

Botany Bay?
Now a suburb of Sydney, it marks the spot from which Captain Cook proclaimed British sovereignty over the eastern coast of Australia on 29 April 1770. Later it achieved notoriety as the name of a penal colony, although this was actually situated a short distance away from the locality where Cook landed.

Electric Brae?
A section of the coast road near Ayr in Scotland where an optical illusion is created giving the impression that the road is descending, whereas the opposite is the case. The effect is brought about by the nature of the configuration of the land on either side of the road in this locality.

Smoo Cave?
One of the more famous caves on the mainland of Scotland, it is situated on the north coast of Sutherland near Durness. The outermost of its three chambers can be readily entered; Sir Walter Scott visited it in 1814. Like many names in this part of Scotland, it probably derives from an old Norse word for rock.

The Blarney Stone?
This feature forms the sill of a machicolation (projecting battlement) of Blarney Castle in county Cork, Ireland.

Little Quiz 26
   When were these major Civil Wars or Revolutions?
1. French Revolution
2. Indian Mutiny
3. Irish Civil War
4. Boudicca's Rebellion
5. Spanish Civil War
6. Russian Revolution
7. American War of Independence
8. English Civil War
9. Civil War between Caesar and Pompey
10. Chinese

In which countries were playing cards first used for games?
China and Japan, probably over 1000 years ago.

What were the earliest symbols used on these cards?
The Chinese reproduced designs from their paper money notes.

What was the Japanese Flower Game?
This was a card game in which the cards used had four flower pictures to represent each month of the year, making 48 in all. This was because the months were known by names of flowers. Each card was assigned a value of a certain number of points. The cards were generally very small, less than 5 cms (2 in) square.

How did playing cards reach Europe?
No one knows exactly, but it is thought they came from India, brought by wandering fortune-telling gypsies.

What is a court card?
Originally called a coat card, it is the clothed or 'coated' figures of the king, queen or jack of any of the four suits in a pack.

Can the game of whist ever be played without a partner?
Whist is a game for four players in which two partners play against another two. In solo or solo whist, however, there is a different set of rules and a player may play without a partner.

What does 'misère' mean?
This is a term used in solo whist, when the bidder contracts to win no tricks, playing a no-trump contract against the other players.

What is a flush?
A run of cards of the same suit. In poker, a hand containing cards from the ace (high) to the ten in one suit is called a royal flush.

What is to revoke?
To fail to follow suit, even if able and required to do so, for which a penalty may be exacted.

Where did playing cards first come to be used in Europe?
In France. There is a record of three sets of playing cards being made up for King Charles IV in the 1390s. Some of the cards have survived and are in the Bibliothèque Nationale in Paris.

What was the origin of the suits in packs of cards as we know them today?
The origin is in the game of piquet, a game of knights and chivalry that was introduced in France in the early 15th century by a French knight, Étienne Vignoles. He devised the suits, namely spades, hearts, clubs and diamonds.

What did the four suits represent?
Spades represented the lance points of the knights, or the knights themselves, hearts represented the Church, clubs were clover leaves representing husbandmen, and diamonds were arrowheads, representing vassals from whom the archers were drawn.

When and where were playing cards first printed in Europe?
In Germany in the late 15th century. The designs were cut into wooden blocks and inked for printing, using a technique said to have been learned from merchants who had visited China where woodblock printing had been in use for centuries.

How did playing cards come to England?
Probably through the lords and knights

who fought in France in the later period of the Hundred Years' War (1337–1453).

Where did the term 'jack' come from?
The third court card used to be called the knave, which meant son or male child, but in time knave came to mean 'rogue', and so 'jack' from 'jack-a-napes' was substituted.

Which king of England actually recorded his losses at cards?
Henry VII, who entered in the royal accounts sums for card debts. The costumes worn by the kings, queens and jacks on cards in Britain today are typical costumes worn in the time of Henry VII.

What is a wild card?
A card that represents any card the holder wants it to, particularly in wild card poker, and wild card rummy.

What is the strongest trick in the game of vingt-et-un (or pontoon)?
A five card trick, which cannot be beaten unless the banker himself has another five card trick, which is extremely rare.

What is a rubber?
It is a match or tournament in cards, the winner being the first to win a fixed number of games. The word generally applies to bridge.

What is the origin of the joker?
The joker, usually two jokers, found in present-day packs of cards is often superfluous. Its ostensible place as a 'wild' card originates in the unnumbered trump of the tarot of the Middle Ages, the fool (le fou) or otherwise jester.

What European country's traditional playing cards were introduced to Japan in the 16th century?
Portugal, with its forty-eight card pack.

What does grand slam mean in the game of bridge?
It is the winning of every trick.

What is 'to throw in the cards'?
It means to give up or admit defeat and the expression comes from some card games, such as poker. If a player is dealt a very poor hand he may throw in the cards and wait for a new deal.

What does 'to meld' mean?
This is to declare a card or a combination of cards that one is holding for a score, usually by placing it or them face up on the table.

English court card c. 1750

Little Quiz 27
   What are the correct names for the following heraldic colours?
   1. gold
   2. silver
   3. red
   4. blue
   5. black
   6. green
   7. purple
   8. orange or brown
   9. blood red
   10. purple red

99

What does 'rep' mean?
It is short for repertory theatre, which is a theatre with a repertoire (or programme) of plays and reviews that are performed by a permanent company of actors and actresses.

Where is the proscenium in a theatre?
It is the space between the front of the stage (where the curtain comes down) and the orchestra pit, usually a huge open space surrounded by an arch (the proscenium arch).

What is theatre in the round?
A theatre where the stage is set in the centre of the area where the audience sits, instead of in front of the auditorium as in conventional theatres. The idea is by no means new: in ancient Greece and Rome, audiences sat round at least three quarters of a stage.

What is an apron stage?
A stage whose front projects beyond the proscenium into the auditorium, sometimes in the shape of a wedge.

What is 'kitchen sink' drama?
It is a derogatory term to describe the sort of plays with working class settings, written and produced in the 1950s to 1970s, in which the principal feature was realism.

What was the play by John Osborne that heralded the arrival of the Angry Young Man cult?
Look Back in Anger, a satire on middle class life and its values, produced first in 1956.

What is Grand Guignol?
A horror or sensational play or other form of entertainment, usually accentuated to the point of absurdity or ridicule. Guignol was the main character in French puppet shows similar to Punch and Judy.

What was a masque?
A form of theatre introduced from Italy into England in the mid-16th century and performed largely on special occasions for kings and courts. It was characterized by fantastic or mythological plots and stories, centred on songs and poetry recitation, and by lavishly designed and decorated sets. The word came from the fact that performers, most of whom were members of the nobility, wore masks.

What 17th century English architect began his career as a masque designer?
Inigo Jones (1573–1652), who introduced Palladian architectural ideas into Britain and designed, among many fine buildings, the Queen's House at Greenwich and the Banqueting Hall at Whitehall.

What is son-et-lumière?
It is an open air entertainment in which lights are directed onto an historic building with dramatic effect, accompanied by a recorded script broadcast through speakers, which tells or acts out a story about the building or the people associated with it.

What was Commedia dell'Arte?
It was a form of Italian drama, first devised in the 16th century, in which performers improvized the words and actions of a pre-determined plot. Performances were often humorous, and mostly centred on some kind of amorous intrigue involving disguises, tricking guardians, and so forth. The form was still popular in the 18th century.

What is the Method form of acting?
Originating in the USA, it means losing oneself completely in the role, in order to convince the audience they are seeing the character from the play rather than the performer.

Where are the footlights of a stage?
They are set in a line or lines in front of the stage and at stage level, usually screened from the audience. They throw light upon the players.

What is to upstage someone?
To affect superiority over someone. It comes from the fault of some actors and actresses of upstaging their colleagues, that is, deliberately manoeuvring them towards the back of the stage during a performance. The back of the stage is known in theatre as upstage.

What are props?
The word is short for properties, and relates to items used on the stage other than scenery and costume. Typical props are items of furniture, china, ornaments, pictures, and these would be borrowed, hired or bought for the production.

What is the principal organization in Britain that represents the acting profession?
Equity.

What was the origin of Punch and Judy?
Punch is short for Punchinello, a hero of puppet plays originating in Italy in the late Middle Ages and performed with glove puppets in a small box theatre. Punchinello was an imaginary character with pronounced physical features, such as hooked nose, hunched back and squeaky, rasping voice, who usually overcame all difficulties and obstacles, and outwitted all opponents.

Who was Will Fyffe?
Will Fyffe (1885–1947) who was a Scot, is best remembered as a music-hall comedian although he had started his career as an actor. He was a brilliant comic and had an extensive repertoire of comic songs. He also played a wide range of parts in pantomime.

Who was Bertholt Brecht?
Bertholt Brecht (1898–1956) was a German poet, playwright and director. He became a Marxist and left Germany in 1933 for Denmark, where he could direct his intellectual energies in a crusade against Hitler. In 1941 he travelled via the USSR to the USA; his political views eventually made him unpopular there, and in 1947 he moved to East Berlin where he set up the Berliner Ensemble, which became a major vehicle for staging his dramatic works. His plays include *Life of Galileo* and *The Caucasian Chalk Circle*. Kurt Weill, the composer, provided the music for some of Brecht's lyrics.

Who was Ellen Terry?
Ellen Terry (1847–1928), D.B.E., was one of the greatest English actresses of all time. Her parents were both actors and she made her own first stage appearance at the age of eight. From 1878 until 1902 she enjoyed a successful stage collaboration with Henry Irving. She is perhaps best remembered for her portrayal of Shakespearian heroines.

What is a Noh play?
A Japanese popular entertainment of the 14th–17th centuries.

Little Quiz 28
   What is the collective noun for a group of – ?
1. young birds
2. chickens
3. cattle
4. angels
5. hornets
6. buffaloes
7. locusts
8. lions
9. dolphins
10. bees

When was the Armourers' Company founded in London?

During the 14th century, but English armourers were not producing armour comparable with European makers in quality or workmanship until the Tudor period.

What was the principal body armour of the Roman legionary during the first two centuries of the Roman Empire?

Known as *lorica segmentata*, it consisted of a flexible system of overlapping strips of metal and two pairs of plates over chest and back. The body portion of strips was held together by leather thongs at the back and fastened in front with hooks and ties, or straps and buckles, loosely enough to allow the wearer to move and bend easily.

What is chain mail?

It is small interlocking iron rings put together to form a garment such as a shirt (hauberk) or a longer tunic, with or without sleeves, enabling the wearer to move freely. The links or rings were made of wire and the ends were generally riveted, though some rings were solid.

How effective was chain mail?

Not as effective as its long period of use (at least three centuries) might suggest. It could be pierced by an arrow and certainly by a lance. It was heavy and uncomfortable. Many wearers first put on one or other of a variety of undergarments as a kind of extra protection, such as thick hardened leather tunic or whalebone vest.

What was a great helm?

A cylindrical shaped helmet with a flat top, having horizontal slits in front of the eyes. It emerged in the late 12th century.

What was a basinet?

An improvement on the great helm, it was close fitting, with a short length of mail hanging from its lower edges to cover the neck and shoulders (the aventail), and it had a hinged vizor to protect the face.

What was the main weapon of the medieval knight?

The sword. It was a weapon made with great skill and craftsmanship. It was treasured by its owner, and if it was not captured in battle or broken, it was often handed down to an owner's son. Many swords were inscribed with the owner's name.

When did plate armour begin to flourish in Europe?

In the 13th century, probably as a result of the ineffectiveness of chain mail, and also because of improvements in swords, particularly the development of sharper sword points which led to swords being used as thrusting weapons as well as cutting ones. The plate armour developed as a series of plates shaped to fit various parts of the body, not all developed at once, and to begin with armour appeared as a mixture of plates joined together with large areas of chain mail. Eventually, plate armour covered the whole body, and there was even armour for parts of the horse on which the armed knight rode.

What is a gauntlet?

A steel glove of mail or plate, which was worn with armour, probably from the 12th century.

What were staff weapons?

They were the weapons used by the infantry in later medieval warfare, such as the halberd, the bill and the glaive. They are also known as pole-arms.

What was a quillon?

A special dagger that resembled a sword, but which was much smaller.

What does 'throw down the gauntlet' mean?

In medieval terms, it was a challenge to a duel. A challenger took off his gauntlet and threw it down on the ground in front of the man he wanted to challenge. If the rival picked up the gauntlet, it meant he accepted the challenge, and a duel followed.

What was a crossbow?

It was a bow placed across a stock that contained a winding mechanism, or a powerful drawing back lever, for pulling back the string and releasing it. The bow fired an arrow known as a quarrel. Crossbows took longer to load and fire than ordinary hand bows, but they were extremely accurate and had a high range.

When was the crossbow introduced and how long was it used?

It emerged in the 11th century in Europe, probably the second half, and it was still being used in the 18th century.

What was the longbow?

It was a development of the simple bow which had been used in war for many hundreds of years (even as far back as ancient Egypt). The longbow was made of yew wood and consisted of a stave over 1.83 m (6 ft) long. This differentiated it from ordinary bows which were only 0.915 to 1.22 m (3 to 4 ft). With a long bow an archer could shoot six arrows a minute with high accuracy and up to 228.75 m (250 yds) or so, nearly twice the range of the shorter bow.

Where did the longbow come from?

It is generally agreed that it was invented by the Welsh in the 13th century, and taken up by both English and Scots early in the 14th century.

What was a halberd?

It had a straight shaft of wood, about 1.83 m (6 ft) long, and at one end was an axe-like blade with a hook on the side opposite the blade.

What is a Scottish claymore?

A big two-handed sword used by the Scottish Highlanders. The word comes from Gaelic *claidheamh mor*, great sword.

Plate armour c. 1500

What was a Todenkopf helmet?

It was a 16th century middle European helmet. The vizor bore a marked resemblance to the front of a human skull.

Which was the first book printed in English?
The *Recuyell of the Historyes of Troye*, printed by William Caxton in English in 1474 at his press at Bruges in Flanders.

Who was the first doctor to be made a peer in Britain?
Joseph Lister (1827–1912), the discoverer of the antiseptic system. He was made Baron Lister of Lyme Regis in 1897. He was also to become one of the original twelve members of the Order of Merit (OM) in 1902.

Who was the first king of Rome?
Romulus, whose dates are generally given as 753–716 BC. He is credited with having founded the city of Rome in 753.

Who was the first Roman governor of Britain?
Aulus Plautius, who was in office between AD 43 and 47. He had led the legions across the English Channel in 43 and defeated the Britons in the south-eastern part of the island.

Who was the first English scientist to write about electricity?
Sir William Gilbert (1540–1603), who in 1600 published a work *De Magnete* which discussed many aspects of magnetism and electric force.

Who was the first general to take an army across the Alps?
The Carthaginian general, Hannibal (247–182 BC). He waged war against Rome and took a huge force over the Alps from Spain in 218, descending into Italy and defeating all armies that the Romans sent against him.

Who was the first archbishop of Canterbury?
St Augustine, who had been sent by Pope Gregory I to spread Christianity in England in 597.

Who was the first reigning queen in Britain?
Cartimandua, queen of the Brigantes tribe, who reigned between the 50s and 70s.

Who was awarded the first Nobel Prize for literature?
René François Armand Sully-Prudhomme (1839–1907), the French poet and philosopher, in 1901.

Who made the first solo voyage round the world in a yacht?
Sir Francis Chichester, 1966–7.

Who was the first president of the Royal Academy of Art?
Sir Joshua Reynolds, the portrait painter, in 1768.

Where was the first castle built in England by William, Duke of Normandy?
On the shore at Hastings, in October 1066. It was an earth and timber structure that was erected in a matter of days. You can see a picture of the construction on the famous Bayeux Tapestry.

Who was the first TT motorcycle rider to achieve a 144.9 kmh (90 mph) average speed for a lap round the Isle of Man TT circuit?
Freddie Frith, OBE, during the Senior TT race of 1937.

Who was the first woman to take a seat as a member of parliament in Britain?
Nancy, Viscountess Astor, in 1919. Her husband William Waldorf Astor, who was MP for Plymouth, succeeded to the title Viscount Astor when his father died in 1919, and so had to give up his House of Commons seat. His wife decided to stand in the by-election that followed, and she won.

Who was the first woman mayor in Britain?
Dr Elizabeth Garrett Anderson, who became mayor of Aldeburgh in Suffolk in 1908. She had also been a pioneer of the movement to allow women to qualify as doctors.

Who was the first footballer to be knighted?
Sir Stanley Matthews (b 1915), one of the greatest footballers of British soccer history.

Who was the first Canadian to be appointed governor-general of Canada?
Vincent Massey (1887–1967), who was in office 1952–9.

What is a first foot?
Especially in Scotland and the north of England, it is the person who first visits a house after midnight on New Year's Eve.

When was the first celebration of the Gunpowder Plot?
Two years after the plot, in fact, when the corporation of Bristol directed the lighting of bonfires on 5 November 1607. Fireworks on these occasions were not recorded until 1660, according to Samuel Pepys's famous diary.

When were old age pensions first introduced?
In Germany, on 1 January 1891. The first Commonwealth country to introduce them was New Zealand, in March (but retrospective to 1 January) 1899. They were not introduced in Britain until 1 January 1909 when, it is recorded, a recipient in Bishops Stortford died as he was signing his first receipt.

Where were the first traffic-lights erected?
At the corner of Bridge Street and New Palace Yard near the Houses of Parliament in London, on 10 December 1868.

Who was the first living person to have his photograph taken?
The unnamed gardener of the Rev Joseph Bancroft Reade of Stone, Buckinghamshire, by his master in 1838.

Little Quiz 29
   In which British counties are the following castles?
   1. Tantallon
   2. Caerphilly
   3. Restormel
   4. Leeds
   5. Arundel
   6. Tattershall
   7. Portchester
   8. Peveril
   9. Dunstanburgh
   10. Beeston
   11. Berkhamsted
   12. St Mawes
   13. Orford
   14. Castle Rising
   15. Castle Acre
   16. Bodiam
   17. Windsor
   18. Rhuddlan
   19. Manorbier
   20. Bothwell
   And in which countries are these castles?
   1. Château Gaillard
   2. Chillon
   3. Krak des Chevaliers
   4. The Boosenburg
   5. Habsburg
   6. Canossa
   7. Sahyun
   8. Gravensteen
   9. Najac
   10. Baños de la Encina

?

What is glass made of?

A mixture of sand, lime and sodium carbonate (soda), which is heated until it produces a clear, bubbling hot liquid that is molten glass. It will have to be heated to about 1500° Centigrade, which is 15 times hotter than a kettle of boiling water.

What is a percussion instrument in an orchestra?

Percussion instruments are those that are struck or shaken to produce sounds, such as drums, triangles, cymbals, tambourines, and castanets. In recent times, more eccentric instruments have been added to the range, such as washboards, xylophones, klaxons and bulb horns.

How is paper made?

Most (though not all) paper is made from wood. Logs are stripped of bark, chopped into very small pieces and then pulped. The pulping stage is important, for at that time various chemicals and things like clay, or old rags, or even straw, are added, which determine the quality, colour and smoothness (or roughness) of the finished paper. Once pulped, the paper is rolled into sheets which are dried out before being cut to required shapes and sizes.

What is shorthand?

It is a means of condensing handwriting to write words almost as quickly as they are spoken. It can be a code of symbols to represent words or a system of shortened words. The idea goes back at least to Roman times. Modern British shorthand derives from an idea by Dr Bright, in the reign of Elizabeth I, who published a book, *The Arte of Shorte, Swifte and Secrete Writing by Character*. This had characters for every word, but it caused many problems for those trying to learn it. Other languages have had shorthand versions, including Persian and Chinese.

106

How is soap made?

Ordinary soap is made by mixing certain animal and vegetable fats with caustic soda (for hard soap) or caustic potash (for soft soap). The fats vary considerably, from coconut oil to clear animal fat. The mixture is boiled and chemicals are added to give the soap scent and colour.

Which famous English diarist used a form of shorthand?

Samuel Pepys (1633–1703), who used Thomas Shelton's system and complicated it with foreign words and his own particular cyphers. Pepys's diary was not transcribed until the 1820s when Dr John Smith, of Magdalene College, Cambridge, deciphered it.

What is a half-timbered house?

A house built of wooden posts (or studs, as they are called) standing on foundations, with the spaces in between filled with plaster applied to lathes of hazelwood or other woods. The studs are left visible. Half-timbered houses were built throughout Europe in the Middle Ages, and the style continued up to the 18th, even the 19th century in some areas.

How is honey made by bees?

It is made from nectar, the thin sweet watery liquid produced in flowers. A bee drinks the nectar and stores it in a special sac where it is mixed with a ferment, or enzyme, produced by the bee. This converts it to honey liquid. When the sac is full, the bee returns to its hive and regurgitates the liquid into wax cells located in the hive.

Is a sponge a plant?

No, it is an animal, and it grows in fresh or sea water. Sponges can be as small as a pin head and as large as a boulder, and come in a variety of colours. Sponges cling to the sea bed or an oyster shell or stone.

What is a barrage balloon?
A balloon of huge size filled with a lighter-than-air gas and allowed to rise into the sky on the end of a cable, to a height of 1000 m (3280 ft) or so. Many of these balloons were used in World War II in and around cities and military establishments in the countryside, to deflect enemy aircraft approaching the site. At night, many enemy aircraft failed to see the cables and flew straight into them and were often brought down.

What is semaphore?
It is an alphabet devised by placing your arms outstretched in a range of different positions, each to represent a different letter. Semaphore signallers hold flags in each hand. It is useful for sending messages over distances when radio or telecommunication has broken down or is non-existent. One signaller stood on a hill or on rising ground and sent a message to another signaller, also on high ground, and so on down to the last man.

How does a bird fly?
A bird flies and glides in the same way as an aeroplane, but whereas a plane needs propellers or jets for take off and to stay in the air, the bird uses its wings to provide what is called lift, that is, upward force exerted by air pressure against the under surface countering the force of gravity. A bird flaps its wings forwards and downwards and then backwards and upwards, first very quickly, and then more slowly as it gains height.

Can hollow trees grow leaves?
Yes, because the vital processes of a tree take place not in the central core but in a band of small tubes, called the cambium, just under the bark. The tubes run down into the roots which draw up the water with the minerals and salts needed for growth.

Is a piano normally one of the instruments of an orchestra?
No, and it only appears if a piano concerto or other composition specially written for piano and orchestra is to be performed.

What is a geyser?
A natural spring that shoots out high into the air boiling water and steam through a crack or hole in the ground. It does so at regular intervals and then dies down. One geyser at Yellowstone National Park in the USA spouts every 66 minutes.

Who invented the steam turbine?
This machine for using the energy built up by steam when it is under pressure to produce rotary motion, was invented by Sir Charles Parsons, fourth son of the 3rd Earl of Rosse, in 1884.

Where was the trolley bus invented?
In Germany, towards the end of the 19th century. It was a road vehicle for passengers, driven by electricity and not by internal combustion engine, and drew its power from overhead cables to which it was linked by a rod that swivelled at each end to cope with corners.

What had a 17th century author of a *History of the World*, the author of *Pilgrim's Progress* and the author of *Mein Kampf* in common?
They all wrote these books in prison: Walter Raleigh, in the Tower of London, John Bunyan, in Bedford Jail, and Hitler in Landsberg prison, in Germany.

What is a kaleidoscope?
Invented in 1817, it is a tube in which three mirrors are set at certain angles to each other. At the bottom of the tube is a heap of tiny sections of coloured glass and metal. By rotating the tube, the sections create an infinite variety of patterns reflected in the mirrors.

What is an antonym?
A word meaning the opposite of another word, such as light/dark, or felicitous/unfortunate.

What is etymology?
The study of the origins of words.

What is a palindrome?
It is a word or phrase that reads the same backwards as it does forwards such as level or Madam I'm Adam.

What do we mean by tautology?
Repetition, in different words, of the same thing, such as 'I have been all alone by myself for hours'.

What is syntax?
It is the part of grammar that deals with the way words are ordered in sentences.

What is accidence?
The study of various forms of words, such as inflexions for gender, number or case.

What is a split infinitive?
It is the error of putting another word or two between an infinitive verb and the word 'to' that should immediately precede it. 'I hope to eventually finish the work', instead of, 'I hope eventually to finish the work'.

What is *oratio obliqua*?
The Latin phrase meaning 'reported speech'. A person may say 'I have paid my bill'. This could be reported by someone else as 'he said he had paid his bill'.

What is bathos?
The same as anti-climax, that is, a figure of speech describing a descent from a higher level of thought to the ridiculous.

What is meiosis?
It is understatement: 'I didn't half enjoy it'.

What is a paradox?
A statement which is true but seems false or self-contradictory, such as, James I was the wisest fool in Christendom.

What is hypallage?
The same as transferred epithet, it means emphasizing an adjective or adverb by using it to describe by its position a word to which it does not belong: such as 'the condemned cell', or 'Melissa shook her doubtful curls'.

What is an innuendo?
It is hinting at a thing without actually saying it. Lord Palmerston once said, 'There is never a good champagne year, unless there is a good apple crop in Normandy'.

What is pathetic fallacy?
This is an extreme form of personification, in which objects are made to sympathize with the emotions of the agent. A good example is a famous description of Cromwell's death: A storm was raging outside as if in sympathy with the mighty soul that was passing from the earth.

What is a rhetorical question?
A question put for rhetorical effect, and not meant to be answered: 'How do I love thee? Let me count the ways.'

What is circumlocution?
A roundabout way of saying things. Winston Churchill once described a lie as a terminological inexactitude.

What is antonomasia?
It is a figure of speech in which an individual person is made to represent a class or attribute. He is a Herod, for a tyrant.

What is inversion?
It is the adoption of a rhetorical instead of a grammatical order of words, to

emphasize a statement, or part of a statement, eg 'Not hard for heroes is this death' instead of 'This death is not hard for heroes.'

What is barbarism?
Using a word that is not in current English usage, such as connexity, teached, connote.

What is a synonym?
A synonym is a word which means the same or almost the same as another, for example, song and air; endure and tolerate, plan and scheme, mistake and blunder.

What is bombast?
Strictly, it is pretentious language. 'I perused the daily chronicle of contemporary events', when you mean 'I read the newspaper'.

Is pleonasm a disease?
No, it is using more words than necessary to express what is meant, eg I saw it with my own eyes. You and I both agree.

What is ambiguity?
It is an idea, or statement, or expression, capable of being understood in more than one sense. He hit a man with a stone on his back.

What is anacoluthon?
This is starting a sentence in one way and finishing it in another way, or giving up one grammatical construction in favour of another in the middle of a sentence.

What is paraphrasing?
It is a restating of an idea, or statement, in different words, or a free rendering of a text or passage.

What is the usual order of words in a sentence called?
It is called the grammatical order. A sentence basically consists of a subject and a predicate.

How many parts of speech are there?
Eight.

What are they?
Noun, pronoun, adjective, verb, adverb, preposition, conjunction and interjection.

What is an elliptical sentence?
It is a sentence in which some words that ought grammatically to be left in are in fact left out, because they do not add to the overall meaning of the sentence. For example; The doctor has done all (that) he can (do).

What is the subjunctive mood?
This states a condition, or purpose, or hypothesis, or wish; such as, *If he should come*, please give him this letter. We eat *in order that we may live.*

What is a diphthong?
A speech sound consisting of two vowels together pronounced as one syllable, as *ae* in Caesar.

What is a diaeresis?
It is the word describing the two dots placed over the second of two vowels together, to show that the vowels are to be sounded separately (eg coöperation). As a matter of fact, diaereses are not so often used nowadays, and when you see COOPERATIVE over a general store, you are supposed to know that the two os should be pronounced separately!

What is a sibilant consonant?
It is one that expresses a hissing sound when pronounced, such as *s, z, sh*.

What is a labial consonant?
It is one that is made with the lips entirely or partially closed, such as *p, b, m, w*.

How many bones form the skull?
Twenty-two: eight bones of the cranium, or top part, and fourteen bones of the face.

Which vertebrae form the spine?
There are thirty-three (top to bottom), seven cervical, twelve thoracic (or dorsal), five lumbar, five sacral and four coccygeal.

How many pairs of ribs has the human body?
There are seven true pairs that are joined to the sternum, or breast bone, and five not joined, usually called false ribs.

What are the English names for: femur, patella, scapula, oscalcis?
Thigh-bone, knee-cap, shoulder blade, heel bone.

What is the cardio-vascular system?
It is the system that maintains circulation of the blood and includes the heart, the blood and the blood vessels.

Where is the medulla oblongata?
It is a stalk, or stem, emerging from the lower part of the brain to join with the spinal cord.

What are the main constituents of human blood?
It consists of a liquid called the plasma, with blood cells, such as red corpuscles, white corpuscles and platelets.

What do arteries do?
They take away the blood from the heart, and with the exception of the pulmonary arteries (in the heart region) all of them carry oxygenated blood.

What are capillaries?
These are minute, very thin-walled blood vessels which separate arterial from venous circulation, taking blood to all tissues in the body.

What are the organs of the alimentary canal?
In order downwards, mouth, pharynx, oesophagus, stomach, small and finally large intestine.

Where is the appendix?
It is a vermiform (worm-shaped) projection from the intestines, and it is situated at the end of the caecum which is a pouch at the end of the small intestine and beginning of the large intestine. The appendix terminates in a sealed end, and appears to have no function.

What is peristaltic movement?
It is the movement by muscular contraction of the intestines, which passes the contents of the intestines along towards the outlet.

What is the main function of the pancreas?
It is a gland lying chiefly in front of the left kidney behind the stomach, which secretes and discharges the enzyme insulin into the circulation, and thus controls sugar metabolism.

How many kinds of muscle are there in the body?
There are three types: i. voluntary muscle, which forms the musculature round the skeleton; ii. involuntary muscle, which is in the visceral organs such as the stomach, intestines, bladder, etc, and iii. cardiac muscle, which is only found in the heart.

What are endocrine glands?
They are glands that have no ducts, but which secrete and discharge into the bloodstream substances which are necessary for the proper operation of certain body functions. These secretions are known as hormones. Among the endocrine glands are the thyroids, the adrenals, the pituitary and the pancreas.

What is a ligament?
A strong band of fibrous tissue connecting bones or supporting organs.

What is the solar plexus?
It is a group of nerve centres in the upper region of the abdomen.

What is the trachea?
It is the wind-pipe.

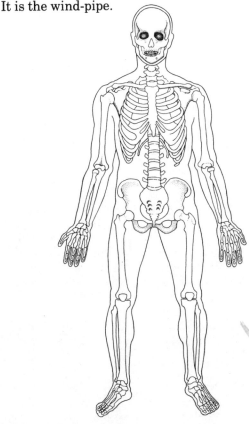

Human skeleton

What is colour blindness?
In the retina of the eye, about one cell in twenty called cones actively transmit colour vision. Three kinds of cones are respectively most sensitive to blue, green and red light. However, about 10% of men and less than 1% of women have genetically defective cones, usually in respect of the ones most sensitive to red

or green. Less frequently, insensitivity to blue, or even to all colours, is inherited. Any of these conditions are referred to as colour blindness. Schoolchildren are tested at an early age with cards designed to reveal any form of colour blindness.

What is the difference between myopia and hypermetropia?
Myopia is short-sightedness; hypermetropia is long-sightedness.

Why are only some twins identical?
Identical twins, which by definition are always the same sex, develop from a single egg which divided shortly after fertilization. Fraternal twins – despite the name they can also be one of each sex or both female – develop from separate eggs which have been fertilized at the same time. Identical twins share a single placenta in the womb, while fraternal twins have separate ones. Twins, incidentally, are born about once in every 85 pregnancies.

What area does our skin cover?
In a normal adult, about two square metres.

How many teeth should an adult have?
Provided that you have looked after them all, 32. This total includes 8 incisors, 4 canines, 8 premolars, 8 molars and 4 wisdom. Wisdom teeth are the last to appear, usually between the ages of 15 and 30.

What is the diaphragm?
This is a domed sheet of muscle which is connected on all sides to the body wall and which forms the floor of the thoracic cavity – the thorax, containing the heart and the lungs. When the diaphragm contracts, the volume of the thorax increases; when it relaxes, the volume of the thorax decreases.

Who are or who were?

Amazons
They were a mythical race whose leaders and warriors were women, and who occupied land to the south and east of the Black Sea. The women had their right breasts removed so that they could more easily use bow and arrow. Amazon warriors fought on the Trojan side in the great battle for Troy.

Thugs
A murderous sect of Hindus in India who flourished in the 18th century and 19th century, and who specialized in violence against travellers whom they ambushed and strangled.

Black Fellows
Another term for the aboriginal peoples discovered in Australia by the early white European settlers of the late 18th century.

Walloons
Modern Belgium is composed of two races, the more northerly Flemings, of Germanic origin, speaking a Germanic tongue, and the Walloons in the south, a people of Celtic origin who speak a French dialect. There are about 3 to 3½ million of them.

Lapps
Lapland is the landmass spreading across the north of the three Scandinavian countries, Norway, Sweden and Finland, and of north-west Russia. In it are several settlements of Lapps, a people of Mongol origin, numbering perhaps 25,000. They live by hunting and reindeer herding.

Druzes
A people of Syria, they were originally a sect who in the 1000s broke away from orthodox Islam and followed a curiously mixed religion containing elements of Christianity and Islam.

Letts
These are the people of the ancient state of Latvia which enjoyed an independent existence for centuries during the Middle Ages. Latvia was absorbed by Russia in the 1720s, but was freed after World War I, only to be absorbed again by Russia in 1939.

Albigenses
This was a heretical sect of Christians who occupied the lands around Toulouse and Albi in southern France, during the 11th to 13th centuries. Their opposition to the orthodox beliefs of the Church was tolerated at first, but in the 13th century the papacy organized a ruthless campaign of extermination, and their district was invaded and ravaged several times with appallingly cruel treatment of the inhabitants.

Buryats
The vast space of Siberia is peopled by many races and tribes. One of the largest is the Buryat people, of Mongol descent, who lived around Lake Baikal. Most of the Buryats are Buddhists. They have been largely absorbed into the Soviet framework of collective farming and state industry, but some of them still retain their ancient custom of wandering off on lengthy trips during hot months to lead a nomadic life in tents.

Micronesians
Micronesia is part of the South Pacific region of the world (also known as Oceania), and it includes in the large sea area the islands of the Marshalls, Marianas and Carolines.

Negrillos
This is the word for the African pygmies, the race of small-sized people who occupy chiefly the areas of the Congo river basin in central Africa. Negrillos are less than 1.525 m (5 ft) tall, indeed 1.346 m (4 ft 5 in) is an average height.

Waldensians
They were a Christian sect founded by Peter Waldo in the 1170s and now known as the Vaudois, living in the Piedmont hills in the Alps. They followed a simple life, rejecting the worldliness of medieval orthodox Christians, and were persecuted for it.

Saracens
Another name for Moslems or Arabs in the Middle Ages. The word was the Greek for an Arab people of the Sinai desert, but was later adopted to cover Moslems of all kinds, particularly those who clashed with the Christians in the Holy Land in Asia Minor.

Moravians
A Protestant sect in Bohemia who were often persecuted for their beliefs over a long period from the 15th to the 18th centuries. Finally, they left Bohemia and many settled in Britain, and some in North America where they worked as missionaries among the Indian races.

Veneti
Nothing to do with Venice, these were a tough, sea-faring Celtic people occupying Brittany in the last centuries before Christ. They were defeated at sea and on land by Caesar during his conquest of Gaul.

Bhils
A group of hill tribes in the central Indian hills.

Young Turks
A militant group of Turkish nationalists who in 1908 rebelled against the ruling sultan and demanded a new constitution.

Jains
A small religious community in India who are notable for their total belief in pacificism and non-violence and whose way of life is one of compassion and understanding for others, men and women alike. Jains follow the teachings of Vardhamana (6th century BC) and they are distinguished for the high degree of literacy and intellectual attainment of their people.

The Alans?
An ancient people, expert horse-breeders, from the area north of the Caucasus, who in the 4th century were overrun by the Huns and driven westwards into central-western Europe. There, they joined up with the Vandals, and eventually crossed into North Africa, in the 5th century.

The Croquants?
These were peasants who rose in well-organized rebellions, three times between about 1593 and 1645, in the Perigord and Saintonge districts of France. Croquant was a colloquial term for nonentity.

Kipchaks?
Turkish tribes who dominated the Eurasian steppes in the 11th century. They controlled the vast district between the Aral Sea and the Black Sea, and fought continuously with Russians, Byzantines and Hungarians. But in the 1230s they were overwhelmed and absorbed by the Mongols.

Little Quiz 30
  In which countries are these cathedrals?
  1. Ulm
  2. Trondheim
  3. Aarhus
  4. Lund
  5. St Isaacs
  6. Hagia Sophia
  7. Cefalu
  8. Coimbra
  9. Albi
  10. Esztergom

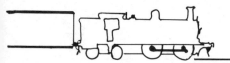

Which was the first passenger-carrying railway in the world?
The Oystermouth Railway, running to and from Oystermouth and Swansea in South Wales. Opened in 1806, its carriages were pulled by horses.

What were the Rainhill Trials?
A competition between locomotive makers to produce the best locomotive for the Liverpool to Manchester Railway. The competition was held in 1829 and was won by the Stephenson locomotive, the *Rocket*.

Which was the first trunk line?
The London to Birmingham Railway line, built by Robert Stephenson in 1838.

Which was the latest of the main lines to be built in the UK?
The Great Central Route, from Nottingham and Leicester to London, in 1898–9.

When were the private railways taken into public ownership?
In 1948 the whole network was divided into six regions, which were: London Midland, Scottish, Western, Eastern, North Eastern, and Southern. Today, there are five, as the Eastern and North Eastern have been merged.

What did Dr Beeching do during his period as chairman of British Railways?
He set in motion the closure of a huge number of little-used railway lines and branch lines.

When did luxury Pullman coaches first appear on British railway trains?
In 1874, when the Midland Railway introduced coaches which had raised roofs with windows along the sides for more light, corridors for walking down, and water-closet compartments. The coaches were also heated.

What was the last steam locomotive to be built for express passenger travel in the UK?
The Duke of Gloucester, completed in 1954 and withdrawn from service in 1962.

What are railway tracks made of?
They were first made of cast iron, but they have been made of steel for well over a century. The first steel rails were laid at and nearby Derby in 1857.

What is welded track?
Rails used to be laid in lengths about 18.3 m (60 ft) long, and at the joins a small gap was left to allow for expansion of the metal in hot weather. The spaces used to account for the 'clickety-click' noise every time a carriage passed over them. Nowadays, rail is laid in 18.3 m (60 ft) lengths and welded in very long stretches, as much as $\frac{1}{3}$ km ($\frac{1}{2}$ mile) or more, and the welded rail is carried on concrete sleepers.

Who built the first steam locomotive to run on a railway?
Richard Trevithick whose locomotive travelled 16 km (10 miles) between Penydarran ironworks and the Glamorganshire canal in 1804.

Which was the worst railway disaster in British railway history?
The three-fold collision between two passenger trains and one train carrying troops, at Quintin's Hill, Dumfries, Scotland, during World War I (22 May, 1915) when 227 people were killed.

Which railway bridge collapsed in a storm in late December 1879, taking a railway train with it?
The Tay Bridge, across the Tay in Scotland, from Dundee to Newtown. It gave way on the night of 28 December, and 73 passengers and train crew were drowned.

What is the highest speed achieved on any national rail system?
The famous French TGV (Train à Grande Vitesse) touched 380 kmh (236 mph) on trials in February 1981.

When were luncheon baskets first provided for passengers on railway trains in the UK?
Probably in 1875 on the Midland Railway network.

Who designed the marvellous Temple Meads railway station at Bristol?
I. K. Brunel. You can see it today. The roof was supported by hammer beams.

Who was the originator of railway guides?
George Bradshaw, an English printer and map-maker (1801–53) introduced the first detailed, comprehensive and accurate railway guides and time-tables. His guides began to appear in 1840 and soon became a byword for accuracy. Years after his death, other guides were often known as Bradshaws.

Which is the longest railway station platform in the UK?
For years it used to be said it was at Colchester in Essex, measuring 604.25 m (1981 ft), but that length has recently been remeasured and found to be only 585.295 m (1919 ft). This has pushed the platform at Gloucester into first place, with its length of 602.985 m (1977 ft).

When was the first railway track laid specifically for a military campaign?
About 32 km (20 miles) of track were laid in the Crimea during the Crimean War (1854–56), from Balaclava to the front line.

In what British city are there still railway stations called Foregate Street and Shrub Hill?
Worcester.

What British city once had railway termini called Buchanan Street and St Enoch?
Glasgow. Both these stations were closed to passengers in 1966.

What famous railway company built the first Pacific locomotive in Britain, and what was it called?
The Great Western Railway, which had the *Great Bear* constructed at its Swindon Works in 1908. Strangely enough, this company never built another Pacific engine and had the *Great Bear* itself converted in 1924 to its favoured 4-6-0 design for express locomotives.

Has a double-decker train ever been designed for use on British railways?
Yes, a two-level electric train was brought into use in 1949 on the London Charing Cross to Dartford service. It was fitted with 1104 seats compared with the normal 772. The seats on the upper deck were so arranged that they were situated over spaces between seats on the lower deck. This experiment was not a lasting success.

Little Quiz 31
  Who was the Oscar winning star in these films?
  1. *One Flew Over the Cuckoo's Nest*
  2. *Gandhi*
  3. *Gone With The Wind*
  4. *Song of Bernadette*
  5. *Ben Hur*
  6. *Hamlet*
  7. *Cabaret*
  8. *On Golden Pond*
  9. *Goodbye Mr Chips*
  10. *Gaslight*

What is a trug?

It is a boat-shaped basket with handle, for use in the garden, and it is made from split and trimmed chestnut straps and willow planks. It was invented in the 1840s by Thomas Smith of Herstmonceux in Sussex. The name is adapted from trog, an old English word for boat.

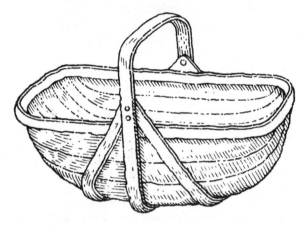

Trug

What is biscuit ware?

A form of pottery (or porcelain) fired but not glazed.

What does Sgraffito mean?

It is a method of decorating pottery or porcelain in which an outer coating is scratched or cut through to expose the colour of the underlying body.

How were the first church bells made?

They were made by monks who took a number of iron plates and hammered and riveted them together into a kind of bell shape. By about AD 700 the first bells had been cast in bronze.

What are bells made of today?

They are generally made of bell metal, which is an alloy of just over 76% copper and just under 24% tin.

How is millefiori decoration of glass made?

Millefiori is Italian for 'a thousand flowers', and this kind of glass decoration is particularly applied to glass paperweights. The patterns of flowers are made up of numerous very small cuttings from coloured glass rods which are set in clear crystal glass.

Which area in Britain is specially associated with flint knapping?

At and near Brandon in Suffolk, about a mile from the Suffolk–Norfolk border. Brandon is near Grime's Graves, the famous prehistoric site of several hundred Stone Age flint mines which were worked by skilled craftsmen from the third millennium BC up to about 1800 BC. Stone Age flint knapping was chopping and shaping flint stone into tools, axes, axe heads and arrow heads.

What is *cuir bouilli*?

It is French for 'boiled leather', and it describes the technique for moulding leather into a variety of shapes. In the Middle Ages, for example, leather was used for many utensils such as bottles, tankards and large jugs (called bombards), and for helmets and footwear. By this process, the leather is soaked, then moulded or pressed into the required shape over some suitable template or pattern. When the leather has set, it is dipped into scalding water very briefly, and dried out with care so that no cracks appear in the material.

What is a glassblower's gather?

It is the blob of molten glass, sometimes called the metal, at the end of a glassblower's blowpipe when ready for blowing.

What is celadon glaze?

It is an old Chinese glaze, greyish to blue-green, the tones depending on the amount of iron used in the mixture.

How was the inside of a leather vessel waterproofed?

Normally, melted pitch was poured into the finished vessel, and then it was flushed out, leaving a very thin coat all over the inside surface. From time to time, the pitching might have to be redone if the vessel sprang a leak.

What is a journeyman?

It is the word for a fully qualified craftsman, who in the days of the craft guilds had been accepted as a member. The word comes from the custom for a man to travel to broaden his experience before settling down in one place and establishing a craft workshop.

What does a broom squire do?

He makes besom brooms. These are a particular type of garden broom, for sweeping lawns and paths. They consist of a head made of a cluster of birch twigs, or of heather, wrapped round one end of a wooden handle.

What is the difference between a carpenter and a joiner?

A carpenter is a woodworker who makes the simpler, plainer things such as fences, gates, and basic cottage furniture. A joiner is more specialized, and makes window-frames, doors, more complex furniture items and may also carry out woodwork repairs.

What is piqué work?

It is a technique used for making small objects such as snuff boxes, spectacle cases, walking-cane heads. The material is tortoiseshell inlaid or overlaid with cut gold or silver sheet or pinheads.

What is champlevé enamelling?

The metal to be enamelled by this method, which produces a raised field, is scored with grooves to a particular design, and the grooves are then filled with enamel. This is polished so that the top is level with the original metal.

What traditionally constructed vehicle was known as a hermaphrodite?

This was mostly made in the Midlands, especially in Leicestershire and Nottinghamshire. It was a two-wheel cart, constructed to allow the addition of front wheels, thus converting it into a four-wheel waggon when required.

What craftsman numbers samsons, boxing engines and travellers amongst his tools?

A wheelwright. He uses a samson to draw adjacent felloes (curved sections of rim) together while fitting a stroke (section of tyre), a boxing engine to bore the axle hole through the naff (hub), a traveller, which is a calibrated wheel mounted on a rod, to measure the circumference of a wheel.

What is change-ringing?

This means ringing a peal of bells in such an order as to form a mathematical permutation. The more bells there are, obviously, the greater the number of possible permutations or 'changes' as they are called. It would hardly be possible to ring the 479,001,600 changes that are possible with twelve bells; 40,320 changes stand as the record, on eight bells, at the Loughborough bell-foundry in 1963.

What is *dalle de verre*?

This French name means 'flagstone of glass'; this craft is concerned with setting slab glass, which can be multi-coloured or patterned, into frames of concrete or the increasingly popular epoxy resins.

What craftsman makes use of oak tree bark?

The tanner.

What is the ILEA?

It is the Inner London Education Authority, the largest education authority in Great Britain, and one of the biggest in Europe. The ILEA is run by a committee of 48 members (with additional co-opted members) and it governs the teaching arrangements and associated responsibilities for about a million children and young students.

What is a mature student?

It is an adult, normally over 25 (and who has held a paid job for at least three years) who goes to a university to study for a degree or diploma. Mature students can claim higher grants than ordinary students.

What is a Public School?

In the UK a public school is a private independent school for which the pupils' parents pay fees. Most public schools are boarding schools, a few are day schools and some are mixed. There are over 1200 such schools in the UK. They got the name public schools because the first ones began as local schools and later opened their doors to people from other districts.

What was School Certificate?

It was an examination taken in England by pupils before leaving school. It prevailed in the education system from the end of World War I up to 1951. A number of subjects were compulsory and pupils could also take extra subjects from choice. It was obligatory to take and pass in English language, and in mathematics, and in three other subjects, in order to obtain the certificate. Good marks earned what were called credits.

What is fagging?

A term to describe the custom in public schools whereby junior boys had to perform jobs, usually of a menial nature for senior boys. The system is dying out.

What did the Robbins Report of 1963 recommend?

Lord Robbins and his committee believed that there should be a significant increase in the amount and choice of higher education. They recommended expansion of university and polytechnic education and the creation of several new universities and colleges.

What is the origin of grammar schools?

The grammar schools probably go back to the days soon after the conversion of England to Christianity by St Augustine, in the last years of the 6th century. The creation of dioceses and the spread of monasteries meant that more people were needed to become priests and monks, and so schools were founded to take young boys in and teach them. The first mention of these schools, which were flourishing in many places in the Middle Ages, is in a document of the 1380s, where the phrase 'gramer schole' appears.

What is a crammer?

It is the word for an individual teacher, or for a small establishment of teachers, who provide special individual teaching privately for young people to help them get through important examinations, where they cannot get such individual help in a school. Crammers began to appear in the UK in the later 19th century, and some of them specialized in helping young men to pass the examinations necessary to get into the army or the navy.

What is a kindergarten?

A school for very young children, between 3 and 6, which helps them to get ready for ordinary school. The name is the German for children's garden and the idea was devised by Friedrich Froebel (1782–1852), a German educational philosopher.

What did the 1870 Elementary Education Act achieve?

It made education compulsory for all young children, and to achieve this it set up special school boards all over the country and allowed funds for building new schools to be raised from the rates. It was a revolutionary improvement in education, and was the work of William Forster.

What was the main achievement of R. A. Butler's 1944 Education Act?

It aimed to achieve 'equality of educational opportunity'. It raised the school leaving age to 15, provided free education for all children at local authority schools, and it established three types of secondary school for children to go to after the age of 11, namely, the grammar schools, (in existence for centuries), technical schools and secondary modern schools (a new creation). Pupils had to take an examination at the age of 11 to determine which type of school they went to. This exam was known as the 11-plus.

What is a prep school?

A preparatory school. This type of school was first introduced in the 19th century specifically to prepare young boys to take the examination necessary to get into public schools.

Which universities offer students the opportunity of taking an external degree?

London University, and the Open University.

What is the Girls Public Day School Trust?

It is a body started in 1872, which founded high schools for girls of the middle classes, where they could be educated to standards enabling them to enter universities. It has a membership of 23 schools.

What is a sandwich course?

It is a scheme whereby a person studies for a degree or diploma or higher certificate and works in a job related to the subject at the same time. That is to say, he or she has the basic job but is given time off to study at a college or other institution.

What does the abbreviation STOPP stand for?

Society of Teachers Opposed to Physical Punishment. Corporal punishment is still allowed in some UK schools. Efforts to get it outlawed are championed by this organization, which consists of teachers and also of parents.

What is the Common Entrance Examination?

At one time, public schools set their own entrance examinations for pupils, in addition to special scholarship examinations for very bright children. In 1903 a common entrance examination system was devised by a group of schools whereby any pupil aiming to get into any of the schools in the group sat a series of papers common to all the schools.

What is the Open University?

An institution created during Harold Wilson's term of office as prime minister (1964–1970), whereby people could obtain degrees by studying at home using correspondence courses organized by the Open University, whose headquarters is at Milton Keynes. Students have to attend one summer course, usually of two weeks, at a recognized centre which is often one of the ordinary universities.

What is the Baccalaureat?

It is an examination, covering a wide field of subjects, taken at the end of one's education at a French secondary school (lycée), which entitles one to apply for a place at a university in France.

Who was Count Basie?
Count Basie (1904–1984) was one of the greatest American jazz musicians and band leaders. He was a favourite before and during World War II.

What is swing?
A popular dance music of the 1930s and 1940s. It came in after the prohibition of liquor was lifted in the USA, when a craze for dancing swept the country. Among the leading swing band leaders were Benny Goodman, Tommy Dorsey and Artie Shaw.

Who was 'The Duke'?
This was Edward Kennedy Ellington (1899–1974), an American jazz pianist and composer who was among the greatest of all jazz musicians.

What is a musical?
It is a development of light opera, emerging in the last year of the 19th century. It is a theatrical performance of popular music, songs and dancing, loosely connected by a story line. It became fashionable in London and New York at about the same time in the 1890s. Later, musicals were specially written for films. Among the composers of musicals were George Gershwin, Cole Porter, Jerome Kern, Rodgers and Hart, Lerner and Lowe, Stephen Sondheim and in the UK, Noel Coward, Ivor Novello, and more recently Tim Rice and Andrew Lloyd Webber.

What is a glockenspiel?
An instrument consisting of a frame of tuned steel bars which is played with two hammers, or by a keyboard.

What is *crescendo*?
It means increasing in loudness.

What is the word for dying down of sound?
Diminuendo.

Who wrote the musical *Annie get your Gun*?
Irving Berlin, the composer who was born in 1888 in Russia and taken to the USA when a baby. He began his musical career as a singing waiter soon after the turn of the century. Since then, he composed over 800 popular songs, one of the earliest of which was 'Alexander's Rag Time Band'. Among the other musicals he composed are *White Christmas* and *Call Me Madam*.

Who was Scott Joplin?
Scott Joplin (1868–1917) was an American pianist and composer, who specialized in ragtime. Among his compositions were 'The Entertainer' and 'Maple Leaf Rag'. Joplin's ragtime has enjoyed a revival in recent years.

What is ragtime?
It is syncopated music for the piano, a forerunner of jazz, and was popular in the 1890s and 1900s.

Who was born Robert Allen Zimmerman?
Bob Dylan, the great folk and rock singer and composer.

Who was Carl Nielsen?
Carl Nielsen (1865–1931) was in his own lifetime recognized as the greatest composer produced by Denmark. His reputation internationally rests largely upon his six symphonies, the last of which he completed in 1925.

What is the nature of the work *Pictures from an Exhibition*?
This is a suite for solo piano by the Russian composer Mussorgsky (1839–1881). It was composed as a tribute to his friend Victor Hartmann, the artist, who died in 1873, and represents ten of his paintings with a 'promenade' as a linking passage. It has adapted well to orchestration by a number of composers, most notably Ravel.

2, 5, 7...

What is the game of fives?
A hard ball game played by two or four players in a court with three or four walls. The ball is hit by the hand, bare or gloved. The game probably began in the 15th century, and may be named from the five fingers.

What was a hundred?
It was a division of a shire of England. Each hundred had its own court which met every month.

What are hundreds and thousands?
They are tiny sugar sweets in different colours, used to decorate cakes and trifles.

How many pounds are there in a hundredweight?
112, though in American measurement, there are 100.

How much is a milliard?
1,000,000,000 (thousand million).

What is one-track?
It is a derogatory term to describe an attitude of someone who is obsessed by one particular idea.

What does 'two-bit' mean?
It is a word meaning worthless.

Who were the two main stars in the film, *The 49th Parallel*?
Leslie Howard and Eric Portman.

What were the Five Articles of Perth (1618)?
These were ordinances by which James I (1603–1625) compelled the General Assembly of the Church of Scotland to restore bishops in their church, to agree to kneel for the Communion, private communion if necessary, private baptism, observing of feast days, confirmation in church, all of which deeply offended the Scots.

Which army commander was affectionately known as One-Leg?
Field Marshal Henry William Paget, 1st Marquis of Anglesey (1768–1854). Paget had been second in command at the battle of Waterloo, where he lost a leg.

What is the Fourth Estate?
The Press.

What is a .22 rifle?
A rifle which fires a bullet whose diameter is 0.22 of an inch.

What railway services serve Seven Sisters station in London?
The Victoria Line of the Underground and the Eastern Region of British Rail.

What was the *Inn of the Sixth Happiness*?
A 1958 film, starring Ingrid Bergman as Gladys Aylward, a missionary in war-torn China.

Little Quiz 32
   In which countries are these cities or towns?
   1. Salamanca
   2. Kirkcaldy
   3. Topeka
   4. Edirne
   5. Nablus
   6. Montreux
   7. Odense
   8. Oaxaca
   9. Rennes
   10. Armagh
   11. Ghent
   12. Omdurman
   13. Wiesbaden
   14. Srinagar
   15. Tbilisi
   16. Tatung
   17. La Plata
   18. Nagasaki
   19. Bury St Edmunds
   20. Ravenna

Which was the earliest commercially successful motorcycle?

The model produced in 1894 by the German inventors Heinrich Hildebrand and Alois Wolfmuller, known as the H & W. It had pneumatic tyres and would achieve a speed of 45.08 kmh (28 mph). There is a surviving example of the machine in the National Motor Museum at Beaulieu.

What is the origin of the TT Races in the Isle of Man?

TT stands for Tourist Trophy, and the first TT race was run in 1907. The circuit was known as the St John's circuit, the village where it started and ended. The Isle of Man was chosen because there was no speed limit on the roads, and because the island's government was willing to close the roads for the race.

What were the two main features of the motorcycles built by the Scott motorcycle firm?

They were powered by two stroke engines of considerable power and the engines were water-cooled. The first model was built in the late 1890s.

Who was the first British motorcyclist to figure in the Honours List?

Freddie Frith, who received the OBE in 1949.

Which world champion motorcyclist once crashed at over 298.8 kmh (180 mph)?

Barry Sheene, at Daytona, USA, in 1975.

What are the four stages of operation of a 4-stroke engine?

i. induction of air and fuel mixture; ii. compression of the mixture into a small space at the top of the cylinder; iii. combustion of the mixture by means of an electric spark across the sparking plug in the cylinder head; iv. exhaust of the gases that have been burnt.

What is a moped?

A motorcycle of 50cc or less, designed to cruise at about 48.3 kmh (30 mph).

Why is the cylinder head of most motorcycle engines provided with fins?

To provide cooling. Air is drawn down between the fins while the motorcycle is in motion, creating cold currents that help to keep the cylinder head cool.

What is the mixture of petrol and air fed into a motorcycle engine by the carburettor?

Usually, 15 parts of air to one of petrol, and this provides the best mix for combustion at an economical level. The engine can work on higher and on lower ratios, but in the case of more air and less fuel, the engine will overheat, and in the case of less air and more fuel, petrol will be wasted.

What does it mean to 'decoke' an engine?

'Decoke' is slang for decarbonize, and all motorcycle engines accumulate layers of burnt carbon on the cylinder head surfaces and on the piston top. After a time, the layers are thick enough to interfere with the engine's performance, and they need to be removed. This is done by taking off the cylinder head and scraping away the carbon.

What does the dynamo do?

It is an electrical motor driven by a gear or a belt from the engine that produces direct current into the motorcycle's battery, keeping the battery charged to perform its functions.

What are the jets in a carburettor?

They are very small components pierced with a tiny hole, which are screwed into appropriate parts of the carburettor and regulate the amount of fuel passing into and out of it.

What was the Black Lightning?
In its time (early 1950s) it was the fastest standard motorcycle in the world, and it was made by the Vincent–H.R.D. stable. The machine could achieve over 241.5 kmh (150 mph).

Which is the longest surviving manufacturer of motorcycles?
The Harley Davidson organization which began to make motorcycles in 1903 and which exhibited models in the 1983 Motorcycle Exhibition.

What is trials riding?
This is an arduous sport involving the riding of a specially adapted motorcycle, non-stop and with the feet clear of the ground at all times over very difficult countryside.

Which motorcycle was T. E. Lawrence (Lawrence of Arabia) riding when he was killed in 1936?
A Brough Superior, given him by a number of friends, including Bernard Shaw.

What does it mean when a motorcycle engine is 'pinking'?
It is an unpleasant metallic noise that sounds like 'pink, pink'. This is caused when the wrong fuel is being used, or if the ignition timing is incorrect, or if the cylinder combustion chamber needs decarbonizing. 'Pinking' is usually accompanied by marked loss of power.

Why do some cylinders require reboring?
When the cylinder lining has become very worn, oil escapes and there is loss of power because the compression is affected. This can be put right by boring out the cylinder to a slightly bigger diameter and relining it with a sleeve of steel, and at the same time fitting new piston rings. Instead of a sleeve, you can fit a slightly larger diameter piston.

What was the most powerful motorcycle built as a normal production machine?
The Kawasaki K2 1300-A1, which had a six-cylinder engine, water-cooled.

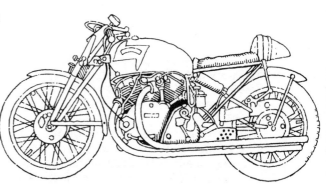

Black Lightning Motorcycle

Little Quiz 33
   In which English counties are these new district councils?
1. Adur
2. Uttlesford
3. Babergh
4. Breckland
5. Dacorum
6. Langbaurgh
7. Holderness
8. Test Valley
9. Waverley
10. Erewash
11. Fylde
   and in which Welsh counties are these?
12. Afan
13. Ynys Mon (Isle of Anglesey)
14. Ogwr
15. Glyndwr
16. Torfaen
17. Ceredigion
18. Brecknock
19. Preseli

What is the generally accepted date of the first Olympic Games held in ancient Greece?
776 BC. Even in those days it was ordained that the Olympiad, as it was called, should be held every four years.

What was the pancratium?
This was a combined wrestling and boxing event introduced to the Olympiad in the middle of the 7th century BC.

Which Roman emperor was the first to compete in the Olympic Games?
Emperor Nero, in the games of AD 65. He entered as a charioteer.

What brought the Olympic Games idea to an end in the ancient world?
Christian leaders decided that the games were undesirable, since they were relics of pagan rituals, and the Emperor Theodosius I banned the games in 393.

When were the Olympic Games re-established?
In 1894, at the instigation of Baron Pierre de Coubertin, the International Olympic Committee was founded. The first games were held in 1896, appropriately in Athens.

What is the ceremony of the Olympic torch?
Before each Games, a torch is set alight and it burns throughout. The torch is ignited by directing on it the sun's rays through a glass at the ancient Greek temple of Altis in the plains of Olympia, and it is carried by a relay of runners all the way to the country in which the Games are being held.

Who was the youngest performer in the Games ever to become an individual champion?
Marjorie Gestring, a US champion diver who won a medal at Berlin in 1936 when she was only 13.

Which member of the British peerage won the 400 m hurdles championship at the Games of 1928?
Lord Burghley, who later succeeded to the title Marquis of Exeter.

What was the amazing achievement of the US athlete Ray Ewry at the Paris Games of 1900?
Ewry had been paralysed as a boy, even confined to a wheelchair. But he was determined to become an athlete, and with tremendous will and application he toughened his leg muscles over many years so that he could compete in standing jump events. In 1900 he won three Gold Medals for the three standing jump events at the Paris Games, did it again at the Games of St Louis in 1904 and won two more at the London Games, 1908.

Which famous US general of World War II competed at the Stockholm Games of 1912?
General George S. Patton, a top American commander in Europe in the closing stages of the war.

Who was the 'Phantom Finn'?
Paavo Nurmi, an extraordinary athlete who, in several Olympic Games, won medals for long distance running, notably Gold Medals in the 1924 Paris Games for 5,000 m and 1,500 m races in the same afternoon.

Which Olympic swimming champion later became a famous film star?
Johnny Weissmuller, best known in the role of Tarzan, won 5 Gold Medals (3 in 1924, 2 in 1928).

Who was the first British woman Olympic Gold Medallist for figure skating?
Jeannette Altwegg won the Olympic title in 1952. She was also World Figure Skating Champion.

What happened to the Olympic champion swimmer Nancy Riach?
Nancy Riach, a Scot, was representing Great Britain in a number of freestyle events at the Olympic Games of 1948 in London. During the Games, Britain was suffering an epidemic of poliomyelitis (infantile paralysis), and between races Nancy Riach contracted the disease. Despite this she continued to compete though in great pain, and won an event. Within two days she died of the disease.

Who was the Flying Dutchwoman?
Fanny Blankers-Koen, who at the London 1948 Games won four Gold Medals, for 80 m hurdles, 200 m, 100 m and her part of a relay race.

Who carried the Olympic torch for the last lap and into the arena at Helsinki at the Games of 1952?
The Phantom Finn, Paavo Nurmi, at the age of 56.

What appalling tragedy occurred at the Munich Games of 1972?
Arab terrorists broke into the Olympic Village on 5 September, and murdered two Israeli competitors. They also kidnapped several others, held them hostage and then killed them that night. Eleven athletes were murdered.

Which four countries have been represented at every summer Olympic Games since they started in 1896?
Great Britain, Greece, Australia and Switzerland.

What are the Winter Olympics?
These were first staged as a separate grouping of events, at Chamonix in 1924. They included figure skating, ski-jumping, bob-sledding, speed skating and ice hockey. Later on, other events were added, such as tobogganing, ski-racing, ice yachting and barrel jumping.

Why did the United States refuse to send their Olympic Team to compete in the 1980 Games at Moscow?
Because the Soviet Union had, in 1979, sent an army into the neighbouring state of Afghanistan and overturned the existing government to install an administration more sympathetic to the Soviet Union.

Why were no equestrian events held at Melbourne, the venue for the 1956 Games?
In these, the first Olympic Games to be held outside Europe or North America, strict quarantine laws did not allow horses to be admitted for equestrian events. To get round the problem, these events were held in Stockholm.

Where would the 1940 and 1944 Games have been held, had they not been cancelled because of World War II?
In Helsinki and London, respectively; locations in reverse order for the first post-war Games of 1948 and 1952. For the record, the 1916 Games cancelled because of World War I would have been held in Berlin.

Little Quiz 34
   Some British titled families have surnames different from the titles: Which are the titles using these surnames?
   1. Villiers
   2. Cholmondeley
   3. Wallop
   4. Marquis
   5. Paget
   6. Wellesley
   7. Curzon
   8. Anson
   9. Bigham
   10. Dundas

$$2 + 5 \times 3 - 1 \div 2 = 10$$

Six times a number increased by 11 is equal to 65. What is the number?
9.

What number multiplied by 11 and reduced by 18 equals 15?
3.

One number is greater than another number by 3, and their sum is 27. What are the numbers?
12, 15.

What are the two numbers whose sum is 30 and one is greater than the other by 8?
11, 19.

If one number is 3 times another and their difference is 10, what are the two numbers?
15, 5.

Which are the two numbers whose sum is 26 and their difference 8?
9, 17.

A, B and C have £72 among them. C has twice B's share and B has £4 more than A. What share has each?
A £21, B £17, C £34.

Divide 75 into two parts, so that three times one part is twice the other.
30, 45.

In 8 hours, C walks 3 more miles than D walks in 6 hours, and in 7 hours D walks 9 miles more than C does in 6 hours. How many miles does each walk in each hour.
C $3\frac{3}{4}$ miles, D $4\frac{1}{2}$ miles.

What number of two digits is 7 times the sum of the digits and if 36 is subtracted from the number the digits are reversed?
84.

Divide £511 among A, B and C, so that B's share equals $\frac{1}{3}$ of A's share and C's share is $\frac{3}{4}$ of A's share and B's share together.
A £219, B £73, C £219.

A is 8 years younger than B and 24 years older than C. $\frac{1}{8}$ of A's age, $\frac{1}{2}$ of B's age and $\frac{1}{3}$ of C's age together amount to 38 years. What are their ages?
A = 42, B = 50, C = 18.

The difference between the squares of two consecutive numbers is 31. What are the numbers?
15, 16.

A has £12 and B has £8: after B has lost a certain sum to A, his money is only $\frac{3}{7}$ of A's. How much did A win?
£2.

How old is a man whose age 10 years ago was $\frac{3}{8}$ of what it will be in 15 years time?
25 years.

Two numbers add up to 54, and there is 12 between them. What are they?
33, 21.

One fifth of the difference of two numbers is 3, and $\frac{1}{3}$ of their sum is 17. What are the numbers?
33, 18.

The digits of a number between 10 and 100 equal each other, and the number exceeds 5 times the sum of the digits by 8. What is the number?
88.

A certain number between 10 and 100 is six times the sum of the digits, and the number exceeds the number formed by reversing the digits by 9. Find the number.
54.

Which number's double exceeds its half by 9?
6.

Two numbers add up to 19. One is twice the other plus 1. What are the two numbers?
6, 13.

Divide £66 between A, B and C, so that B may have £8 more than A, and C £14 more than B.
A £12, B £20, C £34.

What would A and B have if they shared £100 so that B had £30 more than A?
A £35, B £65.

What is the number whose double exceeds its half by 9?
6.

How do you divide 48 into two parts, so that one part is three-fifths of the other part?
18, 30.

Jack is 16 years younger than Fred, and one half of Jack's age is the same as one third of Fred's age: how old are Jack and Fred?
Fred is 48, Jack is 32.

Frances is twice as old as Joan, ten years ago she was four times as old: what are their present ages?
Frances is 30, Joan is 15.

A father is four times as old as his son: in 16 years he will be only twice as old: what are their ages?
Father is 32, son is 8.

George is 20 years older than Mary; five years ago, George was twice as old as Mary. How old are they?
George is 45, Mary is 25.

A father is 24 years older than his son: in seven years the son's age will be two-fifths of his father's age: what are their present ages?
33 and 9.

Two boys have 240 marbles between them; one arranges his in piles of six each, the other in piles of nine. There are 36 piles altogether. How many marbles has each boy?
168, 72.

The sum of two numbers is 97 and their difference is 51. What are the two numbers?
74, 23.

Half Edward's age exceeds a quarter of Cyril's by twelve months, and three quarters of Cyril's age exceeds Edward's age by 11 years. What are Edward's and Cyril's ages?
Edward, 28; Cyril, 52.

In eight hours, Fiona walks three miles more than Jean does in six hours, and in seven hours Jean walks nine miles more than Fiona does in six hours. How many miles does each walk per hour?
Fiona, $3\frac{3}{4}$ and Jean, $4\frac{1}{2}$.

A certain number of two digits is seven times the sum of the digits, and if 36 is subtracted from the number, the digits will be reversed. What is the number?
84.

Find a number which is less than its square by 72.
9.

Divide the number 16 into two, so that the sum of the squares of the two parts is 130.
7, 9.

What is the highest known flight speed of a bird?
170.67 kmh (106 mph), by a white-throated spinetail swift.

Which is the tallest mammal in the animal kingdom?
The giraffe, which can be as tall as 6.1 m (20 ft).

Which is the world's smallest breed of horses?
The Falabella horse, from the Argentine. Some are only 38.1–40.64 cm (15–16 in) tall, weighing as little as 18.16–20.83 kg (40–45 lb). There are Falabella horses at Kilverstone Park Zoo in Norfolk.

Which is the tallest cooling tower in Europe?
Uentrop, in West Germany, at a nuclear power plant. It is 180.25 m (591 ft) high and was built in 1976.

Which is the largest residential palace in the world?
The Vatican, in Vatican City, Rome. It covers 5½ hectares (13½ acres), and has over 1400 rooms, chapels and halls.

Where is the longest pleasure pier in the world?
At Southend-on-Sea, Essex, England, and it is 2.15 km (1.34 miles) long.

What is the biggest pearl ever found?
The Pearl of Laotze, a 6.63975 kg, 24.13 cm long × 13.97 cm thick (14 lb 1 oz, 9½ in long × 5½ in thick) stone found in the shell of a clam in the Philippine Islands in 1934.

Which has been the longest running theatrical performance or show anywhere in the world?
The Mousetrap, a play by Agatha Christie, which was first put on in London in November 1952 and is still running today (1984).

128

What is said to be the highest temperature achieved by scientists artificially?
Inside the centre of a thermonuclear (hydrogen) bomb, temperatures of 300 to 400 million degrees Centigrade are estimated to be reached, i.e. 3–4 million times as hot as boiling water.

Which is the biggest painting in Britain?
Probably the oval picture of *Triumph of Peace and Liberty* by Sir James Thornhill (1676–1734) on the ceiling of the Painted Hall at the Royal Naval College at Greenwich.

Where is the largest art gallery in the world?
The Winter Palace and the Hermitage in Leningrad (formerly, St Petersburg). The two buildings which are one gallery hold over 3,000,000 objects and it requires a walk of more than 24 km (15 miles) to see them all.

Which was the largest passenger liner to sail the seas?
The *Queen Elizabeth*, built in Clydebank in Scotland and launched in 1938. It was 314.45 m (1031 ft) long and displaced 83,673 tons.

Which was Britain's biggest battleship?
The *Vanguard*, which was in service for only 15 years (1946–60). It displaced 51.420 tons and was 248.27 m (814 ft) long. It mounted eight 15-inch guns. The *Vanguard* was never used in war and was eventually scrapped. It was also the last British battleship ever built.

Where is the highest capital city in the world?
Lhasa, Tibet, though Tibet is now part of China. It is 3,686.23 m (12,086 ft) above sea level. The next highest is La Paz, Bolivia, at 3,634.38 m (11,915 ft).

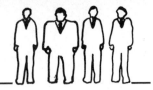

Which British person was awarded the highest number of freedoms of cities and towns?
Sir Winston Churchill, who received 42 freedoms.

Who was the longest reigning European monarch?
Louix XIV of France, 1643–1715 (72 years). Known as the Sun King, Le Grand Monarque, and other nicknames, he was one of the greatest of all European sovereigns.

Which world statesman has held office as foreign minister for the longest period of time this century?
Andrei Gromyko (born 1909), who has been foreign minister of the USSR since 1957.

Who was the longest serving British MP?
Sir Winston Churchill, with a total of 63 years, 10 months.

Where is the largest man-made mound of earth in Europe?
It is thought to be Silbury Hill, a few miles to the west of Marlborough in Wiltshire, just beside the old A4 road to Bath. It is about 39.65 m (130 ft) tall, with a base area of 2¼ hectares (5½ acres), and was raised in the first half of the 3rd millennium BC.

Where is the tallest lighthouse in the world?
A steel tower at Yamashita Park, Yokohama, Japan is 106.445 m (349 ft) tall, and you should be able to see it at least 32.2 km (20 miles) away.

What is the tallest mountain in the world which has yet to be climbed?
Zemu Gap Peak, 7.780m (25,526 ft) in the Sikkim region of Northern India, and a part of the Himalayan range.

What is the loudest noise ever produced naturally by a human being?
A scream of 120 decibels, emitted by Susan Birmingham who lived in Hong Kong in March 1982.

What is the world's most infectious disease?
Pneumonic plague; moreover, only one person in about every 10,000 who contract the disease would be likely to survive it. Fortunately, its occurrence is extremely rare, more so than the related bubonic plague which last claimed a British victim in 1926.

What living creature possesses the largest eye?
The giant squid, with an eye 38cm (15in) in diameter.

What living creature has the most legs?
Millipedes in general have the most legs, though never as many as one thousand, as their name might suggest. Specifically, an unidentified South African millipede has the greatest number, 710 (ie 355 pairs).

What is the most remote land in the British Isles?
Rockall, in the Atlantic Ocean 307km (191 miles) west of St Kilda, the furthest outlying group of the Western Isles of Scotland.

Which is the biggest desert in the world?
The Sahara, in North Africa, which covers over 777 million hectares (3 million square miles).

Which is said to be the hottest place on earth?
Dallal, in Abyssinia (Ethiopia), where the average temperature throughout the year is over 94° Fahrenheit (34.5° C).

What was a sabretache handbag?
A large handbag deriving in design from a military bag carried by a cavalry officer on his left side. It was fashionable in the early 19th century, and was generally heavily embroidered.

When would you wear a mantilla?
Only if you were female, and as a rule over your head and shoulders when you went into a church. A mantilla is a veil or scarf, often with lace trimming, or even entirely of lace, and it is carried over the arm when not worn.

What is a chemise?
It is an undergarment, of cotton or linen as a rule, worn by women under a dress or coat and skirt.

What are cami-knickers?
Popularly worn before World War II and for some years after it, they are a combined garment of petticoat top and a pair of knickers.

What was the bustle?
It was a small stuffed cushion arrangement set underneath a woman's skirt at the back, to create a puffed out shape. The fashion began to emerge in the mid-19th century and lasted, with one or two short periods of being out of fashion, to the end of the century.

What is a cummerbund?
It is a sash worn round the waist, by both sexes but more generally by men today with evening dress.

What is a deerstalker?
A special cap of tweed for men, with a peak at both front and back, and with ear flaps which, when not tied under the chin, are folded and tied on top of the cap.

What was a pelerine?
A shoulder cape with pronounced elongated ends at the front.

What was a dormeuse?
A French nightcap worn in the later 18th century, with a loose-fitting, ribbon-trimmed crown over the head and lace flaps, rounded over the ears and curved back to expose the forehead.

Who used to wear a redingote?
Most men, usually of the upper classes, in the 18th and here and there in the early 19th century. It was a long, double breasted overcoat, narrowed at the waist, with large collar, and long cut-away tails.

What was a toque?
A close-fitting cap without brim, usually worn by women.

Day dress with bustle c 1884

What was a banyan?

This was a loose coat of the 18th century worn by men indoors. It reached to the knees, had a shortish vent at the back and was fastened by buttons or a sash. The banyan was generally made of simple washable material.

When did women's bathing suits begin to appear in western Europe?

In the later 19th century, probably about 1870. The early style was made of flannel, serge, or alpaca, usually blue or black. The garment stretched from neck to mid-thigh and was tied round the waist, the short leggings also were tied with ribbon.

What was the 'princess line'?

This is a phrase to describe a manner of dress-making in which the back of the garment is close-fitting and has no seam.

Why was the Ulster overcoat so called?

Because the design came from Northern Ireland. It was a double-breasted overcoat, sometimes belted in the middle, with a cape or two capes over the shoulders.

Would you wear galluses today?

You might wear the modern equivalent, which is braces. Galluses first appeared in the 1780s and were of soft, silky material, finely decorated but without elastic which was not then known. They held up the breeches.

What were the characteristics of the dress of the Incroyables?

The Incroyables were a group of dandies of the 1790s who wore their smart clothes in a deliberately messy and unkempt manner, grew their hair exceptionally long and straggly, and sported ear-rings. They wore enormous scarves round their necks, the front bows of which covered much of their faces.

What was a buffon?

It was a square of lace or linen worn like a scarf round the neck and tied into a huge bow at the front, known also as a neckerchief.

What was the trollopee?

A mid-18th century sack-type dress worn indoors by women, generally in the morning only. It hung down below the waist in pleats.

What is a caftan?

A caftan, or kaftan, is a long-sleeved coat, often worn loose. It originated in the Middle East, becoming popular in Britain in the late 1960s.

What is a kimono?

A wrap style of robe with full-cut sleeves and a sash, originating in Japan. The best kimonos are made of silk and often have exquisite designs.

What is a pea jacket?

This is a heavy, double breasted navy blue woollen jacket worn by sailors. The term originates from the Dutch word *pij*, a coarse woollen material.

What is a Basque beret?

A peakless round-crown cap, often made of felt, and originating in the Basque country of France and Spain. It is a garment that will always be associated with the artist, Pablo Picasso.

What is a stock?

A stock is a made-up neckcloth, taking the form of a piece of lawn, silk or muslin pleated into a stiffened band which fastens at the back of the neck. It enjoyed its heyday throughout the 18th century, then fell into a decline for general wear. However, it has remained as part of the huntsman's traditional attire.

Who was the first of the Habsburg royal line in Europe?

Rudolph I (1218–1291), Count of Habsburg, who became emperor of the Holy Roman Empire in 1273 and made his son duke of Austria in 1282. From 1438 to 1806, with one exception, the title Emperor of the Holy Roman Empire was held by a Habsburg.

How did Harold II become king of England in 1066?

He was chosen by the Witenagemot (the English Council), although he was not a member of the royal family. Harold was the son of Godwin, Earl of the West Saxons, and was the most suitable person to rule on the death of Edward the Confessor.

Why was William I succeeded by his *second* son as king of England?

Because the Conqueror left his empire divided between Robert, the eldest who was to have Normandy, and William, the next son, who was to have England.

Who was Pedro the Cruel?

Pedro the Cruel (1334–1369) was king of Castile and León (part of Spain). During the first part of his reign he ruled well, tending to side with the people against the nobility, but he was faced with many baronial revolts, some led by his half-brother Henry of Trastamara. This led him to commit many unjust and severe acts, some against his own family, and in the end he lost his popularity. Pedro died in a duel with his half-brother.

When did the king of Prussia become the emperor of Germany?

Wilhelm I, king of Prussia from 1861, was chosen as first emperor of Germany in 1871 and died in 1888.

When was Queen Victoria proclaimed empress of India?

In 1876.

Why did George I, a cousin of Queen Anne, succeed her in 1714 when there were closer relatives?

Because George, elector of Hanover, was a Protestant. The closer relatives were Catholics and so barred from the succession.

Why was Charles II succeeded by his brother James when he had several sons?

Because all of Charles's children were illegitimate.

Which Scottish king was killed by an exploding cannon?

James II (1437–1460), at the siege of Roxburgh Castle.

What was the relationship between Elizabeth I, and James VI of Scotland who succeeded her?

Elizabeth's father Henry VIII was brother of James's great-grandmother Margaret Tudor (wife of James IV).

Where did John II of France die, and why?

John II (1319–1364) became king of France in 1350. In 1356 he was captured at the battle of Poitiers by the victorious English under the Black Prince and taken to London. Four years later, he was allowed to go back to France, leaving one of his sons as a hostage. But the son escaped in 1363. John thereupon chivalrously volunteered to go back to London in his place, and died in London soon afterwards.

Who was Shakespeare's 'time-honour'd Lancaster'?

John of Gaunt (1340–1399), Duke of Lancaster, fourth son of Edward III and virtual ruler of England during part of the minority of Richard II (1377–1399). The phrase comes from Shakespeare's play, Richard II.

Which English king defeated his brother in battle and then kept him in prison for nearly 30 years?
Henry I (1100–1135) defeated his elder brother Robert, Duke of Normandy, at the battle of Tinchebrai in 1106 and put him in prison in Cardiff Castle where Robert stayed until his death in 1134.

Was George V the eldest son of Edward VII?
No, Edward VII's eldest son was Albert, Duke of Clarence, who died in 1892, without heir.

What happened to Louis XVII of France?
He was the second son of Louis XVI and became heir to the French throne in 1789 when his elder brother died. Louis XVI was deposed in 1792 and executed by guillotine in 1793. The young Louis XVII, who had been born in 1785, was kept in prison where he died in 1795. Many legends arose as to his fate, and some said that he was spirited out of prison to safety. There were even claimants in later years.

Who was the first king of the Belgians?
Leopold I (1831–1865), who was elected in 1831. He was an uncle of Queen Victoria.

Who was the first Stewart king of Scotland?
Robert II, son of Marjorie Bruce (Robert Bruce's daughter) and her husband, Walter the Steward. Robert II reigned from 1371 to 1390.

Has there ever been a king of Finland?
No, though there have been one or two regents, and a number of viceroys and governor-generals – and even some grand dukes. Finland now has a president.

Who was the youngest son of George V?
It is usually said to have been the Duke of Kent, who was killed in an air crash during World War II (1942). But George V and Queen Mary had a younger son, Prince John, born in 1905 who died in 1919.

Has there ever been a king of Brazil?
Yes. Brazil was a monarchy from 1815 to 1889. The first monarch was Queen Maria (1815–1816), who was also Maria I, Queen of Portugal. She was succeeded by her son, John, who was also John VI of Portugal. John handed Brazil to his son Pedro in 1822. Pedro elevated himself to Emperor Pedro I in that year, but abdicated in 1831 and was succeeded by his son Pedro II who was to rule until he was deposed in 1889. Brazil then became a republic which it still is.

Who was the last Emperor of the Holy Roman Empire?
Francis II (1792–1806), who was also Archduke of Austria. The Holy Roman Empire was abolished by him at the insistence of Napoleon, in 1806, and Francis became Francis I, Emperor of Austria, a new title. He reigned until 1835. The last Austrian emperor abdicated in 1919.

Little Quiz 35
What do these phrases mean?
1. Blowing your own trumpet
2. Crying for the moon
3. Building castles in the air
4. Looking a gift horse in the mouth
5. Playing to the gallery
6. Turning over a new leaf
7. Tilting at windmills
8. Flogging a dead horse
9. Keeping one's feet on the ground
10. Drawing the longbow

Who was the first woman to be elected a head of state?
Mrs Vigdis Finnbogadottir, who was elected president of Iceland on 30 June 1980.

Who was the first woman to address the House of Commons?
It was not Viscountess Astor, the first woman MP, but Mrs Elizabeth Robinson (1695–1779) who came from Gibraltar to give evidence about the slave trade.

Which was the first university in England?
Oxford, which is generally said to have been founded in about 1167, and whose first college was University College, opened in 1249.

Which was the first university in Scotland?
St Andrews, founded by Bishop Wardlaw in 1412. Its first curriculum was based on that of the university of Paris.

Who was awarded the first Nobel Prize for physics?
Wilhelm Röntgen (1845–1923), the discoverer of X-rays, in 1901.

Who was the first pope?
Traditionally, St Peter, one of the twelve disciples, was the first pope, and his term of office is usually given as 42 to 67. He was martyred in 67.

Who was the first president of the USSR?
Mikhail Kalinin, who held office from 1923 to 1946.

When was the first non-stop transatlantic air flight?
In 1919, when Sir John Alcock and Sir Arthur Whitten Brown took a Vickers Vimy bomber from Newfoundland to Ireland, nearly 3200 km (2000 miles) in just over 16 hours.

Who was the first Ottoman Sultan?
Othman (or Osman), who ruled from about 1299 to 1326. The word Ottoman is taken from him.

Who was the first president of the Royal Society?
An Anglo-Irish mathematician, William, Viscount Brouncker, from 1662 to 1677.

When was the first English Prayer Book issued?
In 1549, in the reign of Edward VI. Much of its matchless prose was written by Archbishop Cranmer.

When was the first public demonstration of television?
On 27 January 1926, when John Logie Baird, its pioneer, revealed it at a gathering in London.

Who was the first Prince of Wales?
Rhodri Mawr (Rhoderic the Great), who was prince of Gwynedd, that is, north Wales, and who was recognized as overlord of Wales between 844 and 878.

Who was the first illegitimate son of Charles II (1660–1685)?
The first known illegitimate son was James Scott, later created Duke of Monmouth. He was the son of Charles and a Welsh girl, Lucy Walter, and was born in 1649, the year of Charles's father's execution. For a time in the early part of Charles II's reign, the king seemed likely to recognize the duke as his heir.

Which Irish king first successfully united the various kingdoms of Ireland?
Traditionally, it was Brian Boru, king of Munster, who was recognized as Ard Ri, or high king, from about 1001 to 1014, when he was killed in battle with the Vikings at Clontarf. He was killed at the moment of victory for the Irish forces.

Who was the first surgeon to stitch arteries while operating?

Probably Ambrose Paré (1517–1590), a French surgeon who became a royal physician and served four French kings.

Who was the first president of Czechoslovakia?

Thomas Garrigue Masaryk, from 1918 to 1935. Czechoslovakia was a new state created out of parts of the old Austro-Hungarian empire after World War I. The principal component was the ancient state of Bohemia.

Who was the first and only Englishman to be elected pope?

Nicholas Breakspear (c. 1100 to 1159). He was elected pope as Adrian IV in 1154.

Who is the first lady?

The wife of the president of the USA, or of the governor of a US state. If the president (or the governor) is a bachelor or widower, the first lady is the person he chooses to act as hostess for him at functions.

When were the first rubber bands made?

Elastic bands made from vulcanized rubber were patented by Steven Perry, a member of the firm of Messrs Perry and Co of London, on 17 March 1845.

When was the passenger lift or elevator first recorded?

This was one which was installed in the private apartments of Louis XV at the Palais de Versailles, France, in 1743. The king used it to communicate with his mistress, whose rooms were on the floor above his. It worked through a carefully balanced set of weights, and could be easily raised or lowered by hand.

When were greeting cards first used?

These were designed for use on birthdays and other anniversaries by William Harvey and engraved by John Thompson of London in 1829.

What was the world's first hotel?

This was Low's Grand Hotel, situated in Covent Garden, London, and opened in January 1774 by David Low. Previously, travellers and others requiring hotel facilities had had to rely exclusively upon inns.

Who was the first person to be killed by a motor vehicle?

Mrs Bridget Driscoll of Croydon was knocked down and killed by a car driven by Arthur Edsell at the Crystal Palace, on 17 August 1896. At the inquest it was said that the car was only travelling at 4 mph when the accident occurred. The verdict was 'accidental death'.

Who was the first ombudsman?

Lars August Mannerheim, who held this office in Sweden from 1810 to 1823.

When was the first restaurant opened?

The first establishment to be called a restaurant was the Champ d'Oiseau (bird's field), established by M Boulanger in Paris in 1765.

Little Quiz 36

What time is it in the following capitals of the world, when it is 12.00 noon (Greenwich Mean Time)?

1. Paris
2. Cairo
3. Singapore
4. Madrid
5. Tokyo
6. Peking
7. Melbourne
8. New York
9. Buenos Aires
10. Auckland, New Zealand

Who discovered the laws of planetary motion?

Johann Kepler (1571–1630), the German astronomer, who between 1609 and 1619 showed that the planets move round the sun in ellipses, that the square of a planet's period of revolution is proportional to the cube of its mean distance from the sun, and other fundamental laws, which were later elaborated by Isaac Newton.

Who discovered the periodic arrangement of the elements?

Dmitri Ivanovich Mendeleyev (1834–1907), one of Russia's most distinguished chemists, who in 1869 produced his table of all the elements, in which he predicted the existence of many not then discovered, but which were later found. No. 101 is named *mendelevium* after him.

Who discovered the electron?

Sir Joseph John Thomson (1856–1940), Cavendish professor of experimental physics at Cambridge from 1884 to 1919.

Who discovered the neutrino?

Wolfgang Pauli (1900–1958), an Austrian physicist, who showed that there must be an electrically neutral particle in the nucleus of an atom, which was later proved by Enrico Fermi.

Who identified quasars?

Quasars, the more popular name for quasi-stellar radio-sources, were first identified in 1963 by the scientists Thomas Matthews and Allen Sandage of the United States.

Who discovered the anthrax bacillus?

Robert Koch (1843–1910), the German bacteriologist, in 1876. This remarkable scientist made many other important discoveries, including the tubercle bacillus (tuberculosis) in 1882 and the cholera bacillus. He was awarded a Nobel Prize in 1905.

Who discovered creosote?

Creosote is a mixture of chemicals resulting from distillation of wood tar. It was discovered by Baron Karl von Reichenbach (1788–1869), a German scientist and industrialist, who also discovered paraffin.

Who discovered the leprosy bacillus?

Armauer Hansen (1841–1912), the Norwegian bacteriologist, in 1879.

Who discovered alpha and beta rays in radioactive atoms?

Lord Rutherford (1871–1937), Cavendish professor of experimental physics at Cambridge, who was also the first physicist to split the atom (1919).

Who discovered ozone?

Christian Friedrich Schönbein (1799–1868), the German chemist, in 1839. Schönbein also invented gun cotton.

Who discovered saccharin?

This sharply sweet white powder, used as a substitute for sugar, was discovered by the German chemist Constantin Fahlberg in 1879.

Who first discovered aspirin?

A French chemist, Charles Frederic Gerhardt (1816–1856), who was professor of chemistry at Strasbourg.

Who discovered the element *neptunium*?

Edwin McMillan and Philip Abelson, both in the United States, in 1940. McMillan shared the Nobel Prize for chemistry in 1951, with G. T. Seaborg who had helped to discover plutonium.

Who discovered that sun spots give out radio waves?

Sir Edward Appleton (1892–1965), in 1946. Appleton discovered the region of the upper atmosphere known as the Appleton layer.

Who discovered streptomycin?
This powerful and effective antibiotic drug was discovered in 1943 by Selman Abraham Waksman (1888–1973), a Russian-born bacteriologist living and working in the United States. He was awarded the Nobel Prize for medicine in 1952.

Who discovered carbonic acid gas?
Dr Joseph Black (1728–1799), the Scottish chemist, who also discovered latent heat. Carbonic acid gas is carbon dioxide.

Who discovered the element chromium?
Louis Nicolas Vauquelin (1763–1829), a French chemist who was professor of chemistry at Paris from 1809.

Who discovered the element selenium, the major component in the photoelectric cell?
The Swedish chemist, John Jakob Berzelius (1779–1848), who discovered other elements, and was also responsible for formulating the present system of symbols for the elements, and laid the basis of chemical formulae.

Who discovered the elements strontium, calcium, magnesium and barium?
Sir Humphry Davy (1778–1829), who also invented the miner's safety lamp.

Who discovered the phenomenon of the super-cooling of water?
Gabriel Daniel Fahrenheit (1686–1736), of temperature-scale fame, discovered that in certain circumstances water can remain as a 'super-cooled' liquid when its temperature is dropped to below freezing-point.

Who discovered the cause of gangrene?
The bacillus causing gangrene was discovered in 1892 by William Henry Welch (1850–1934), the American pioneer of scientifically organized pathology.

Who discovered latent heat?
It was discovered by Joseph Black (1728–1799), the Scottish physicist and chemist, in 1760.

Who discovered the cause of malaria?
The discovery that malaria was transmitted by mosquitoes was due to the collaboration of two British physicians, Sir Patrick Manson (1844–1922) and Sir Ronald Ross (1857–1932). Manson, known as the 'father of tropical medicine', advanced the hypothesis in 1894 that the malaria parasite used the mosquito as its transmitting agent. He then inspired Ross to make the actual discovery that this was indeed true in 1897–98. In addition to Ross's talents as a physician for which he was awarded the Nobel Prize for medicine in 1902, he was also a distinguished poet.

Who discovered Prussian blue?
This was an accidental discovery, made by a German dyer named Diesbach in 1704.

Little Quiz 37

How do the following archbishops and bishops sign their names? They write their Christian names and then add:

1. Canterbury
2. York
3. Oxford
4. Chester
5. Peterborough
6. Rochester
7. Carlisle
8. Salisbury
9. Ely
10. Exeter
11. Durham

When was the first internal combustion-engined car, fuelled by petroleum, driven successfully along a road?
In 1859 by Étienne Lenoir, in Paris.

Which was the first four-wheeled petrol driven car of wholly British design?
It was a car made by Frederick George Lanchester at his Birmingham factory in 1895.

What was the Red Flag Law?
The Road Locomotives Act of 1865 which said that each locomotive powered by steam on the road was to have three persons in attendance, one to stoke, one to steer and one to walk in front with a red flag to warn oncoming horse traffic. The maximum speed was 3.22 kmh (2 mph) in towns and 6.44 kmh (4 mph) in the country.

In which country are car number plates permanent from the day of initial registration to the day of scrapping?
Great Britain. In other countries, plates may be changed on crossing from one state or province to another.

Who designed the best-selling Mini-Minor first produced in 1959?
Sir Alec Issigonis (b 1906), of British Leyland. He also designed the famous and highly successful post-war Morris Minor, which first appeared in 1949.

What was the Silver Ghost?
It was the first car produced by the Rolls Royce partnership, and was so called because it was so well silenced that it was difficult to hear it moving along the road. This high degree of engine silencing has always been one of the characteristics of Rolls Royce motor cars.

How did the great firm of Rolls Royce originate?
C. S. Rolls (son of Lord Llangattock), one of Britain's earliest aviators, met Henry (later, Sir Henry) Royce, an engineer who had a factory in Manchester where he made electrical equipment, cranes, etc., and who had built himself a car. Rolls was so impressed with Royce's car that he offered to market it, and the famous partnership was formed in 1906.

Who is often ranked as second only to Fangio, and cherished as Britain's greatest driver?
Stirling Moss (b 1929). Though he has never won a world championship, he has won numerous international and national races, often with tremendous élan and at colossal speed. Though appallingly badly injured at Goodwood races in 1962 and had to retire when he recovered, he has nonetheless remained by far the most popular motor ace in Britain.

When was the Automobile Association founded?
1905.

206 GT Ferrari

Only three men have held both world land speed and water speed records. Who were they?
Sir Malcolm Campbell (1885–1948), his son Donald Campbell (1921–1967), and Sir Henry Segrave (1896–1930). Both Donald Campbell and Henry Segrave were killed attempting to increase the water speed record.

What is a V-8 engine?
It is an engine which has eight cylinders in two opposing banks of four, set in a 'V'. A few cars were made and fitted with these engines, which were very powerful, but which were heavy on petrol consumption.

Which was the first three-letter car registration?
ARF for Staffordshire, in July 1932.

Which pope was the first to use a motor car regularly?
Pope Pius XII. Pope Pius X had been presented with a motor car in 1909 but he refused to ride in it.

Which was the first mass produced British car?
The small Austin Seven, first produced in 1922. It cost less than £100, could reach about 80 kph (50 mph), was supplied with either a hard top or a canvas folding-down top, and more than a quarter of a million of the cars were made. You can still see the occasional Austin Seven of the 1920s on the roads today, but they are rarity items.

Who is regarded by many as the greatest racing driver of all time?
Juan Manuel Fangio (b 1911), the Argentine driver who was world champion driver five times. He is remarkable for not having started serious car racing until he was nearly forty, an age at which many others retire.

What were the record speeds achieved by the three?
Malcolm Campbell (land: 481.8 kph (301.13 mph), water: 228.2 kph (141.74 mph); Donald Campbell (land: 652.77 kph (405.45 mph), water: 444.89 kph (276.33 mph); Segrave (land: 362.62 kph (231.44 mph).

What German company had made bicycles and typewriters before marketing their first car in 1900?
Adler, which had also made components for Benz before that date. They made private cars until 1939, but only resumed production of motor cycles after the war.

What is peculiar about the French Arola cars?
This firm has made three-and-four-wheeled minicars since 1976; the former having a 47 cc engine, the latter a 50 cc engine. Both have automatic transmission.

What Yorkshire firm with a Lancashire name once made cars?
The Blackburn Aeroplane and Motor Co Ltd of Leeds had made aircraft, but produced the Blackburn 20 hp tourer from 1919 to 1925. They also made bodies for other car makers.

What top class British driver was killed while flying his own aircraft?
Graham Hill, who crashed while returning to Elstree airfield from a test session at the Paul Ricard circuit on 29 November 1975. Among his many successes, he won the Monaco Grand Prix five times.

What hat-tricks were scored at the 1974 Le Mans 24 hour race?
The Matra-Simca team won for the third successive year; Henri Pescarolo achieved his personal hat-trick of wins.

What were the principal musicals composed by Cole Porter?
Cole Porter (1892–1964) produced many musical successes, including *Kiss me Kate, Can-Can, Anything Goes, High Society,* and also numerous hit songs, such as 'Begin the Beguine' and 'Night and Day'.

How long did the Beatles dominate the Pop Scene?
From 1963 to 1971 when the partnership of the four was disbanded. They were John Lennon (murdered in December 1980), Paul McCartney, George Harrison and Ringo Starr. Their themes were simple, the lyrics direct and caring, and they were set to fine harmonies.

What is reggae?
It is a West Indian style of popular music generally played on makeshift instruments. It is closely associated with Rastafarianism, a 'back-to-Africa' movement in the West Indies. The music borrows from calypso and from rhythm-and-blues, emphasized with an insistent, repetitive beat, and is currently very popular in Europe.

What two famous composers tried but never succeeded in meeting each other?
Johann Sebastian Bach and George Friedrich Handel. Both were born in 1685, both went blind in the last years of their lives. Bach and Handel dominated the musical scene in Europe from the second to the fifth decade of the 18th century.

What was Mozart's favourite wind instrument?
The clarinet.

For whom did Purcell write the opera *Dido and Aeneas*?
It was written in 1689 to be performed by the pupils of a London girls' school.

Which dictator loved the music of Wagner?
Adolf Hitler who was friendly with the Wagner family and patronized the Bayreuth Festival.

In 1958, Shostakovich won a Lenin Prize for his Eleventh Symphony. What was the subject of the symphony?
The October Revolution of 1905 in Russia.

Which of Gustav Mahler's symphonies is a choral work?
The Eighth symphony.

What three rock 'n roll stars were all to die young?
Buddy Holly, killed in an aircraft, 1959; Gene Vincent, who died in 1971; Eddie Cochran, killed in a car crash, 1960.

Which pop group of the 1960s smashed up their instruments as part of their performance?
The Who.

Which guitarist has been named by Segovia as his 'heir' and described by him as having bridged the gap between classical and popular guitar music?
John Williams.

In 1913, the Diaghilev Ballet Company performed a work at the Théatre des Champs-Elysées in Paris, which caused a riot. What was the work, and who wrote it?
The Rite of Spring by Igor Stravinsky.

Indian music began to become very popular in the West in the 1960s. Which musician advanced this popularity and what instrument did he play?
Ravi Shankar, playing the sitar.

Which of these composers set Shakespeare's *Romeo and Juliet* to music – Tchaikovsky, Prokofiev, Berlioz, Bernstein?
All of them.

What is the origin of Handel's *Water Music*?
Handel was court composer to the elector of Hanover, later George I of Great Britain and Ireland, 1714–27. He stayed away from court for long periods and on one occasion, it is said, when the king remonstrated with him, Handel composed the *Water Music* to placate him.

What are the drums called in an orchestra?
Tympani.

What is the common name for the flageolet?
The penny whistle.

What is a Jew's harp?
It is a small metal frame which is pressed against the teeth, while the fingers twang a steel wire or strip attached to it.

What does pastiche mean in musical terms?
A piece of music deliberately written in another composer's style.

What is an aubade?
A song of the dawn.

What was the song that really put Cliff Richard at the top of his profession as a pop singer?
Living Doll, in 1959.

What is a rhapsody?
In musical terms it is a single movement composition of no defined form, based on a theme taken from elsewhere or written by the composer himself, and generally having a romantic strain.

What is *Rhapsody in Blue*?
One of the best known compositions of George Gershwin (1898–1937), it effectively bridges the gap between classical music and jazz. It was composed in 1923, was an instant success and is among the most popular pieces of music of the 20th century

Who is the Master of the Queen's Musick?
An Australian composer, Malcolm Williamson, who was born in 1931. He succeeded Sir Arthur Bliss in 1975.

Three very famous English composers died within a few months of each other in 1934: who were they?
Sir Edward Elgar, OM (1857–1934), Frederick Delius, CH (1862–1934) and Gustav Holst (1874–1934).

What is the recapitulation in a composition?
Where the original theme is restated in much the same form but much later on in the work.

What is the difference between a trombone and a sackbut?
Basically none – the sackbut is the earlier English version of the trombone.

What is bebop?
A curious name for a musical style of jazz of the 1940s, made popular by artists such as Dizzy Gillespie and Charlie Parker. Bebop depends largely upon improvization, and features a strong double bass emphasis to maintain beat, allowing the drums to 'star' as it were as a solo instrument.

What was Sir William Walton's only full length opera?
Troilus and Cressida, originally written in 1954. It was put on again in the mid 1970s and was a great success.

Who discovered the Mississippi river?
Fernando de Soto (1496–1542), a Spanish explorer who, while governor of Cuba in the late 1530s, took an expedition from the island to the mainland of Florida. He found the Mississippi but died of fever before he could reach Mexico.

Who found the Bering Strait?
Vitus Bering (1680–1741), a Danish navigator who was invited by the Russian government to explore the area where Russia appeared to join with North America. Bering found the strait of water between the two land masses but died before he could get back to Russia to report his findings.

Who discovered Venezuela?
Alonso de Ojeda (1465–1515), one of the earlier Spanish navigators who followed Columbus into the West Indies and Central America.

How was Brazil discovered?
By accident in 1500. Pedro Alvarez Cabral (1460–1525), a Portuguese navigator sent by Emmanuel I of Portugal in 1500 with a fleet to sail to the East Indies, was blown off course in the Atlantic and landed in Brazil which he declared a territory of Portugal. How much of it he explored we do not know, but he went back to sea, carried on with his voyage down to the Cape of Good Hope and reached India.

Who discovered the Rio de la Plata?
Juan Diaz de Solis (1470–1516), a Spanish navigator, who set out in 1515 to explore the River Plate estuary. He was killed by natives in 1516.

Who wrote *The Worst Journey in the World*?
Apsley Cherry-Garrard who accompanied Scott to the Antarctic on his expedition to the South Pole when Scott, Evans and Oates perished.

Who first explored the Amazon river?
Francisco de Orellana (c. 1500–1549), a Spanish navigator who had been on the staff of Gonzalo Pizarro in South America, and who traced the Amazon all the way from the Andes mountains to the Atlantic on the east coast in 1540–41.

Who was Sir Humphry Gilbert?
Brother-in-law of Sir Walter Raleigh, Gilbert (1540–1583) took an expedition to North America to found a colony. He landed at Newfoundland and set up a colony at St John's. On his return journey, however, his ship was sunk and all aboard were drowned.

Who discovered Spitsbergen?
Willem Barents (d 1597), a Dutch navigator who was searching for a passage over the top of Europe to the East.

Who were the first white men to cross Australia from north to south?
Robert O'Hara Burke (1820–1861), an Irish explorer from Galway, and William John Wills (1834–1861), an English explorer who had emigrated to Australia from England when he was eighteen. They managed the expedition to the south but were overcome by starvation and illness on the way back and both died.

Who first crossed the ice fields of Greenland from east to west?
Fridtjof Nansen (1861–1930), the famous Norwegian explorer, zoologist and later on, statesman, in 1888.

Who was St Brendan?
Brendan (c. 484–577) was an Irish monk who founded the monastery of Clonfert in the 550s. He is credited also with having led an expedition across the Atlantic that reached Greenland and even North America, a belief that arose from stories written in later medieval times.

Who was the first navigator to round Cape Horn?

Willem Cornelis Schouten (c 1567–1625), a Dutch navigator employed by the East India Company. He called the cape after his native town, Hoorn.

What did the Roman fleet under Agricola achieve?

Agricola was governor of Britain from AD 77 to 84. In the last year of his term he sent his ships round the top of Scotland down to the Clyde, perhaps even to the Solway, and this proved what had been believed, namely, that Britain was an island.

What are Hakluyt's Voyages?

This is the abbreviated title of a book, *Principal Navigations, Voyages and Discoveries of the English Nation*, written in 1589 and enlarged at the end of the 16th century by Richard Hakluyt, an English geographer who at one time was archdeacon of Westminster. It still makes thrilling reading.

Who first opened up Japan to trade with the West, in modern times?

Captain Matthew Calbraith Perry (1794–1858), in 1853, was sent by the US Government with a fleet of ships. He delivered a formal request for trading rights to agents of the Japanese emperor, and a few months later, returned to Japan to collect the answer. The US were granted trading facilities at two ports Hakodate and Shimoda.

What was the book *The Kon-tiki Expedition* about?

Written by Thor Heyerdahl (b 1914), the Norwegian explorer and anthropologist, it was an account of his attempt to show that the Polynesian Islands in the Pacific could have been first settled by Peruvian Indians from South America. To prove it he built a raft like those which were in use thousands of years ago in Peru and sailed it across the Pacific from Callao.

What did Necho, king of Egypt, organize in about 600 BC?

A voyage by Phoenician mariners through the Red Sea down the east coast of Africa, round the Cape and back to the Mediterranean via the straits of Gibraltar. He also considered cutting a canal between the Nile and the Red Sea.

Who was Gil Eanes?

Gil Eanes (15th century) was a Portuguese navigator who took a ship round Cape Bojador for the first time, in about 1533. It was a landmark in the gradual exploration of the African coastline by the Portuguese in the 15th century.

Who discovered Tristan da Cunha?

The Portuguese admiral, Tristão da Cunha, in 1506.

For what was Ibn Battuta noted?

This Arab traveller (1304–1377), a native of Morocco, was apart from Marco Polo the greatest explorer of the Middle Ages. His journeys, which occupied more than twenty years of his life, took in Northern and Eastern Africa, and the Near, Middle and Far East, including China and Indonesia. He dictated his account of these travels to a scholar called Ibn Juzayy, this work being completed in 1357.

Who was Camillus?

Marcus Furius Camillus (d 365 BC) was one of the earliest of Roman great heroes. He was a soldier and statesman, led the Romans against the armies of Veii and besieged their city for ten years. Then, in the 390s he saved Rome itself from destruction by the Gauls. To achieve this he had to be elected dictator for a hitherto unprecedented five terms.

Who was Mohammed Ali Jinnah?

Jinnah (1876–1948) was a Moslem Indian statesman who during the long campaign for self-government for India worked for the partition of Hindu India and Moslem India into two separate states. When independence was granted in 1947, India was divided into two states, Hindu India and Moslem Pakistan (a new state). Jinnah became Pakistan's first governor-general.

Who was Che Guevara?

Ernesto 'Che' Guevara (1928–1967) was an Argentine doctor and writer who had immense compassion for the underprivileged in South America. He became a revolutionary, mastered the arts of guerrilla warfare, and put them into practice with great skill and daring on behalf of revolutionary movements in several parts of the world. He helped Fidel Castro to win Cuba in 1959, held high posts in Castro's government but then moved on to central Africa to help revolutionaries in the Congo. Guevara was captured while trying to organize a revolt in Bolivia, and shot.

Who was Cardinal Fleury?

André Hercule de Fleury (1653–1743) was a French statesman and cleric who was tutor to the boy king Louis XV (1715–1774) in the first years of his reign. Fleury had a strong influence on French domestic and foreign policy of the 1720s and 1730s and from about 1726 to his death was virtual prime minister.

Who was Martin Luther King?

He was an American Baptist Minister who led the movement for civil rights for black people in the USA. Born in 1929, he worked for much of his adult life for this cause, advocating passive resistance and non-violence, and for his high example he was awarded the Nobel Peace Prize in 1964. He was assassinated at Memphis in Tennessee in 1968.

Who was Andreas Hofer?

Andreas Hofer (1777–1810) was a Tyrolese guerrilla leader who organized a revolt in 1809 among peasants in the Tyrol, against the government of Bavaria. At first he defeated government forces sent against him, but in 1810 he was himself defeated and executed.

Who was Jawaharlal Nehru?

Nehru (1889–1964), one of the greatest of India's statesmen was for years a leading figure in the independence movement and went to gaol several times for his activities. When independence was granted, Nehru was appointed first prime minister of the new India and he led India until his death in 1964. His daughter Mrs Indira Gandhi is prime minister of India today (1984).

Who was Count Tilly?

Count Johan de Tilly (1559–1632) was Flemish by birth. He was appointed to restructure the armies of Maximilian, Duke of Bavaria, in the period 1610–1618, and at the outbreak of the Thirty Years' War in 1618, he was made commander of the Catholic League's forces. He won several major victories, but was defeated at Breitenfeld in 1631 and again the next year at Lech, where he was killed. His opponent was Gustavus Adolphus, king of Sweden, the leading general on the Protestant side in the Thirty Years' War, who was himself to die on the battlefield, at Lutzen, only a few weeks after Lech.

What was the Dreyfus case?

One of the sorriest slurs on the history of the French nation, this case rent the country into two major factions and almost resulted in civil war. Alfred Dreyfus (1859–1935) was a Jewish officer in the French army. In 1894 he was accused of passing secrets to a foreign power and court-martialled. Stripped of his rank, he was condemned to life imprisonment on Devil's Island. The trial was a scandal, for the evidence against him had been forged by anti-Semitic elements in the army. Although the actual perpetrator of the forgery confessed to the crime, Dreyfus was not immediately pardoned. Instead, he was retried, found guilty again, and then offered a pardon. Senior statesmen and generals were found to have been corrupt, to have lied and to have manipulated witnesses. Finally, Dreyfus was properly acquitted on appeal and restored to his rank, and in the end was awarded the Legion of Honour.

Who was Thebaw?

Thebaw (1858–1916) was the last king of Burma, from 1878 to 1885. Thebaw resented the interference of Britain in his dealings with France, particularly over trading activities, and in the war which followed, he was completely routed and deposed.

Who was Pugachev?

Emilion Pugachev (c. 1741–1775) was a Russian Cossack soldier and revolutionary leader. In the 1770s he organized a revolt of peasants against Catherine the Great, czarina of Russia, and had much success against several of the armies she sent against him. He pretended to be her husband, Czar Peter III who had been murdered (at her instigation) in 1762. But in 1775 Pugachev was defeated and taken, and in front of a huge crowd in Moscow was hanged.

Who was Catherine Parr?

Catherine Parr (1512–48) was the sixth and last wife of Henry VIII and survived him by one year.

Who was Josephine de Beauharnais?

Josephine de Beauharnais (1763–1814) widow of a general who was executed during the Reign of Terror in France, married Napoleon Bonaparte in 1796. She became empress when Napoleon was crowned emperor, but in 1809 was divorced by Napoleon who wanted a son.

Who was Nell Gwynne?

Nell Gwynne (c. 1650–1687) started life as an orange girl, went on the stage at Drury Lane where she was a talented comedienne and became mistress of Charles II to whom she remained faithful until his death.

Who was Kublai Khan?

Kublai Khan (1216–1294) was a grandson of Genghis Khan and was the first Mongol emperor of China, from about 1259 to his death. He set up his capital at Peking and created a magnificent court at which the artistic and craft skills of the Chinese flourished. He was visited by travellers from many parts of the world, including Marco Polo who stayed for seventeen years and served him in several high positions before returning to Italy and publishing an account of his experiences.

Why was Georges Danton put to death in 1794?

Danton (1759–1794) was a French lawyer and powerful orator who early in the French Revolution (1789–1794) became one of its leading lights. Danton was not an extremist, although he worked for major changes in French society and government. By 1794 he had excited the fear of the extreme elements who thought he might 'betray' the Revolution, and he was executed.

When was the first game of rugger played?

Traditionally, two teams were playing football at Rugby public school one day in 1823, when a player, William Webb Ellis, decided to pick up the ball and run towards the opposing goal and put it down in the goalmouth. The idea of picking up the ball spread to other schools and clubs, but it was nearly half a century before the game of rugby football was formalized.

When was the Rugby Union formed?

In January 1871, and in the same year England and Scotland played their first international match.

What is the Five Nations Championship?

It is an annual series of rugby matches played by teams from England, Scotland, Ireland, Wales and France, and it grew out of the first matches between England and Scotland.

What is the origin of roller skating?

The pastime seems to have begun seriously in the USA in the mid-19th century, when the manufacturer James Plympton introduced a four-wheeled skate and also opened what is believed to be the first public roller skating rink, at Newport, Rhode Island. Roller skates were greatly improved when the wheels were fitted with ball bearings in the 1880s.

What are the three main weapons used in fencing?

The foil, a light, thrusting weapon with tapering, quadrangular section blade and a small bell-like hand guard; the sabre, a flat V-section bladed cut-and-thrust weapon with a half-round guard; and the épée (the duelling sword), a heavier bladed weapon with triangular fluted section, much stiffer than the foil, and which has a large bell-type guard.

What are the familiar names of the rugby teams of New Zealand, South Africa, Australia, and of the combined travelling team of the countries of Britain?

All Blacks, Springboks, Wallabies, British Lions.

Who was the 1983 world champion snooker player?

Steve Davis (b 1957).

Who was probably the greatest snooker player of the 20th century?

Joe Davis (1901–1978) who won 15 world championships between 1927 and 1946, and who in his time also held the world's highest break. Joe Davis was also world champion billiards player four times.

What is the origin of billiards?

There is a record of Louis XI of France (1461–1483) owning a billiard table. The game was certainly enjoyed by Louis XIV of France (1643–1715).

Who is Reg Harris?

Probably the finest and most successful cyclist ever to emerge from Great Britain. He won several championships before World War II and was Britain's fastest amateur cyclist. During the war he served in the army and was badly wounded, but still returned to cycling afterwards and for several years dominated the cycling scene, turning professional and winning the world sprint championships in 1949, 1950, 1951 and 1954. He also set several world records which stood for a generation or so.

What is coursing?

One of the oldest of field sports, and a forerunner of greyhound racing, it is the chasing of hares by greyhounds using sight rather than scent. It is organized today in enclosures and parks.

Who is Mark Spitz?
Born in 1950 in the USA, Mark Spitz won 9 Olympic Gold Medals for swimming events in the Games of 1968 and 1972. Six of the medals were for events in which he also established world records.

What is octopush?
A relatively new sport consisting of a kind of hockey played in swimming pools by swimmers under the water, using snorkel tubes.

Who was the first British woman to succeed in swimming across the English Channel?
Mercedes Gleitz in 1927. It was her eighth attempt.

When did croquet become fashionable in Britain?
In England in the mid-19th century, after some years of popularity in Ireland where it was known as 'crokey'. The game derives from a similar sport in France, probably from late medieval times.

Is karate an ancient Japanese martial art?
No, it was introduced into Japan by Funakoski Gichin after World War I from the island of Okinawa where it had been practised for centuries by the islanders against their Japanese oppressors. They had developed its form from an ancient Chinese style of boxing.

Who invented the game of cribbage?
Sir John Suckling (1609–1642), the English poet and supporter of Charles I.

What is a trampoline?
Invented at the beginning of the 20th century, it is a sprung, webbed bed slung between a frame, from which an athlete – or anyone else – can jump, twist, bounce, somersault.

What is the Royal and Ancient?
The game of golf. It is also the name adopted by the St Andrews Golf Club, founded in 1754 and is the world (excluding USA) authority on the game.

How long has fencing been an international sport?
Since just before World War I when the Fédération Internationale d'Escrimé (FIE) was founded, in 1913. But fencing has been practised by individuals as a recreation, for duelling and for individual combat in warfare, almost since the invention of bronze weapons 5000 or so years ago.

When did the *News of the World* darts championships begin?
In 1927–28 for the London area. The tournament was gradually extended to other areas, a process interrupted by World War I. It resumed in 1947–48 as a national competition.

What is the origin of bullfighting in Spain?
A mural dating back to 3830 BC found at Catal Huyak in Turkey, provides the first evidence for the sport of bullfighting. It had some following in Roman times, but it was the Moors who brought it to Spain from Africa in the 8th century. An enclosure for bullfighting was made in Seville in 1743, although the first rings bearing a resemblance to those in use today were not constructed in Spain for a further eleven years.

In what European country is association football only played in the summer?
Iceland, where for climatic reasons the season lasts from May to October.

What is marine ball?
This is a variation of water polo, played in a shallow pool.

When was Goodwood Racecourse laid out and opened?
In 1801. Racing at Goodwood was introduced by the then Duke of Richmond and Gordon on his Goodwood estate, near Chichester in Sussex, and it is still held there at the end of July every year.

Where is the St Leger run?
At Doncaster Races in September. The St Leger is the oldest of the flat race classics, and was first run in 1776. It was named after Colonel Barry St Leger. The distance of the race is 2.938 km (1¾ miles 132 yd).

What is the leading racecourse in France?
Longchamp, in the Bois de Boulogne north-west of Paris, on the site of a medieval nunnery. Here, the greatest international event of the world, the Prix de l'Arc de Triomphe, is held. The course was opened in 1856.

Where are the One Thousand Guineas and the Two Thousand Guineas run?
The 1000 Guineas and the 2000 Guineas are run at Newmarket.

Which horse has won the Grand National three times?
Only one, and that was *Red Rum*, in 1973, 1974 and 1977. *Red Rum* also came second in 1975 and 1976.

What is a thoroughbred horse?
It is an English breed of horse used for racing or hunting, and is bred from English mares crossed with Arab stallions. All English thoroughbreds are descended from one or other of three famous Arab horses brought to England in the 18th century.

What were the three Arab horses?
The Byerly Turk, the Darley Arabian and the Godolphin Arabian.

Where are the Oaks and the Derby run?
Epsom.

Which king was the first to sponsor racing at Newmarket?
James I (1603–1625), but it was his grandson Charles II (1660–85) with whom one associates royal interest in racing here. He had one horse called Rowley, which he raced at Newmarket. He himself came to be known by many as Old Rowley.

Who was the first jockey to be knighted?
Sir Gordon Richards (b 1905). He began riding in 1920, and by the time he retired in 1954 he had ridden 4870 winners and had been champion jockey in 26 seasons.

Which was the race that always eluded Gordon Richards, until his last full year as a jockey?
The Derby. But in 1953, Coronation Year, he won on Pinza, at his 28th attempt. He had been knighted only a few days earlier. When he retired he became a trainer.

What is the Grand National?
A national steeplechase which is run at Aintree near Liverpool in late March or early April every year. The course is 7.245 km (4½ miles) long and has 30 jumps. It was first run in 1839, though it was not called the Grand National until 1843.

What is point-to-point racing?
Small-scale cross-country steeplechasing for amateur riders.

Who was Fred Archer?
He was the most famous and the most successful champion jockey in the 19th century. Champion for thirteen seasons in a row he rode 2748 winners, including five in the Derby.

What is the totalizator?
It is a system on horse-racing courses (and also on greyhound racing tracks) which records bets and pays out winnings without the intervention of bookmakers. It is known for short as the tote.

What is the Horse-race Totalizator Board?
Founded in 1963 to take over the responsibilities of the previous Racehorse Betting Control Board, it operates totalizators at approved courses in Britain, and it also provides cash and credit offices in places away from courses.

Where is the Horse-racing Museum?
In Newmarket, on the premises of the Jockey Club.

Which was the best known racehorse owned by Winston Churchill?
Colonist II, which won more than a dozen races. In one race, he apparently turned his head to one side to try to bite a rival coming up beside him.

What was so special about the Irish horse Arkle?
Generally regarded as the greatest steeplechaser in the history of racing, Arkle was also the most popular. He won numerous races, often against top competing steeplechasers with such seemingly effortless grace and speed that every time he raced he was greeted with roars of applause. When he broke a foot in 1966 during a race – but still went on to win – he had to retire. He received sackfuls of Get Well Cards, most of them addressed simply to – Arkle, Ireland.

What is the origin of the National Hunt Chase at Cheltenham?
This was instituted in 1859 by 'Fogo' Rowlands with a view to providing a race for steeplechasing hunters over a challenging course which local hunts would both subscribe to and support. The race then became peripatetic, although returning to Cheltenham on occasions until it finally settled there in 1911.

Who said of racing: 'I consider this to be a national sport – the manly and noble sport of a free people, and I deeply feel the pride of being able to encourage these pastimes, so intimately connected with the habits and feelings of this free country . . .'?
William IV. Despite the fact that he felt no personal enthusiasm for the turf, the king acknowledged its worth as a social institution which united all classes.

What religious leader built up one of the world's greatest racing empires?
Aga Khan III (1877–1957), who became the spiritual leader of the Ismaili sect of Shiah Muslims upon the death of his father in 1885. He was raised in India where he acquired his love of racing mainly through his close social contacts with the British raj. He first visited Britain in 1898, and France shortly afterwards; then in 1904 he started to build up his racing interests in those countries. Subsequently, he had 17 successes in classic races, including the Derby on five occasions.

Little Quiz 39
   What colour are these gemstones or minerals?
1. amethyst
2. ruby
3. malachite
4. citrine
5. serpentine
6. lapis lazuli
7. emerald
8. moonstone
9. bloodstone
10. zircon

When was St Isaac's Cathedral in Leningrad built?

It was started in the mid-18th century by the Italian architect Rinaldi, in what was St Petersburg. But the huge gilded domed building you can see today was not finished until the later 19th century, to designs by Richard de Montferrand, a French architect who won a competition for the cathedral's completion. It is 111 m (364.08 ft) long, 98 m (321.44 ft) wide and the central dome is 100 m (328 ft) tall. There are 562 steps to the top.

Who designed the splendid cathedral at Brasilia?

Brasilia, the new capital of Brazil, was begun as a new city soon after World War II. It is about 1207 km (750 miles) from Rio de Janeiro. The cathedral was designed by the Brazilian architect, Otto Niemeyer, and it was started in 1959. It is circular in plan and the main floor is sunk about 3.05 m (10 ft) below ground level. The building is shaped like a sheaf of corn, with 16 equidistantly spaced ribs rising from a wide base, narrowing in the centre and splaying out again like a corona at the top, the ribs interspersed with glazed grids.

What are the principal features of Aachen Cathedral in West Germany?

It is really a cluster of chapels set round a central chapel which is known as the Palatine Chapel. It was built in the time of Charlemagne (768–814), and the additions were spread over the next six centuries. It is also where Charlemagne is buried.

What is Fontainebleau?

A palace built for the royal family of France by Francis I (1515–1547) over the remains of an old castle. It was decorated and furnished in Renaissance style (much of which survives) and was refurbished in the time of Napoleon and of Louis Philippe (1830–48).

150

What is a duomo?

It is the Italian word for a cathedral in an Italian city. It means House of God.

What is the Bull Ring in Birmingham?

It is the new city centre, opened in 1964. The principal feature is a huge drum-shaped building rising out of a vast complex of concrete and glass which is offices and shopping centre.

What is the longest single span suspension bridge in the world?

The Humber bridge which crosses the Humber between Humberside (East Yorkshire) on the north side and South Humberside (N. Lincolnshire). It is 1410 m (4624.8 ft) long and it was opened in 1981. It can cut almost an hour off the car journey from London to Hull and the east of Yorkshire.

Where is the palace of Split?

Split, on the Adriatic coast of Yugoslavia, known also by its Italian name of Spalato, is a port founded by the Roman emperor Diocletian in about AD 300. In the modern town is a huge square-plan palace built by Diocletian, to which he retired in 305 in order, as he said, to grow cabbages.

Where is Coca Castle?

This vast 15th century castle-palace for the archbishops of Seville was built by Moslem workers for Christian masters. Though enormously strong and heavily fortified, it has never been involved in warfare.

Where is the Palace of the Nations?

In Geneva, Switzerland. It is a complex of large buildings which once housed the League of Nations, founded in 1920 after World War I but superseded in 1945 by the United Nations Organization. The Palace of Nations today houses several organizations including the World Health Organization (WHO).

What is Trajan's Column?

It is a monument erected by the Roman emperor Trajan (AD 98–117), to celebrate his various military victories, especially those against the Dacians in south-east Europe. The base is a cube of stone, of 5½ m (18 ft) with a bronze gate in one side. The column is of marble, 3.70 m (12.136 ft) in diameter and reaching a height of 29.77 m (97.64 ft). Inside is a spiral staircase of white marble, with 185 steps. On the top it once had an eagle, then after his death a statue of Trajan replaced it, and this in turn was replaced by a statue of St Peter in 1588. The outside of the column is decorated with a continuous spiralling relief sculpture, depicting various events in Trajan's career, and is a valuable source of evidence for several aspects of Roman military activity.

Which is the tallest building in Britain?

Currently (1984) it is the new National Westminster Bank headquarters building in Bishopsgate, in the City of London. It is 183 m (600 ft) tall and is served by 21 lifts. It is roughly triangular in plan, like the logo on the bank's cheques and cheque book covers, that is, a triangle with flattened corners. It was completed in 1979.

Who built Hampton Court Palace?

Originally, it was built for Cardinal Wolsey in the earliest years of the reign of Henry VIII (1509–1547). In 1526, Wolsey gave the palace to the king who added the Great Hall and other features. The palace remained a royal residence for several generations, and it was restored and enlarged by Christopher Wren for William III.

Where is the Eiffel Tower?

It is on the south bank of the Seine in Paris, near the Champ de Mars. The tower is an astonishing structure, almost 300 m (985 ft) tall, and built of iron in a grid form between 1887 and 1889 – itself a marvel of technology. Much of the ironwork was prefabricated and bolted together on the site. The tower weighs over 9,700 tons, 7,000 tons of which are the ironwork. It was designed and supervised by Gustave Alexandre Eiffel (1832–1923).

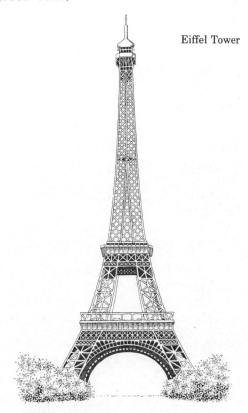

Eiffel Tower

Little Quiz 40

These were the Nine Muses in Greek Mythology. What were their arts?

1. Calliope
2. Clio
3. Urania
4. Terpsichore
5. Thalia
6. Euterpe
7. Erato
8. Melpomene
9. Polyhymnia

What is a tabloid newspaper?
A small size newspaper, about half the size of *The Times*, and which is profusely illustrated with photographs and cartoons, many of the photographs taking anything up to a whole page each.

What does a sub-editor of a newspaper do?
He or she gets the copy (text) ready for printing, which means marking the typed sheets of text with directions as to how it is to be set in print. He or she also decides how long the article or news item is to be and cuts the text to fit the amount of space. In this the sub-editor is guided to some extent by the importance of the story in relation to other stories and articles on the same page.

What is newspaper layout?
This is a sketch of a particular page, or set of pages, done in pencil by the sub-editors' department, so that the printer is given a good idea of what the finished page ought to look like when printed.

What does the term freelance journalist mean?
He or she is a journalist who writes for a newspaper or magazine, but is not on the paper's staff. They get paid fees for particular contributions. Many freelance journalists write for a number of papers and magazines.

Which trade unions protect the interests of journalists and other contributors to newspapers and magazines?
The Institute of Journalists, founded in 1884, and the National Union of Journalists, founded in 1907.

What does a press agency do?
It gathers news stories and circulates them to newspapers all round the country, generally by means of a teleprinter.

What is a giveaway newspaper?
Something relatively new in newspapers in Britain, it is a paper whose production costs are entirely paid for by the advertisers who buy space in the pages, and which also makes a small profit for the owners. The paper is given away to readers.

What does the Press Council do?
Briefly, it exists to ensure the continuation of the freedom of the Press in Britain, and to ensure that the Press maintains its standards. It also investigates complaints made against individual papers and journalists. The Press Council is also supposed to draw attention to possible dangers from mergers or take-overs among newspaper proprietors.

Why would a newspaper use a picture agency?
Picture agencies take photographs of events, personalities, disasters and other newsworthy items, and circulate them to newspapers and magazines which may be glad not to have to send their own staff photographers out to the scene. Such agencies usually keep a library of pictures on which newspapers and magazines and other people can draw at short notice.

How old is *The Times*?
Almost two hundred years. It was founded by John Walter in 1785.

Who is reported as having said, 'Publish and be damned'?
The first duke of Wellington.

What does a copy taker do?
Sometimes known as a telephone reporter, he or she is a journalist who sits at a typewriter in a newspaper office, usually wearing headphones, and types out the stories dictated over the phone by reporters from outside.

Who was Cassandra?
Sir William Connor, the famous columnist wrote under the name Cassandra a daily column for the *Daily Mirror* from 1935 to 1967. He was one of the best known journalists of the present century, and often produced the perfect single-line sentence to sum up a personality or an event. On the death of Pope John XXIII in 1963, he wrote, 'He put his arm round the heart of the world'.

What is a newspaper's masthead?
It is the title of the newspaper printed in large letters at the top of the front page. The word also means the title where it appears on the page that carries leading articles.

Where is *The Scotsman* newspaper printed?
Edinburgh.

What is offset lithography?
It is a method of printing used for books, some magazines and newspapers from a flat surface using the principle that grease (in this case ink) and water will not mix.

What does a leader writer do?
He or she writes a column expressing the views of the newspaper on one of the day's main items or some other topic of major interest. The views are those of the editor of the paper or the proprietor but not necessarily of the leader writer.

What daily newspaper reflects the views of the Communist Party in Britain?
The Morning Star.

When did the English provincial press start?
With the *Norwich Post*, founded by Francis Burgess in 1701, probably on 8 November, although there is no copy of the first issue in existence.

What is the only daily morning newspaper to be published in Wales?
The *Western Mail*, published in Cardiff.

What is the name of the editors' professional association?
The Guild of British Newspaper Editors, which has about 500 members.

When did photographs first appear in newspapers?
The first ever appeared on the back page of the *New York Daily Graphic* for 2 December 1873; it was a halftone illustration of Steinway Hall in New York.

Little Quiz 41

To what parts of the body or aspect of medicine do these prefixes refer – eg gastro = stomach?

1. derm-
2. cerebro-
3. haema-
4. sclero-
5. ophthalmo-
6. myo-
7. psycho-
8. thorac-
9. entero-
10. arthr-

and what do these word endings suggest?

11. -itis
12. -tomy
13. -rrhea
14. -lapse

Which organs do these complaints relate to?

15. astigmatism
16. cholecystitis
17. hepatitis
18. nephritis
19. mastoiditis
20. sinusitis
21. cystitis
22. pneumonia

What was the principle behind the first mariner's compass?

In the 11th century it was noted that the black stone which attracts iron, magnetic stone, would if floated in a vessel on the surface of a bowl or a pond of water always come to rest with its longer axis pointing in north and south directions.

Who first measured the electrical conducting power of various substances?

Henry Cavendish (1731–1810).

What is the principle of the conservation of energy?

It states that the sum total of all energy in the world is constant. If energy apparently disappears in one form, an equivalent amount of another form of energy will appear somewhere else, at the same time. In other words, no energy is ever lost or created.

Who first suggested that sound travels through the air in waves?

Leonardo da Vinci (1452–1519). He also showed that an echo reflected (or sent back) waves of sound from a hard surface.

What was Avogadro's hypothesis?

That equal volumes of all gases at the same temperature and pressure contain the same number of molecules. This was stated by Amadeo Avogadro in 1811.

What did Oersted prove about magnetism and electricity?

Hans Christian Oersted (1777–1851), a Danish physicist, discovered that magnetism and electricity were closely connected, and he proved it by holding a wire carrying electric current over a pivoted magnetic needle and parallel to it, and the magnet was deflected. When he reversed the direction of the current in the wire, the needle was turned in the opposite direction.

What does a catalyst do?

It is a substance which alters the rate of a chemical reaction but which itself is unaffected chemically by the process.

What is the critical temperature of a gas?

The temperature above which a gas cannot be liquefied, however great the pressure that is applied.

What is radioactivity?

It is the emission of radiation in the form of alpha rays, beta rays or gamma rays from unstable elements by the spontaneous breakdown of their atomic nuclei.

When did Aristotle live?

About 384 to 347 BC. He was tutor to Alexander the Great, as well as one of the fundamental thinkers and natural philosophers of all time.

What were the Aristotelian theories of matter?

Anything that occupies space consists of matter of some sort. Aristotle stated that there were four kinds of matter, earth, fire, water and air, and these were the elements. Solids consisted of earth but also contained smaller amounts of other elements which could be expelled by heat. Liquids consisted chiefly of water.

How did Aristotle describe the arrangement of the universe?

Aristotle, the famous Greek natural philosopher, who lived from about 384 to 347 BC, said that the earth was the centre of the universe, and that round it the sun, moon, stars and planets revolved, in their own orbits. He was for a time tutor to Alexander the Great.

Who first calculated the speed of light?

The Danish physicist Olaus Roemer

(1644–1710), from observing the eclipses of Jupiter's moons.

What was dephlogisticated air?
This was Dr Joseph Priestly's name for oxygen.

What is the Quantum Theory?
Advanced by Max Planck (1858–1947) in 1900, it states that radiation is given out in packets, or quanta, of energy and not in a continuous stream.

What did the ancient Greek philosopher Thales discover about the stone, amber?
He found that if he rubbed a lump of amber briskly against his hand, it would pick up small objects off the ground or off a table. This was the earliest known experiment in electricity. Thales lived from about 640–550 BC.

What did Dr Joseph Black discover about heat?
Joseph Black (1728–1799), a Scottish physicist, noted that when a solid melts or a liquid boils, some of the heat disappears as energy. This he called latent heat, and he devised a method of measuring it.

Who discovered the positively charged particle found in the nuclei of all atoms, the proton?
Lord Rutherford (1871–1937), Cavendish professor of experimental physics at Cambridge, and the first man to split the atom (1919).

Who discovered the element uranium?
Martin Heinrich Klaproth (1743–1817), professor of chemistry at Berlin University.

What was a Voltaic pile?
Devised by Alessandro Volta (1745–1827), Italian professor of natural philosophy at Pavia University, it was a series of zinc plates separated from a series of copper plates by pieces of cardboard soaked in dilute sulphuric acid. The plates were arranged in the order zinc, cardboard, copper, in series. A wire joined at one end plate brought close to another wire at the other end plate would produce a spark. The sparks were continuous, which indicated a continuous flow of electric current. In other words, Volta had produced the first battery.

What was the Phlogiston Theory?
It held that all inflammable substances contained something called phlogiston which was burned off during the combustion. From this, no inflammable substance could be an element, except the phlogiston itself. The theory was believed by many leading chemists for much of the 18th century.

What is the nature of the effect known as electro-photoluminescence?
This is the flash of light or luminescence which occurs in certain materials, such as zinc sulphide phosphorus, when an electric field is applied or removed while the material is exhibiting phosphorescence.

What is the Weldon process?
This is a process for making chlorine which is dependent upon the action of manganese dioxide on hydrochloric acid, and which is still used in industry to a limited extent. The resulting manganese chlorides are mixed with lime in iron towers, then air is blown through for a number of hours until the manganese reoxidizes to form manganese dioxide. This is then allowed to settle and may be reused in the first stage of the process.

When and where was the first World Cup?
In Uruguay, South America, in 1930. The winners were Uruguay.

When did England win the World Cup?
In a sensational match against West Germany played at Wembley in 1966. The England side was captained by Bobby Moore.

Where was football first played?
In China, in the 3rd century BC. The Chinese played a game called Tsu chu (which means: kick (tsu) ball (chu).

What is the origin of Association Football as we know it?
It began in England in 1863 when a number of London football clubs formed the Football Association and drew up a set of rules. The earliest years saw a number of changes in the rules, partly because clubs outside London did not agree with all the London rules. The game has evolved over the years since then, and there are still occasions when rules are amended.

When was the Football Association (FA) Cup competition inaugurated?
In 1872.

How many people turned out to watch the match between Brazil and Uruguay for the World Cup Final in 1950 at Rio de Janeiro in Brazil?
199,850 the highest number ever to attend a major football match.

Who is Sir Alf Ramsay?
Alf Ramsay was manager of the FA World Cup Team from 1963 to 1974, and this included the great year 1966, when England won the World Cup. Ramsay himself had played for England more than thirty times. He was knighted in 1967.

What was the appalling disaster that struck Manchester United Football Club in 1958?
The first team, with its manager Matt (now Sir Matt) Busby, was returning from a successful game in the European Cup competition, in Yugoslavia, when the aircraft carrying the team crashed on taking off from Munich airport. Eight of the team were killed, Busby and others (including Bobby Charlton) were seriously injured.

Which world famous goalkeeper was compelled to give up playing after a road crash?
Gordon Banks, 73 times player for England and regarded as one of the world's greatest goalkeepers. He was badly injured in a road crash in 1972, which left his eyes permanently affected.

Who holds the record number of goals scored while playing for England?
Bobby Charlton, who in thirteen seasons (1958–1970) scored 49 goals. He was awarded an OBE.

What is the Cup Winners' Cup?
This slightly confusing phrase relates to an international football competition held every year for national cup winners, or runners-up if the winner already qualifies as holder or is in the European Cup.

What is the world governing body of association football?
FIFA (the Fédération Internationale de Football Associations). This was founded in 1904 with six nation members, and now has over 150 members.

What are the recognized dimensions of a football pitch?
The dimensions are variable, between 100.65 and 109.8 m (110 and 120 yd) × 64.05 and 24.4 m (70 and 80 yd) for international matches.

Who is Pelé?
The world famous nickname of one of the greatest footballers, Edson Arantes do Nascimento, a Brazilian who was born in 1940. Pelé was already playing international football by the time he was seventeen, and when he retired from international playing in 1971, he had played 110 matches for Brazil, scored 97 goals in international football, as well as 1216 goals in 1254 matches of all kinds.

What is a *catenaccio* line-up on the football field?
It is a system of tactics of a defensive kind, by which one player (known as the sweeper) operates behind a row of four backs, three midfield players and two strikers (goal scorers).

What does it mean if a player is 'capped'?
It means he is included as a representative of an important team.

What does CONCACAT stand for?
Confederacion Nortecentroamerica y del Caribe de Futbol, which governs football in North and Central America and the Caribbean.

Which famous player was told when young that he would never make a footballer?
Billy Wright (b 1924) by Wolverhampton Wanderers' club management. He went on to captain Wolves (as the team is known) and also England. He played 105 matches for England, 90 of them as team captain, and he did not retire from football until 1959.

Which football team is often described as White Hart Lane?
Tottenham Hotspur (affectionately known as 'Spurs'), whose home ground is in White Hart Lane, Tottenham, in North London.

Which national team has won the World Cup three times?
Brazil, in 1958, 1962 and 1970.

What is the derivation of the name 'Spion Kop', given to parts of certain British football grounds?
This was the name of a hill in South Africa where, in January 1900, the British suffered a bloody defeat at the hands of the Boers. Troops from Lancashire suffered the highest number of casualties, and later the mounds where the spectators stood at football grounds in that country became known as Spion Kops as a tribute. The name is first recorded as having been used in Britain at Anfield, the ground of Liverpool FC, in 1906, then its usage spread rapidly.

What was the worst disaster ever to have occurred at an English football match?
This occurred at Bolton Wanderers' ground, Burnden Park, on 9 March 1946. Because of the sheer size of the crowd already in the ground, or their actions in trying to get in, 33 people died through being crushed or asphyxiated and 500 more required first aid.

What ground was built before the team whose home it became was created?
Stamford Bridge, the home of Chelsea FC. This site which had been a market garden until 1876 then became the headquarters of the London Athletic Club. Twenty years later, the two Mears brothers started negotiations to take over the ground and turn it into a prestige football stadium, but did not succeed until 1904. Having tried with no success to attract another team to play there, one of the brothers, Gus, eventually set up his own team, Chelsea, in 1905.

What is PAYE?

The letters stand for Pay As You Earn, a scheme whereby numerous employees in Britain pay their income tax. Their salaries or wages are assessed for a year's tax, and each pay cheque, or envelope with cash, contains the pay less the amount of tax worked out as a proportion of the year's tax. The amount deducted is determined from a set of tax tables provided to all employers by the Inland Revenue.

What is a franking machine?

A machine that prints the postage rate on a sticky slip of paper or directly on the envelope. This is called 'franking'.

What is collating?

If you have a report, or a catalogue of products, or any multi-page document, and if it is to be duplicated or photocopied for circulation to a number of people inside and/or outside the firm, the sets of papers have to be sorted and then stapled. This is called collating. It can be done by hand, which takes time. It can also be done by collating machines which do the job very quickly.

What is a typing pool?

In larger firms, government departments and other big organizations, there is generally enough typing work every day for a number of typists. It is often convenient for the typists to work together in one room, under a supervisor, and this is generally called the typing pool.

What is an 'Action' slip?

These are internal communications that take various forms, but generally have some kind of arresting feature calculated to encourage the receiver to take some action quickly upon the matter discussed in the communication such as a bright colour for the lettering, or a large printing of the word ACTION.

What is a golf ball typewriter?

A typewriter that does not have the usual type bars (levels with individual letters at one end) but has all the characters mounted on a small typing head which is ball-shaped and approximately the size of a golf ball. This moves across the machine when the keys are pressed.

What international paper sizes are likely to be used in the average office?

A 4, which is 297 mm × 210 mm ($11\frac{7}{8}$ in × $8\frac{3}{8}$ in) and A5 which is half that size. The A 4 size replaces the old foolscap size.

What is filing?

It is the storage of letters, records, documents, carbon copies of letters, etc., kept in folders, binders, wallets, in drawers or cabinets specially designed for the purpose.

What is an 'In' tray?

A rectangular wire-net tray, or a tray made of plywood or plastic, which rests on an office desk. All correspondence, files etc., that are to be dealt with by the person who occupies the desk are put into this tray.

What does a document shredder do?

Papers and documents that are no longer needed but which you don't want other people to read are put into a shredder which reduces them to very thin, unreadable shreds.

What is flexitime?

Staff can choose their own working hours within a basic framework. They have to do a 'core' of work, which is a period of about 4 hours, when everybody works, say from 10.00 am to 12.00 noon and 2.00 pm to 4.00 pm. The other hours may be done more or less when the worker likes.

What is the most valuable contribution of flexitime to people outside the firm where it is operated?
Flexitime means that a workforce does not go into work at one fixed time, thus adding to the crowding on commuter trains, Underground trains etc. It helps to spread the travelling over a much wider range of time. The same applies to finishing work on flexitime principles.

What is a consignment note?
When goods are sent by outside transport firms, they should be accompanied by a consignment note. This is provided by the firm and it gives details of the goods being sent (consigned), the name and address of the sender (consigner), the date of despatch and any other instructions, and the name and address of the firm or person to whom the goods are being sent (consignee).

What is O and M?
It stands for Organization and Methods department of a firm, which is devoted to examining and maintaining checks on the efficiency (or otherwise) of the firm. The O and M department recommends ways to speed up production, cut down waste and improve working conditions.

What does an audio typist do?
Types letters, reports and documents from a tape, or tapes, on which they have been previously recorded by dictation. The tape is played back on the dictating machine through ear phones.

What is Red Star delivery?
It is a fast delivery service for letters and parcels, which is operated by British Rail and which guarantees delivery the next day at any station in the UK.

What is an open plan office?
It is an office arrangement whereby a huge space is not broken up into a lot of partitioned offices but is left open, and laid out with desks and furniture. The furniture and equipment are arranged in groups for each worker, and each working area may be separated by soundproof screens.

What does the abbreviation Ltd mean?
Limited Liability Company, which is a form of business in which a number of people known as shareholders have invested money and have elected directors to run it for them.

What is a status inquiry?
This is one which is, for instance, addressed to a bank by a person or business wishing to discover the credit-worthiness of a prospective customer.

What is a bad debt?
A bad debt is a term used in accounting for one which is known to be irrecoverable, and is therefore treated as a loss.

Little Quiz 42
  In the Bible, who was?
  1. Abel
  2. Abednego
  3. Benjamin
  4. Melchizedek
  5. Belshazzar
  6. Elizabeth
  7. Jonathan
  8. Uzziah
  9. Zadok
  10. Lot
  11. What happened to Lot's wife?
  Who were?
  12. The Pharisees
  13. The Amalekites
  14. The Jebusites
  15. The Scribes
  16. The Rechabites
  Who?
  17. 'cared for none of these things'
  18. had the fatted calf killed for him
  19. was cured of 'seven demons' by Jesus
  20. wore a coat of many colours

Who introduced the first adhesive postage stamp?

Sir Rowland Hill (1795–1879). He had written a pamphlet entitled 'Post Office Reform' in 1837, in which he had suggested the idea of a prepaid post, with postage stamps to indicate the payment. Up to then, letters were conveyed to the recipient who paid on receipt the cost which was calculated on the distance covered. The first stamps were introduced in 1840.

What was the very first mark of stamp?

A penny stamp, which was the new standard price for up to one ounce weight of postage anywhere in the country. The first stamp was black and carried a picture of Queen Victoria. Actually, these stamps were not issued until four months after the introduction of the Penny Post, because there were delays in getting the printing ready in time.

Who suggested the stamp design?

The design was put out to public competition, and over 2000 people submitted ideas, some of them fantastic. But in the end the postmaster general adopted the simple rectangular shape with the portrait of the queen – which had been suggested by Rowland Hill in the first place.

What happened if you did not prepay postage on your letters?

Your letter was delivered but the recipient had to pay double the postage rate – which still obtains today.

What are the Cinderellas in stamp collecting terms?

They are the once ignored philatelic items that are now collected with great enthusiasm by thousands of collectors. They consist of fakes, forgeries, duty stamps, propaganda labels, registration stamps.

What is a watermark?

In stamps it is a device used on the printing paper to prevent stamp forgery. There are several types of watermark and they can generally be seen if the stamp is held up to a bright light. British watermarks have included the royal crown and the royal monogram.

Have stamps always been perforated along the edges?

Not to begin with. The earliest stamps had to be cut from sheets. Perforation began in about 1852, following experiments by Henry Archer.

Which country produced a stamp which carried as its illustration a few bars of its national anthem?

Venezuela.

What were the Charles Connell Canadian stamps?

Charles Connell was postmaster general for the state of New Brunswick in Canada in 1860, and he had a 5c stamp printed bearing his own portrait. This caused a stir because it was customary to print only the portrait of Queen Victoria in Britain and in the countries of the Empire. Connell portrait stamps are valuable for there were not many run off.

What is a first day cover?

It is an envelope with a new issue of stamp, or stamps, postmarked on the day of issue. Covers are collectors' items. They can be obtained by buying the stamps and sticking them on an envelope addressed to oneself and posting it on the same day.

Where is Britain's National Postal Museum?

It is in St Martin's le Grand, in London's City. It contains vast quantities of material from the archives of the Post Office.

Stamps have generally been printed on paper. What other materials have been used?
Hungary printed commemorative stamps on wax cloth in 1958, metal foil has been used by Tonga, Sierra Leone and the USSR (which has also used silver paper). Bhutan printed stamps on silk. And the state of Latvia, restored to independence after World War I, printed some of its first new stamps on the backs of old German war maps.

Which were the first of the other countries in the world to introduce prepaid postages?
The USA in 1842, Brazil in 1843 and Switzerland, also in 1843.

What was the official cancellation mark for the earliest Penny Post?
A Maltese cross, the design of which varied in some small detail in many of the towns of issue.

Which is the only stamp of the USA to have been printed outside the USA?
During the Civil War (1861–1865), the Confederate states of the South, which had withdrawn from the Union and were at war with the other states, printed their own stamps. One was a 5c of 1862, bearing the portrait of the Confederate president, Jefferson Davis. The stamp was printed by the English firm, De La Rue.

What is Stampex?
It is an annual postage stamp exhibition held in London, at the Royal Horticultural Hall in Westminster, or the Central Hall, also in Westminster.

When did people start to collect postage stamps seriously?
It is not possible to say precisely, but certainly within twenty years of the introduction of stamps there were catalogues of new and used stamps, and there were several philatelic societies and clubs. In 1856 Edward Stanley Gibbons, who was working as an assistant in his father's pharmacy in Plymouth, started to deal in used stamps as a sideline, and thus founded the now world famous firm of stamp dealers.

Which is considered the most distinguished philatelic society in the world?
The Royal Philatelic Society in London, which was founded in 1869 and has about 1000 members who include the majority of the world's best known stamp collectors.

Who has been commemorated with the largest number of mourning stamps?
If we understand by a mourning stamp one issued within one year of a person's death, those issued after the death of Sir Winston Churchill in January 1965 totalled 287 plus 14 miniature sheets.

What are the oldest stamps still valid for postage?
The United States definitive series issued on 17 August 1861.

Have stamps ever been issued for an uninhabited island?
Uninhabited Redonda in the West Indies, has had stamps issued for it since 1979. They were issued in anticipation of the island's commercial and tourist development; this has not, however, so far materialized.

What area of the globe has been simultaneously depicted on the stamps of three nations as belonging to each country exclusively?
A slice of Antarctica shown on stamps of the (British) Falkland Islands Dependencies, Argentina and Chile.

What is a tithe barn?
A long rectangular building of late medieval date (or occasionally a little later) in which the parish priest stored his tithes (that is one-tenth of the produce of the land which were paid to the church). Several very fine tithe barns have survived, including the well-known one at Great Coxwell, Oxfordshire, built in the 14th century.

What is rotation of crops?
The order of growing different crops so that each one contributes to the soil constituents needed by the next, corn one year followed by root crops the next year is an example.

What is strip cropping?
This is the planting of crops in strips in such a way as to prevent erosion.

How did fairs begin in Britain?
A fair is a gathering for the sale of products, and fairs are held from time to time and generally include amusements and sports. The earliest fairs appear to have been held in Roman times.

What was a mop fair?
An autumn fair at which farm-hands and house servants paraded themselves in the hope of being engaged for a year's service with a local farmer.

What is the Forestry Commission?
It is a government-sponsored organization founded in 1919 to encourage growth and protection of forestation in Britain. It now owns about 3 million acres of land, over 2 million of which are planted with trees.

What was a pinfold?
An enclosure inside a village in medieval times in which stray animals were rounded up and held until their owners came to retrieve them on payment of a fee.

What is the Countryside Commission?
It was set up in 1968 to promote conservation and enhancement of the landscape of the countryside in England and Wales.

What is the official definition of a footpath?
A highway over which the public has a right of way on foot only, other than such a highway at the side of a public road.

What is ecology?
It is the study of living organisms within their environment, and this includes human beings and their habitats.

What were turnpikes?
They were gates that had spikes, and they were erected on certain roads for the authorities to use to collect tolls from travellers. These were erected after 1663 and the money was meant to be used to help maintain the condition of the roads.

Why was charcoal-burning an important activity?
Charcoal-burning took place for centuries in areas such as Sussex and Kent, and in Gloucestershire, where the charcoal was used by ironsmiths for their forges. The charcoal-burning industry declined with the gradual move over to the use of coke.

Who was William Cobbett?
William Cobbett (1763–1835) was a Surrey-born journalist and political reformer who championed the distressed labouring classes, particularly those in rural industries and on farms. He owned a newspaper and got into considerable trouble with the authorities for his attacks on abuses. He published his famous *Rural Rides* in 1830, a book of collected articles written over the previous years, in which he illustrated the best and the worst aspects of rural life.

What are the Fens?
They are flat, low-lying tracts of land in East Anglia and south Lincolnshire, particularly round the area of the river Wash. These tracts have been drained by means of a network of canals, started in the 17th century, and this has resulted in the production of a substantial area of extremely fertile land. The Romans made efforts to drain the Fens during their occupation of Britain, but the work was not continued by the Anglo-Saxons.

What is a deserted village?
This is a village abandoned by its inhabitants over the course of a period of years for one reason or another, often because of a plague visitation and resulting depopulation. Interest in these villages, of which there are several hundred, has been growing in recent years as aerial photography has revealed more and more evidence. Villages were also destroyed or allowed to decay by landlords of farms and great estates who wanted extra land for pasturing sheep.

Who are the crofters?
They are Scottish small-holders who rent and cultivate holdings known as crofts in the Highlands and Islands of Scotland. They are protected by acts of Parliament.

What was a hollow way?
An ancient form of boundary marking created by digging a deep ditch between two properties and heaping the earth along each side to form a double line of banking. It was also known as a two-fold ditch.

When was the first Ordnance Survey prepared?
Begun in 1791, under the title of the Trigonometrical Survey, its main concern was to map Great Britain on a scale of one inch to one mile (1/63360), a task completed in 1873.

What is a bridle path?
This is a path over which the public has the right of way on foot and on horseback, and from which vehicles are legally barred.

Little Quiz 43

Who are the patron saints of these?
1. actors
2. archers
3. art
4. beggars
5. blacksmiths
6. bricklayers
7. candlemakers
8. carpenters
9. children
10. cripples
11. domestic animals
12. expectant mothers
13. fishermen
14. glassworkers
15. greetings
16. learning
17. librarians
18. lost articles
19. messengers
20. motorists
21. pilgrims
22. porters
23. scholars
24. shepherds
25. tax collectors
26. teachers
27. watchmen
28. widows
29. writers
30. cabinet-makers

and of these towns or countries?
31. Paris
32. Wales
33. Madrid
34. West Indies
35. Norway
36. Austria
37. Belgium
38. Cyprus
39. Romania
40. Genoa

What is the origin of the marathon?
The ancient Athenians defeated the Persians at a great battle at Marathon in 490 BC. A messenger ran all the way from the battlefield to Athens, about 40 km (26 miles) to bring the news to the city. A similar long distance run was included as an event at the first modern Olympic Games held in Athens in 1896, and there has been a marathon event ever since.

Which England cricketer also held the world record for the long jump?
C. B. Fry, who played for the England cricket team many times between 1895 and 1912, including several matches as captain, and played for the England soccer team as well. He set a world record for the long jump in 1893 at 7.180 m (23 ft 6½ in) which remained unbroken for years.

What is the present world record for the long jump?
8.908 m (29 ft 2½ in) by Bob Beamon of the USA, in 1968.

What is putting the shot?
It is throwing a metal ball weighing about 7¼ kg (15.95 lb) as far as you can, holding it in a prescribed manner and having a limited distance in which to swing yourself into the throwing position.

Who was the first runner to break the 4-minute mile barrier?
For a long time, runners had been trying to run a mile in under 4 minutes. Many had got very close to it, including Britain's Sidney Wooderson, but not until 6 May 1954 was it achieved – by Roger Bannister, at Oxford, who ran a measured mile in 3 mins 59.4 seconds.

What is the best time for the mile run now (1984)?
3 mins 48.8 seconds, by Steve Ovett, in 1980.

What is the discus event in an athletics competition?
Competitors throw a heavy disc of wood edged with metal, about 18 cm (7½ in) across and weighing about 2 kg (4¼ lb). They are confined to a circle of about 2.5 m (8.2 ft) in diameter in which to take their stance and twist themselves into the best posture for swinging to throw the discus.

Which South African president at one time claimed to hold the world record for the long jump?
Paul Kruger, who was president of the Transvaal Republic, 1883–1902, and who jumped 7.015 m (23 ft) in 1845.

What great athletic events were the subject of the British film *Chariots of Fire*, made in 1981?
The winning of gold medals at the 1924 Olympics by Harold Abrahams (100 m) and Eric Liddell (400 m).

What is White City's connection with athletics?
The stadium was built for the 1908 Olympic Games held in London, and it accommodated over 90,000 spectators. In 1934 it was refurbished and used for the staging of the British Empire Games. White City continued to be used for athletics (as well as other events) up to 1970.

Where are the Scottish Amateur Athletics Association Championships held?
At Meadowbank, Edinburgh, which was opened in 1970.

Which woman long jump champion won two Olympic medals?
Elzbieta Krzesinska of Poland, who in 1956 jumped a world record of 6.354 m (20 ft 10 in) for women's long jumping, and in 1964 came second with 6.277 m (20 ft 7 in).

What is the world record for the discus throw?
71.192 m (233 ft 5 in) in 1978, by Wolfgang Schmidt of East Germany.

What is the world record for the javelin throw?
96.786 m (317 ft 4 in) by Ferenc Paragi of Hungary, in 1980. Imagine what it might have been like when a whole regiment hurled their javelins in battle, as they did in Greek and Roman times.

Which is the best time recorded for the marathon by a woman runner?
2 hours, 25 mins 29 secs, by New Zealand's Alison Roe, at New York in 1981.

When was the first time that two runners in the mile event both broke the 4-minute barrier?
In the Commonwealth Games of 1954, when Roger Bannister and John Landy came first and second respectively, at 3.58.8 and 3.59.6.

What was the most outrageous act of cheating in an Olympic marathon?
At the St Louis Games of 1904, the early leader, Fred Lorz of New York, was taken some of the distance by car. Not surprisingly he finished first, but was subsequently banned for life by the Amateur Athletic Union (USA).

When were the Commonwealth Games started?
They grew out of the old British Empire Games which were first held in Canada in 1930.

When and in what sports were women first allowed to compete in Olympic Games?
In tennis and golf at the Paris Games of 1900; in swimming at the Stockholm Games of 1912; in track and field events at the Amsterdam Games of 1928.

Who was the first black athlete to win an Olympic title?
William De Hart Hubbard of the USA, who won the long jump at the Paris Games of 1924. Hubbard also took the world record for this event from his fellow countryman, Robert LeGendre, in the following year.

Discus thrower

What is a bonsai tree?

It is a potted tree or shrub which has been rendered almost a miniature version of the original by severe pruning of the roots and stem. The technique is a Japanese one, and bonsai is the Japanese word for it.

What are hardy plants and half-hardy plants?

Hardy plants can survive frost in the open everywhere and every year. Half-hardy plants are those which can survive a normal winter outside but in a sheltered place or in milder areas, such as parts of the UK affected by the Gulf Stream.

Why do you put mulch round the bottom of a flower stem?

Mulch is organic matter such as rotted manure, compost, decayed grass cuttings, and if you put it round a flower stem or rose bush stem it keeps the moisture in and provides food for the plant. It also keeps the weeds down.

What is so remarkable about the rose called 'Peace'?

It is a hybrid rose created in the 1930s in France, which has a huge pale yellow flower with a pink tint on the petal edges. It was given the name 'Peace' in 1945 to celebrate the end of World War II.

Why are tea roses so called?

They were originally grown in China and they have a scent of tea.

What are bedding plants?

These are planted in beds for short term display in the garden.

What are alpine plants?

Strictly, they are plants native to the alpine zone, but the term is nowadays used to cover all small plants that are suitable for a rock garden.

What is so special about orchids?

There are many thousands of species of orchid, and also many thousands of artificial hybrids, but to the expert eye each of the differences is detectable. Orchids are almost always very beautiful flowers. They have been cultivated seriously in the western world for the last two and a half centuries, but the Chinese were growing orchids about 500 BC.

How long ago is it thought that the first flowering plants appeared on Earth?

About 200,000,000 years ago.

What is humus?

A black substance in the earth that is formed out of decaying vegetable and animal matter, and which is the most natural form of fertilizer.

What does cultivar mean?

It is a word meaning a new plant variety cultivated from a natural plant.

What do you plant in a kitchen garden?

Vegetables and herbs and also fruit bushes.

What is a tap root?

The long, central root which goes down vertically into the ground, and which is the principal root of the plant.

What is pollarding?

It is the procedure by which you cut back a tree to the top of its main trunk so that a new and thick head of branches is formed by fresh growth.

Who introduced the first systematic classification of the plant kingdom?

Carl Linnaeus, or Linné, who lived from 1707 to 1778, and who was a Swedish botanist. He visited many countries and studied gardens and botanical collections in great detail.

Are algae plants?
Yes, they are water plants which contain chlorophyll, and range from tiny forms too small to be seen by the naked eye to seaweeds.

What is the death cap?
Said to be the most poisonous of all fungi of the toadstool variety, it looks very like a mushroom.

What is coral spot?
It is a dangerous fungus that affects trees, and if it gets into the living shoots it can kill branches, eventually killing the whole tree. It is detectable by its tiny coral-red coloured spots accumulating in clusters often, though not only, at or near where branches fork, or on branches that have been damaged or broken.

When did the first greenhouses come into use in Britain?
In the mid-17th century, special houses in the garden were erected for plants and vegetables. They are mentioned by the great diarist and gardening enthusiast, John Evelyn (1620–1706).

What is a perennial plant?
A plant that flowers every season, as opposed to an annual plant that begins from a seed, reaches maturity and then dies, all in one year.

What is a cloche?
A cloche is a portable cover used to protect delicate plants and encourage their growth. The Romans are recorded as having dug pits for plants which were protected by sheets of mica, talc or glass; cloches, especially bell-shaped covers from which the name is derived, may have evolved from these Roman covers. They became common in the 17th century and were made of glass. In fact it is only quite recently that plastic and polyethylene have been substituted.

How did grafting originate?
Nobody knows for sure, but a probable explanation is that ancient peoples acquired the technique from observing examples of natural grafting which may happen when neighbouring trees rub together. In Classical times both Geeks and Romans were familiar with several grafting procedures; there is also a reference to grafting in St Paul's *Epistle to the Romans*.

What is topiary?
This name is derived from the Latin word for general gardener. By the first century Roman gardeners were trimming cypress and box trees and shrubs into fanciful shapes, and it was this specific activity which eventually acquired the name of topiary. Following the Dark Ages, topiary again became popular in 15th century Italy and, along with many other Renaissance fashions, spread to England by the time of Henry VIII. The best examples of English topiary are seen in box and yew hedges.

What is a cold frame?
It is a frame made of wood and covered with glass used for protecting young plants from the cold.

Little Quiz 44
  What are the trade unions represented by these abbreviations?
  1. TGWU
  2. NUJ
  3. NUT
  4. CPSA
  5. USDAW
  6. NUPE
  7. COHSE
  8. ASLEF
  9. ASTMS
  10. NGA

What does an actuary do?
In brief, a skilled mathematician and statistician who applies estimates based on mathematical probability upon all kinds of financial risks, problems and calculations, notably in things like life assurance, other insurances and even gambling. It is highly skilled and most actuaries have a qualification from the Institute of Actuaries.

Are Scottish barristers different from English and Welsh barristers?
Scottish barristers are called advocates. They normally have had at least nine months' pupillage with a practising member of the Faculty of Advocates.

Is there a future for the bookbinding craft?
Perhaps not a lot for new books which are nowadays bound by machines, but for specialized limited editions and, of course, for repairing old books, there is a very great need for this ancient skill.

If the bursar of a school or university college asked to see you, what would you expect to discuss?
Probably – though not of course for certain – a financial matter, for a bursar is the person who runs the financial side of a school or college. Bursars are also experienced in general administrative and personnel matters.

What is the main role of the clerk of works on a building project?
Ensuring that the work is being done according to the specifications of the architect and/or consulting engineers. There are other names in use for this job, such as site supervisor.

What is a stock jobber?
A person who works on the Stock Exchange, buying stock at low prices and selling it at higher prices, making a living from the profit.

Would you expect canteen meals to be more appetizing and better prepared if there was a qualified dietician on the staff?
You would be right to expect it, for a dietician is a specialist in the nutritional aspects of food and would normally ensure that your diet was well-balanced and with proper allowance made for vitamin content. Dieticians are employed at schools, universities, hospitals, and in industry.

Why is the factory inspector's role so important?
An inspector ensures that the machinery in a factory is safe for the operators and conforms to the stringent standards demanded by various regulations. He also sees that conditions of work for the staff are up to the required levels. Inspectors make random checks as well as attending to specific complaints.

What does a hydrographer do?
Nowadays a hydrographer is called a hydrographic surveyor and is a specialist in the study of seas and other waters, particularly as to what use can be made of them for industry. He or she also keeps checks on their navigability, or otherwise, and is responsible for producing and up-dating navigational charts.

If you invent a new process or tool, you will need to obtain a patent to protect the idea from being stolen, or copied without your agreement. Why use a patent agent?
Obtaining a patent is not an easy thing to do, because of all the research that has to be done to see that your idea has not already been thought of and registered by someone else. If you want to introduce a new trade mark, that also requires considerable searching, and a patent agent can do this probably better and certainly more quickly.

Architects are associated with buildings, so what is a landscape architect?

Buildings need to be designed in relation to their environment, which means considering things like the garden, roads, and so forth. A landscape architect plans gardens, parks, other land lay-outs, for new building projects such as housing estates, factory and other industrial sites, and also works out ways of improving the landscape of existing structures.

What does a medical laboratory technician do?

He or she performs a vital function in diagnosis and treatment of disease (and in medical research too) because they are an essential part of the medical laboratory where specimens of fluid, tissue, bone and so forth are sent down for swift and accurate investigation and analysis. They work in hospitals, universities, blood transfusion units, veterinary establishments, even some government departments, and also in police laboratories and commercial laboratories.

What is the probation officer's role?

Probation officers look after offenders who have been put on probation by the courts as an alternative to being imprisoned, advise them and help them to get to grips with the reasons for having broken the law and find ways of not doing so again. They are in the unusual position of being part of the judicial process, that is, representing authority, and at the same time giving active support to those who have offended against that authority. They also help other people, such as parties to divorce cases and prison welfare cases.

What does a genealogist do?

He or she traces your family tree, if it is possible to do so, and prepares it in detail.

What is a municipal engineer?

This is a local government officer who is responsible, according to rank, for one or more of a range of public engineering works such as building and planning control, roads and bridges, drainage and sewerage, public buildings, traffic engineering and so forth. There is an essential qualification, associate membership or fellowship of the Institution of Municipal Engineers.

How does an occupational therapist help a person recovering from a major physical illness or injury, or from mental illness?

The recovery process, especially if it is going to be lengthy, is greatly helped if the patient can concentrate for some of the time on creative or constructive work of some kind. Occupational therapists devise schemes for individuals and for groups and then supervise them.

What is a Queen's Messenger?

A courier working for the Foreign Office, or perhaps another government department, who conveys messages, documents etc. all round the world.

Interpreters and translators work with languages. But is there any real difference between their jobs?

An interpreter may well have to deal with translations from time to time as does a translator, but a professional interpreter will be employed mainly in international conference work by organizations such as the United Nations making instantaneous verbal translations of spoken words. A translator's work covers a wider range and deals mostly with the written word.

Do librarians belong to a special professional organization?

Most people who take up librarianship as a career become members of the Library Association, which was founded in 1877.

What is equity?

It means fairness and justice, and refers to that common fairness which follows the spirit rather than the letter of justice. It is a legal system in England which supplements statute or common law and corrects, if necessary, its failure to accord with what is morally just and fair.

What is an injunction?

It is an order of a court which restrains someone from doing something injurious to or likely to injure another's interests, or which orders something to be done for the protection of another's interests.

What is an affidavit?

A statement in writing verified by oath or solemn affirmation of the person making the statement, made for the purpose of production in evidence in legal proceedings.

What is affirmation?

Some people refuse to swear an oath when called upon to do so in a court. They are entitled to refuse but have instead to make a solemn declaration, as allowed by Act of Parliament.

What was benefit of clergy?

An ancient privilege, long since abolished, which was granted to ecclesiastics, and later on, to clerks (that is, all persons who could read and write), exempting them from trial in the secular courts in criminal cases.

What does *caveat emptor* mean?

Latin for 'let the buyer beware', it is a maxim that is applied in cases of sale or bargain, where the buyer takes no guarantee from the seller as to the seller's right to sell, or as to the quality or suitability of the thing bought.

What is a peppercorn rent?

A yearly or other kind of rent of purely nominal amount.

What does it mean when it is said that, for example, a local authority has acted *ultra vires*?

It means that the local authority has acted beyond the powers given it by law. This applies also to companies or other incorporated bodies.

What is a deposition?

It is a statement made by a witness on oath in court. It is also a sworn statement made by a witness and used in court in his absence.

What is a curtilage?

An old word for a piece of land that adjoins a dwelling house. It is still used in legal documents concerned with the transfer of property.

What is an Act of God?

For the purposes of a legal document, it is an inevitable event without the intervention of man, such as a flood or tempest. The phrase is used as a get out clause in some contracts, particularly those with insurers and carriers.

What is a codicil to a will?

A document that makes additions to, or alterations to, the provisions in a will. It has to be executed with the same formalities as the will itself.

What is battery?

It is unlawful beating of another person. It is worse than an assault which can be no more than an attempt at battery.

What are letters of administration?

If a person dies intestate, the court may authorize someone to administer the estate of the person who has died intestate.

What are ancient lights?

They are windows or openings which have uninterrupted access to light for not less than twenty years, and which are therefore to be respected when adjoining buildings are put up.

What is intestacy?
The state of being intestate, which means dying without having made a will.

What is alimony?
It is an allowance made by order of the court out of a husband's estate for the support of his wife when a judicial separation or a divorce is decreed.

What are the two main offences of contempt of court?
1 Failure to comply with an order of a superior court, or resistance or insult to the court or the judges. 2 Conduct likely to prejudice the fair trial of an accused person. Offences are punishable by fines and/or imprisonment.

What is a wayleave?
It is a right of way over or through land for the carriage of minerals from a mine or quarry.

What is a test case?
It is an action in the courts, the result of which is applicable to other similar cases that are not taken to the courts.

What is circumstantial evidence?
A series of circumstances which lead to the inference or conclusion that a person is guilty when there is no direct evidence available.

What is to turn queen's (king's) evidence?
An accused person who, instead of being put on trial, is allowed by the Crown to give evidence against persons associated with him in an alleged crime on the understanding that he is not put on trial himself, is said to turn queen's evidence.

What does the queen's proctor do?
He is the Treasury solicitor who represents the Crown in probate, matrimonial and Admiralty cases. In matrimonial cases he can intervene at any stage if he thinks that there has been collusion between the parties or that material facts have not been disclosed, and he can ask for the decree *nisi* of the divorce not to be made absolute.

What was manbote?
It was compensation paid for the unlawful killing of a man or woman particularly if the person was the villein (serf) of a lord.

What is messuage?
Messuage is a term meaning a house, including gardens, courtyard, orchard and outbuildings.

What is a conveyance?
It is a deed or other document by which property is conveyed from one person to another.

When would you be said to be insolvent?
When you have not enough money or other assets to pay your debts.

What are rights of estovers?
They are rights of taking from woods or waste lands a reasonable portion of timber or underwood for use in the home.

Little Quiz 45
  Of which country were these president?
  1. Jomo Kenyatta
  2. Archbishop Makarios
  3. Juan Peron
  4. Field Marshal von Hindenburg
  5. Marshal Pilsudski
  6. J. K. Polk
  7. Adolphe Thiers
  8. Sun Yat-Sen
  9. Douglas Hyde
  10. Chaim Weizmann

What is Viewdata?
This is an information system, available like CEEFAXand ORACLE, on the home TV screen by means of a control box, but it is linked also with the telephone, enabling it to retrieve all kinds of information from a network of computers all over the country. The scheme is under development, but before the end of this century it may be possible to use the system as an instant telephone directory, a 'what's on' list, for full sets of prices in local shops, for menus in restaurants, and a hundred and one other things.

What is autocue?
It is a device that allows a TV performer, whether actor, interviewer or speaker, to give the viewers the information or speaking lines he or she would have memorized if on a stage or read out if in a studio in earlier TV history. It enables him or her to speak as if the words have been memorized but they in fact are being read from a screen just below the TV camera.

What does a stunt artist do?
Actors and actresses often have to appear to be involved in a variety of scenes of violence, as part of the story they are acting, such as fights, duels, struggles with wild animals, shoot-outs, bad car crashes and so on. The average actors are not trained to do these things and a special kind of artist known as a stunt man or stunt woman stands in for them. With careful editing afterwards, it is possible to make the shots look as if they really did involve the actor or actress.

What is Channel 4?
It is the second independent television channel to be launched in the UK and began transmission of programmes in November 1982. Channel 4 does not make programmes, but commissions or buys them ready-made from independent television producers.

What is a roller caption?
When you see the list of stars, followed by the names of those who helped to make the film or play (list of credits), it is often run through on a dark background. This is done by a machine rather like a mangle, which can be hand-operated or motor driven, and it is rotated horizontally or vertically, as desired. There are considerable variations in presenting these credits.

What does a set designer do?
On TV he designs and supervises the building of the sets for a programme, whether play, serial or film. Unlike a theatre set which is seen by the audience only from the front, TV sets are filmed from several angles, and the set designer has therefore to plan his sets so that they cater for cameras filming at these different angles. He must know about the light-reflecting properties of the buildings and furnishings and the sound dampening characteristics as well.

What is Eurovision?
It is the organization of the European Broadcasting Union which coordinates television and radio programmes in the Common Market countries of western Europe plus some of those that are not in the EEC. It gathers and circulates programmes from member countries to each other and to countries outside the union. It is administered from Geneva and the technical base is in Brussels, at the top of the Palais de Justice building.

When was the first official TV service in the world opened?
In March 1935 at Alexandra Palace in London. Before that, however, a number of programmes and broadcasts had been put out on a haphazard basis from various transmitters over the previous six years. Baird, the inventor of television, started outside broadcasting on BBC transmitters in 1929.

What is the IBA?

The Independent Broadcasting Authority, which originated as the Independent Television Authority in 1954 specifically to supervise the provision of an independent TV broadcasting service to the nation, and to compete with the BBC. The name was changed to IBA in 1972 to take in commercial radio.

What is audience research?

It is the process by which the BBC and IBA attempt to keep track of the opinions of their viewers and listeners, and to get their response to the programmes that are put out on national and local networks. Opinions are sought regularly by a variety of techniques, from individuals for the BBC and from family groups for IBA.

What is Teletext?

The system for displaying printed information with diagrams where needed on TV screens in the home. Two main systems are operating in Britain at present: the BBC's CEEFAX and the IBA's ORACLE.

What do CEEFAX and ORACLE stand for?

CEEFAX means Seeing Facts, and ORACLE stands for Optical Reception of Announcements by Coded Line Electronics.

How is the information conveyed?

It is made available on ordinary household TV screens by means of fitting an adapter for decoding, and specific information is called up by a small key pad hand controller. There is also a directory which lists the services that can be called (a list that is in a continuous state of growth). Information available includes weather forecasts, latest news statements, City prices, sports scores and results, etc.

What does a floor manager of a TV studio have to do?

First he has to be good at handling all kinds of people, many of whom may be on the set at one time. He has to translate commands from a director into effective orders. He has to know what is going on in the studio all the time, and to ensure that everyone else involved understands their roles too. He generally walks about with headphones on, which connect with the control room outside the studio, so that he can listen to what the control people are saying and at the same time give orders or advice to people on the set.

What is dubbing?

It is preparing certain film sequences in advance by mixing sound effects and commentary into the film to create a unified presentation of a sequence. For example, much outdoor filming of news is done in silent pictures, and so sounds have to be added in the sound effects room afterwards. This is dubbing, and it is a great skill, for it has to appear as genuine as possible.

What is video tape recording?

It is an alternative to film. A VTR apparatus receives signals directly from a TV camera and stores them on special magnetic tape. The process is similar to audio tape recording, except that the tape for video is much wider. The advantages are that the pictures can be played back instantly and they do not have to be processed.

What is Sianel Pedwar Cymru?

It is the Welsh language television service provided for Welsh speaking areas in Wales. Known for short as S4C, it also broadcasts for a number of hours on Channel 4.

Who were the Goodies?

Tim Brooke-Taylor, Graeme Garden and Bill Oddie.

Who was Marshal Turenne?

Probably the greatest general ever produced by France. Even Napoleon acknowledged Turenne's supreme military genius. Henri de la Tour d'Auvergne, Vicomte de Turenne (1611–1675), was the son of the Duc de Bouillon and grandson of William the Silent. Turenne was born a Protestant, but this did not interfere with a spectacular career in the French army in the closing years of the Thirty Years' War (1618–48) or afterwards, though it may have stood in the way of his being made constable of France. He became marshal in 1643, when he was only thirty-two: he had led huge armies into great victories by the time he was thirty. In the wars of Louis XIV against the Dutch and the Imperial armies in the 1670s, Turenne was the French supreme commander. In one assault, he was killed by cannon shot. Louis XIV was grief stricken, and said he would rather have lost two whole armies than Marshal Turenne.

Who was Pericles?

One of the greatest of all Athenian statesmen in the long history of Greek civilization, Pericles lived from about 490 to 429 BC. From about 460 to his death, he was leader of the democratic party and dominated the city state, improved its buildings (it was he who commissioned and had built the Parthenon, among other great buildings), encouraged the arts and literature, and also proved to be a sound and successful war leader when the occasion arose. Pericles died of plague in 429.

Who was Sennacherib?

He was an Assyrian king who ruled from about 704 to 681 BC. His reign was one of conquest of neighbouring lands, but he also initiated great building projects, including the rebuilding of the city of Nineveh. He was murdered by one of his sons in 681.

Who was prime minister of Britain when he was only twenty-four?

William Pitt, the Younger (1759–1806), and he remained prime minister for an unbroken period of seventeen years (1783–1801). Pitt was a genius. He went to Cambridge at fourteen, was called to the bar at twenty and entered the Commons at twenty-one. Within two years he was chancellor of the Exchequer. He had already demonstrated remarkable talents as a parliamentarian, and in 1783 was asked by George III to be prime minister. He returned to office in 1804 and was prime minister again until his death in 1806.

Who was Pitt the Younger's father?

An equally celebrated statesman and orator, William Pitt, the Elder (1708–1778) was virtual prime minister and war leader during the Seven Years' War (1756–1763), managing the war effort with great skill, enabling the allied cause to triumph over France and in particular to win Canada and India for the British Empire. In later years, Pitt, created Earl of Chatham in 1766, came to support the cause of the colonists in America against the British government.

Who was Chairman Mao?

Mao Tse Tung (1893–1976) was for many years between the two World Wars a communist political leader in a China which had, first, a strongly anti-communist government, and then was invaded and partly occupied by the Japanese. When the Japanese were finally defeated in 1945, the old nationalist government (Kuomintang) returned, but Mao led a powerful movement to drive them out and build a new China. In 1949 he cleared the nationalists out of the mainland and declared the formation of the People's Republic. For the next twenty-seven years Mao governed China on Communist lines.

Why was the Chinese emperor Wang Mang murdered?

Wang Mang reigned from about AD 9 to 23. He was one of the Han dynasty rulers. He conceived a highly revolutionary programme of reform that included new methods of tax raising, nationalizing of land and distributing it to peasants, fixing prices and incomes, and curbing monopolies. But his ideas, commonplace today, were too advanced for his time and he was murdered.

Which Dutch admiral is said to have sailed up the English Channel with a broom tied to the mast of his flagship, to show he had swept the seas of English ships?

Maarten van Tromp (1597–1653), a great Dutch naval commander who had inflicted several defeats upon Spanish fleets during the Thirty Years' War (1618–48). In 1652 he defeated the English fleet under Admiral Blake.

Who was Solon?

Solon the Lawgiver (c. 640–c. 560 BC), was chief magistrates of Athens in the 590s, and in that time he reconstructed the constitution of Athens, dividing the population into four classes, allowing each class the right to send delegates to a popular assembly to govern the state. He has been called the founder of democracy.

Marlowe wrote a play about Tamberlaine the Great. Was there such a person?

Yes, Timurlaine, as he is alternatively known, was a Mongol chief, born about 1336, a descendant of the great Genghis Khan. Timurlaine spent much of his life attempting to recreate the huge empire that Genghis had built in the early 13th century. In 1398 he captured Delhi in India, then overran Asia Minor in 1402, capturing its ruler Bayazid I. He planned to march upon China, but during the early stages of the march he died, in 1405.

Which Welsh prince was known as 'The Good'?

Hywel Dda (Howell the Good), prince of all Wales from about 920 to 950. He was grandson of Rhodri Mawr, the first prince of all Wales. Hywel kept the peace with England, whose system of government he admired, and towards the end of his reign he brought many of the varied Welsh customs and laws together into a unified system.

Who was 'The Tiger'?

This was Georges Clemenceau (1841–1929), the French statesman, so called because of his toughness, particularly towards the end of, and after, World War I. Clemenceau had a long career as politician in France, had survived the siege of Paris, had been a physician and even worked in the USA. From 1906 to 1909 he was prime minister, and when France was in dire trouble in 1917 in World War I he was asked to take office again. He made a major contribution to restoring French morale and mobilizing the French war effort to final victory in 1918.

Who was Coligny?

Gaspard de Coligny (1519–1572) was the leader of the Huguenots in France during the wars of religion in the mid-16th century. He had had a distinguished army career, was then made an admiral and organized voyages of Huguenots to the New World to found colonies. In 1572, he was murdered, along with thousands of other Huguenots in Paris, on the night of St Bartholomew's Day.

Who was Maecenas?

Gaius Maecenas (70–8 BC) was a friend of Octavius (later, Augustus) probably from an early age. He was an entrepreneur in ancient Rome, and for years acted as a sort of private adviser to Augustus. It was he who suggested that Octavius should accept the position of first emperor of Rome in 27.

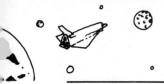

What is a turboprop aero engine?
In full, turbo-propeller engine, it is a jet engine which has a turbine-driven propeller, which is given extra thrust from the expulsion of hot gases.

What is a hydrofoil boat?
It is a fast boat which has a set of 'wings' or hydrofoils attached to the hull and mounted under water. As the speed of the craft is increased, the foils create an upward thrust that lifts the hull out of the water. Eventually the craft skims across the surface with only the foils and propeller in the water.

What is the Safège monorail?
A type of monorail developed in France. An experimental track was built near Orléans. The train hangs from rubber-tyred wheels on bogies running inside a box girder.

How did the autogiro work?
Invented by Juan de la Cierva in Spain in 1926, it had an aeroplane body of conventional shape with a normal propeller-driven engine at the front. Over the pilot and passenger compartment, however, was a motor mechanism with long blades on top. These blades rotated freely when the craft travelled forwards and had no independent power of their own. The turning of the blades provided lift for the aircraft to rise and to stay in the air, while the propeller provided the forward movement.

Which was the largest airship ever built in Britain?
The R101, built by the Royal Airship Works at Cardington in Bedfordshire in 1929–30. The airship crashed on its maiden flight in October 1930. It was on its way to India, carrying among others, the secretary of state for air, Lord Thomson. The crash occurred at Beauvais in France. R101 was 236.8 m (258 yd) long.

What was a bubble car?
In the 1950s, one or two German firms that had manufactured war planes in World War II (such as Messerschmidt and Heinkel) started to make very small vehicles, with bubble Perspex hoods, accommodating two people, either side by side or one behind the other. These cars were three-wheeled, and were about a quarter of the size of the average family car. They could park in half the space, but they were so small that they were frequently not seen by drivers of huge lorries and other vehicles, and many accidents happened. They were also underpowered for the work that most of their owners expected of them.

Who invented the hovercraft?
Sir Christopher Cockerell (b 1910), an electronics engineer who turned to boat-building. The first models were tried out in the 1950s and the first cross-channel hovercraft service was opened in 1966.

When was the first mail-carrying coach service introduced in Britain?
In August 1784, by John Palmer, a theatre owner from Bath in Somerset. He obtained a contract from the Post Office to open a regular service of mail-carrying coaches between London and Bristol. The coaches also took passengers. Each coach had an armed guard. The service was maintained reasonably efficiently by means of frequent changes of horses along the route.

Why was a hansom cab so called?
It was a two-wheeled, hooded carriage pulled by one horse and which carried two people inside, with a driver seated on a perch behind the carriage body, the reins passing over the hood. It was introduced by Joseph Hansom (1803–1882) in 1836, and because of its light-weight construction, was a fast means of getting about. It was the forerunner of the taxi.

How were the German V-1 flying bombs powered?

These flying bomb terror weapons, produced by the Germans in 1944 and directed against England, were powered by a crude form of jet engine called the pulse jet. They were also called 'buzz bombs' after the characteristic noise they made.

What is a Jumbo Jet?

A very large passenger airliner or freight carrier, particularly the Boeing 747. Jumbo Jets can carry up to about 500 passengers, or more than 380 tons of cargo, and can do so over 1000 km (7000 miles).

What is the amphicat?

A Swiss-invented amphibious 'runabout' vehicle that is produced in a range of sizes and forms for a variety of duties. One model can go up ski slopes carrying several passengers, another can cross rivers and lakes using an outboard motor.

Where and when did the last London tram finish its final journey?

At New Cross depot in South London in July 1952.

What is a travelator?

It is a moving pavement. Passengers stand on the special 'conveyor belt' which is a horizontal path, and are carried along while they stand still. Some travelators are set absolutely level, some are slightly raked. A travelator at Bank Underground station in London takes you from the station down to the City-Waterloo line going under the Thames.

How fast does Concorde cruise?

This splendid Anglo-French supersonic airliner, which carries up to 100 passengers, cruises at over 2160 kph (1200 mph) which is over Mach 2, twice the speed of sound.

What is a turbo-train?

It is a train with a gas-turbine powered locomotive. The idea was conceived in Switzerland during World War II, and turbo-trains are used for passenger and freight transport in several countries, including France, Canada, the USA, and Russia.

Hovercraft

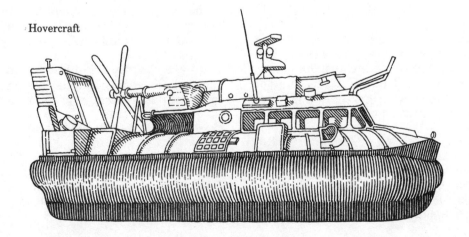

What is the origin of the teddy bear?
It is said to have first appeared in 1902 in the USA as an animal modelled on a cartoon of the then president, Theodore (Teddy) Roosevelt (1901–1909), who was a famous hunter.

What two famous military surrenders of the 20th century happened in the same place?
In World War I, the German surrender to the Allies in 1918, and in World War II, the French surrender to the Nazi Germans in 1940 both took place in the same railway carriage at Compiègne in France.

Where are the Western Ghats?
They are mountains down the western side of the Indian subcontinent, beginning about 160 km (100 miles) north of Bombay, down to near Calicut.

What is a grandmother clock?
A smaller version of the grandfather (long case) clock, usually not more than about 2 m (6½ ft) tall, sometimes less.

How can you locate south during the day by using your watch?
Hold your watch flat with the hour hand pointing towards the sun. A line drawn half-way between the hour hand and the figure twelve on the watch face will point south.

What is an encyclical?
It is a letter written by the pope and addressed to all the archbishops and bishops of the Roman Catholic Church, dealing with some ecclesiastical, moral or social question, or questions.

How many living organisms are there in the world?
It has been estimated that human beings share the earth with 3,000 quintillion (3,000,000,000,000,000,000,000,000,000, 000,000) other living organisms.

Who invented lithography?
Aloys Senefelder, a German printer, in 1796. He drew a picture using an oil-based crayon on a smooth, flat stone. Then he covered the stone with a film of water and passed an ink-filled roller over the area. The water did not mix with the oil (the two don't mix), but the oil marks made by the crayon did, and by laying a sheet of paper over the stone he was able to get a print of his drawing. The word comes from two Greek words, *lithos*, a stone, and *grapho*, I write.

What is a periscope?
It is an upright tube with an opening at the top set at 45°, and a similar arrangement at the bottom. A mirror is set in each angle, and enables the person at the bottom to see what is going on outside at the top. A periscope is used in a submarine cruising or stationary just under the surface of the sea or river, to enable the captain to see what surface ships are nearby and may be threatening.

What is the common English word of three letters that spelled out makes a proper number in Roman numerals?
MIX (1009). M = 1000, IX = 9.

What were the names of the six wives of Henry VIII?
Catherine of Aragon, Anne Boleyn, Jane Seymour, Anne of Cleves, Catherine Howard, Catherine Parr.

What are the plurals of these words: gene; genie; genus; genius; genesis?
genes; genies; genera; geniuses; geneses.

How deep is the Pacific Ocean at its deepest?
At the Mariana Trench it is 11,041 m (36,200 ft) deep, which is over 2135 m (7000 ft) greater than the height of the highest mountain, Everest 8708 m (29,028 ft).

Where was Dixieland?
It was a farm on Manhattan Island, New York, once owned by Johann Dixie. The term came later to refer to those states south of the Mason and Dixon Line in the USA, the boundary between Maryland and Pennsylvania states, marked in 1763–7 by Mason and Dixon. It was the dividing line between the free and the slave states in the American Civil War, 1861–5.

What is a plectrum?
A piece of bone, ivory, tortoiseshell, wood or plastic with which to pluck the strings of some musical instruments, such as a mandolin or banjo.

What is the last sentence in the famous Hippocratic Oath, still taken by doctors when they graduate?
'Whatsoever things I see or hear concerning the life of men, in my attendance on the sick or even apart therefrom, which ought not to be noised abroad, I will keep silence thereon, counting such things to be as sacred secrets.'

Which was the first motor car race?
It took place in France in 1894 and was won by Count de Dion who drove one of his own de Dion steam cars from Paris to Rouen at a speed of 18.67 kmh (11.6 mph).

What is the largest butterfly native to the British Isles?
The swallowtail, which has a wing span of 7.6–8.89 cm (3 to 3½ in) and can weigh up to 0.509g (0.018 oz).

When is the festival of Martinmas?
The feast of St Martin is on 11 November, and in the Middle Ages fairs were held, at which farm workers gathered hoping to be hired. It was also a day on which cattle were killed and put away for winter storage and eating.

What is the Balfour Declaration?
A letter written in 1917 by the British foreign secretary, A. J. Balfour (1848–1930) to Lord Rothschild, a prominent Jewish banker and chairman of the British Zionist Federation, saying that the British Government viewed 'with favour the establishment in Palestine of a national home for the Jewish people'. It eventually led to the creation of the state of Israel in 1948.

Before the reorganization of local government of 1 April 1974, how many counties was Wales divided into and what were their names?
Thirteen: Monmouth, Glamorgan, Carmarthen, Pembroke, Cardigan, Brecon (or Brecknock), Radnor, Montgomery, Merioneth, Caernarvon, Anglesey, Denbigh and Flint.

What are the names of T. S. Eliot's *Four Quartets*?
Burnt Norton, East Coker, The Dry Salvages and *Little Gidding*.

What is the capital of Nepal?
Katmandu.

Little Quiz 46
What were the Latin names for these places in Roman times?
1. Lyons
2. Lincoln
3. Alexandria
4. Trier
5. St Albans
6. Cadiz
7. Marseilles
8. Paris
9. Segovia
10. Milan
11. Geneva
12. Istanbul
13. Cologne
14. Budapest

What was the Holocaust?

Holocaust means destruction by fire on a large scale, and the Holocaust is a phrase used to describe the attempted wholesale destruction of the Jewish people by the Nazi Germans in Germany, 1933–45, and in occupied Europe 1939 onwards. About 6,000,000 Jews perished.

What was the Kuomintang?

It was the Nationalist Government in China under the leadership of Chiang Kai-shek (1887–1975), from about 1926 to 1949. In that time, it struggled with attempts to overthrow it, then with Japanese invasion and partial occupation of China, and it was finally brought down by Mao Tse Tung when he won control of the Chinese mainland in 1949. The Kuomintang continues to rule in Formosa, now Taiwan.

Who were the Spartacists?

They were left-wing revolutionaries in Germany who formed a party in 1916 during World War I and were opposed to the continuation of the war. When Germany was defeated, the Spartacists became the German Communist Party and attempted to seize power, but were crushed and their leaders put to death.

Who were the Octobrists?

They were the right wing of the liberal movement that organized the 1905 Revolution in Russia, a revolt whose demands were issued in the October Manifesto.

When did the old kingdom of Ceylon, for a time a British colony, become Sri Lanka?

Ceylon was a British colony from the early 19th century to 1948 when it was granted self-government and Dominion status. In 1972 the Ceylon government declared the country a republic and changed the name to Sri Lanka, which means Resplendent Island.

What is Comecon?

It is a kind of common market of Eastern European countries. The letters stand for Council for Mutual Economic Assistance, and it was set up in 1949 by the USSR. Members now include Cuba and Mongolia.

What had the Boxer Rebellion to do with boxing?

It was a revolt by nationalistic Chinese in 1898 against the continued presence in China of various foreign embassies, trade delegations and commercial centres, missionaries and other 'intruders'. The rebels were known as boxers because they exercised by means of a form of shadow boxing, which helped to integrate mind and body and make them strong enough, they believed, to withstand bullets and sword cuts.

Which event in the Russo-Japanese war of 1904–5 finished the war?

The great naval victory of the Japanese fleet over the Russian Baltic Fleet at Tsushima in May 1905. The defeat of Russia precipitated the 1905 October Revolution. (See also p 24.)

What happened to President Allende of Chile?

Salvador Allende (1908–1973) was a left-wing radical statesman in Chile who succeeded in winning election to the presidency in 1970 by democratic means, without bribery, force or underhand methods, in a part of the world where presidents were usually right wing dictators. For three years Allende tried to introduce many much-needed reforms, but the army overthrew his liberal régime and Allende himself was murdered.

Which country formally declared itself to be an atheist state in 1967?

Albania, in south-east Europe, one of the Eastern European bloc countries.

When did the Isle of Man get self-government?

In 1866, the Isle of Man was granted home rule, that is, self-government. It had its own parliament, the Tynwald. One of the Tynwald's assemblies, the House of Keys, is among the oldest legislative assemblies in the world.

Why was the French government during World War II known as the Vichy Government?

The German army defeated the French army in June 1940, and the French Government under Marshal Pétain surrendered. Northern France including Paris was occupied, but the southern part was run by Pétain in collaboration with the Germans. Pétain set up his seat of government at the health resort of Vichy, famous for its mineral waters since Roman times.

Where is Andorra?

It is a tiny semi-independent republic at the eastern end of the Pyrenees, between France and Spain. It has a population of about 20,550 (1971) living in an area of nearly 453 sq km (175 sq miles). It is governed by a Council of twenty-eight members, who hold executive power under two co-princes, nowadays the French president and the Spanish bishop of Urgel.

What happened at Pearl Harbor in December, 1941, to bring the USA into World War II?

On 7 December 1941, Japanese aircraft attacked the US naval base at Pearl Harbor in Hawaii, sinking several ships and killing hundreds of people, thus starting a war with the USA. Germany, Japan's ally then declared war on the USA, thus turning the two struggles, USA v Japan and Germany and its allies v Britain and Russia, into one global conflict.

Who were the Mau Mau?

Mau Mau was the popular name for a secret society associated with the Kenya national independence movement which from 1952 to 1960 dominated the Kenya political scene, while the country was still a British colony. The activities of the Mau Mau were characterized by violence, kidnapping, murder and destruction of farms owned by white people and killings of black people who worked with the whites or who refused to support Mau Mau.

Who owns Heligoland?

This is an island off the mouth of the Elbe, in the North Sea. It had for long been German, but in the 18th century it became Danish. In 1807 it was taken from the Danes by the British, and held until 1890 when it was returned to Germany. During both World Wars the Germans fortified it and used it as a naval base, but after World War II the fortifications were destroyed.

What happened to the Portuguese province of Goa in India?

This little enclave on the Malabar coast of India about 322 km (200 miles) south of Bombay, was founded by the Portuguese in 1505. When India won its independence from Britain in 1947, moves were made to absorb Goa. In 1950 India formally demanded its surrender, but Portugal refused, whereupon India set up a blockade and then invaded. The Portuguese gave in and withdrew in 1961.

What is the origin of the name Zimbabwe, chosen for the new state formed when Southern Rhodesia became fully independent in 1980?

Zimbabwe was the name of an ancient Bantu civilization that flourished from the 8th century to the 15th century in Rhodesia and extensive remains of its centre were found at Zimbabwe.

Why did the Russian prince, Felix Yusupov, sue the famous MGM film studios for libel in 1934?

In 1916, Yusupov had helped to murder the corrupt and evil monk, Rasputin, whose influence upon the court of the last czar of Russia, Nicholas II, had been disastrous for the Russian war effort in World War I. Several years later, MGM produced a feature film purporting to tell the story of Rasputin. In it the suggestion was made that Yusupov (whose name was changed in the script to Chegodiev) was engaged to a princess Natasha who was Rasputin's mistress. Yusupov was in fact married to a noblewoman who had never had anything to do with Rasputin, and he regarded the story of the film as libellous. He won substantial damages, but during the hearing he had to tell in some detail the full story of the killing of Rasputin.

What happened to the Reverend William Sawtrey in 1401?

Sawtrey was rector of King's Lynn. He was a Lollard, that is, a follower of the teachings of John Wycliffe. In 1401, Lollards became victims of a government persecution campaign, and when Sawtrey travelled to London to preach in favour of the Wycliffe teachings, he was taken and burned to death at Smithfields. It was the first such punishment for heresy in England.

What was the Great Train Robbery of 1963?

On 8 August 1963, a Post Office mail train on the way from Glasgow to London was ambushed in Buckinghamshire by a gang. About 120 mail bags were taken, with £2,631,784 worth of old bank notes. The train guard was injured. Most of the gang were caught and received long prison sentences. One, Ronald Biggs, escaped to Brazil. Only £343,448 worth of notes were recovered. It was the biggest train robbery in British criminal history.

Who was Horatio Bottomley?

Bottomley was one of the most extraordinary rogues of the 20th century. Born in 1860, he was a journalist and financier who also had an extraordinary knowledge of the law and a first rate aptitude as a speaker. He promoted companies, made fortunes and lost them, was prosecuted for fraud but acquitted by brilliantly conducting his own defence, entered Parliament but had to retire after another financial scandal. He also founded the magazine *John Bull*. During World War I he organized schemes for raising war bonds and a gullible public invested thousands of pounds – which he pocketed. In 1922 he was again prosecuted for fraud, and this time, despite his eloquence, was convicted and sentenced to seven years in prison. He died in 1933, in poverty.

What was the Assassination Plot of 1696?

By the middle of the 1690s, many Englishmen who had at first welcomed the accession of William III (1688–1702) had become disillusioned. In 1696 a number of them, led by Sir John Fenwick and Sir George Barclay, plotted to murder the king at Turnham Green, near Chiswick in London. The plot was betrayed and the leaders were arrested and executed.

Who murdered the French Revolutionary leader, Jean Paul Marat?

Jean Paul Marat was one of the most extreme of the French revolutionaries, notorious for calling for large scale massacres of opponents. On 13 July 1793, he was stabbed to death while in his bath by a noblewoman, Charlotte Corday, who supported the Revolution but hated Marat's extremism. Charlotte Corday was arrested and tried, and went to her execution a few days later with great calm and dignity.

Whom did Sherlock Holmes describe as the Napoleon of Crime?

Professor James Moriarty, a brilliant mathematician who turned his talents to planning and supervising a series of major crimes. Moriarty appears in the Holmes story, *The Final Problem*, in which the two men fought a life-and-death struggle in the Reichenbach Falls in Switzerland.

Who invented the guillotine?

Once said to have been invented by Dr Joseph Ignace Guillotin (1738–1814), the French doctor and revolutionary, it is now known that it was in use as an instrument of execution in several other countries before the French Revolution, though of course under different names. Dr Guillotin knew of its existence and recommended its use to the authorities, and it came into service in 1791.

Who was the last person to be hanged in public in Britain?

Michael Barrett, sentenced for his part in a Fenian bomb attack in 1867. He was hanged on 26 May, 1868 at Newgate prison in front of a big crowd.

Why was Admiral Byng shot at Portsmouth in 1757?

In the first year of the Seven Years' War (1756–1763), things were not going well for Britain. Admiral Byng led a squadron in an attempt to relieve the garrison on the island of Minorca, off the east coast of Spain, which was under siege by the French. His force was severely mauled by the French and he withdrew. There was an outcry in England, and Byng was court-martialled for cowardice and neglect of duty. He was acquitted of cowardice but found guilty of neglect of duty, and because the nation seemed to want a scapegoat, he was sentenced to death and shot. This was the occasion which prompted Voltaire to say it was done 'pour encourager les autres'.

Why did Lord Alfred Douglas receive a six-month prison sentence for criminal libel in 1923?

He had published a broadsheet accusing Winston Churchill of having made money on the Stock Exchange by delaying the full report of the battle of Jutland. It was untrue and Douglas was charged with a criminal libel of which he was not able to prove the truth, and sentenced.

Why was George IV's queen, Caroline, tried in Parliament in 1820?

Caroline was married to George IV in 1795, when he was prince of Wales. It was an unhappy match and eventually Caroline went abroad to Italy. When George succeeded to the throne in 1820, Caroline claimed her rights as queen. But the king got the prime minister to introduce a bill in parliament petitioning for the marriage to be dissolved, on the grounds of Caroline's adultery. She was defended superbly by Lord Brougham, and the case was dropped amid tremendous public enthusiasm.

What was the main effect of the criminal law reforms of Sir Robert Peel, the home secretary, in 1828?

Peel abolished the death penalty as the punishment for more than 100 crimes, many of them minor offences like sheep-stealing.

What was the Cato Street Conspiracy?

It was a plot to murder Castlereagh and other members of the Cabinet in 1820. Led by Arthur Thistlewood, the plan was to attack the ministers as they dined at Lord Harrowby's house in London. The plotters were betrayed and surprised while making final preparations in a loft above a stable in Cato Street, Edgware Road, London. They escaped for a time but were later put to death.

What is humanism?
A term meaning belief in the idea that an honest and useful life is possible without its being geared to, or motivated by, any religious beliefs.

What, then, is Humanism?
It is the name given to the cultural movement that prevailed during the Renaissance period in Europe, which was characterized by the revival of interest in things Greek and Roman, and which enlarged the interests of people beyond the limits previously determined by the Christian religion.

What is Apartheid?
It is a policy prevailing in South Africa, and it means 'separate development' for the coloured races, on different terms from the development of the ruling white races. In practice, it means discrimination against non-European groups, to their disadvantage, even to the extent of refusing them the right to vote. As such, the policy is almost universally condemned.

Who were the Nihilists?
Nihil is the Latin for nothing, and Nihilists were a mid-to late-19th century group of Russian political activists who sometimes resorted to murder or bomb throwing in an attempt to undermine Russian society without offering anything in its place. One notable Nihilist crime was the murder of Czar Alexander II, in 1881, the first czar to alleviate the lot of the peasantry in Russia and who abolished serfdom.

What is the Bahai faith?
A religion founded in Persia in the middle of the last century by two teachers, Mirza Ali Mohammed and Mirza Husain Ali, who advocated belief in the spiritual unity of mankind and who encouraged their followers to devote their lives to the service of others.

Were the Shakers anything to do with the Quakers?
They were a small American sect of people who in the 1740s broke away from the Quakers and settled in New York State. They continued to accept most of the Quaker beliefs but added several of their own, such as that God was both man and woman, that the manifestation of man was Jesus Christ and the manifestation of woman was Mother Ann, who was a convert from England called Ann Lee. The name Shakers came from the fact that some of their rituals involved intense shaking of the body.

What is yoga?
It is an ancient Hindu philosophy which teaches the integrating of body, mind and will into a union with an Absolute Being, a state that can be achieved through a system of progressive mental and physical exercises.

What have the British Israelites to do with Israel?
Nothing strictly, but they are an English Protestant sect that believes that white Anglo-Saxon people are descendants of the lost tribes of Israel – those that were deported from Israel in the 8th century BC. This they say, makes them God's Chosen People.

Who are the Christadelphians?
An American Protestant sect, founded in 1848, who claim to practise what they say is original 1st century Christianity according to the earliest followers of Christ. They believe that only they know how to interpret the Scriptures properly.

What is the ecumenical movement?
Basically a movement among all Christians – Catholics, Protestants, Non-conformists, etc., to unite all believers. The movement was given a significant boost in 1982 when Pope John Paul II visited Britain.

Who were the Levellers?

You could say they were the first English communists. They were a left wing sect of the Parliamentarians in the Civil War, whose membership was drawn from small farmers, workmen, traders, many of them serving in Parliament's New Model Army, and they campaigned for a republic with one representative assembly elected by manhood suffrage. While Cromwell had some sympathy with some of their aims, he had to suppress them in the army because of the threat they posed to good order and discipline.

Who were the Muggletonians?

This was a religious sect emerging in the Civil War in England and continuing during the Commonwealth period. It was founded by Ludovic Muggleton who issued a new interpretation of the Book of Revelations. The sect believed that it was the Father (God) not the Son (Jesus Christ) who had died on the Cross, that God himself had been in human form.

What is the transmigration of souls?

It is a belief that after death the soul enters the body of another living creature. The belief has been a tenet of several faiths, including those of some Hindu sects, of Buddhism, and it was also held by some of the ancient Greeks.

Who were the Christian Socialists?

Originally, they were a group of Christian clerical and lay leaders in the mid-19th century in Britain, who campaigned for major social reforms. They believed in the principles of socialism that were developing in Europe, but wanted to temper them with Christian teachings. They encouraged cooperative workshops, education classes for workers and other charitable activities for the benefit of the poor. They also gave support to the newly growing trade union movement.

What is anthropomorphism?

It means the attribution of human form and character to God or to gods, and also to animals or even plants. It is a tendency in most human beings at some time, instanced perhaps most obviously by regarding domestic animals as having human personalities and desires. Another form of anthropomorphism is the belief that God is some mystical human being in the sky looking down towards Earth, His creation.

What are Baptists?

They belong to a religious sect which believes in total immersion and do not approve of the baptism of infants.

What was the Oxford Movement?

This was initiated in 1833 by a group of scholars and divines at Oxford University. The movement was characterized by a desire to restore to the Church of England certain pre-Reformation principles which had been lost. Prominence was given to the Catholic character of the Church, without implying the necessity of union with Rome. When many of its leaders, notably Cardinal Newman, did become Roman Catholics the movement foundered.

Little Quiz 47
  Where are these lakes?
  1. Great Slave
  2. Van
  3. Koko-Nor
  4. Great Bear
  5. Titicaca
  6. Onega
  7. Issyk-Kul
  8. Manitoba
  9. Bala
  10. Loch Ness

Who invented the telescope?
There are various claimants, but perhaps the one with the most widely recognized claim is Hans Lippershey, a Dutch spectacle-maker who died in 1619. He is said to have invented his telescope in 1608.

Telescope

Who invented the cylinder lock?
Linus Yale (1821–1868), a locksmith who founded the Yale company.

Who invented the safety razor?
King C. Gillette (1855–1932), in 1895.

Who invented the blast furnace?
The Scottish engineer James Neilson (1792–1865), who was for nearly thirty years foreman and manager of Glasgow gasworks.

Who invented the metronome?
Johann Nepomik Maelzel (1770–1838), a German musician and instrument-maker who settled for a time in Vienna and taught music. He later moved to Paris and finally emigrated to the USA. He produced the metronome in 1816.

186

Who invented the mercury thermometer?
The mercury thermometer was invented in 1714. Up to then the fluid used in thermometers had been alcohol. It was Gabriel Fahrenheit (1686–1736), a German physicist who was the first to use mercury (or quicksilver) in the thermometer tube, and he fixed the freezing point at 32 degrees and the boiling point at 212 degrees.

Who invented the safety pin?
Walter Hunt (1796–1859), an American, invented the safety pin in 1844 and it was patented in 1849. He was responsible for other new ideas, including the paper collar.

Who invented the lathe?
The lathe for metal turning and screw cutting was invented by Henry Maudslay, an English engineer (1771–1831).

Who invented the gyroscope?
The distinguished French physicist Jean Bernard Léon Foucault (1819–1868), invented the gyroscope in 1852 with which he showed how the Earth rotates on its axis.

Who invented the passenger lift?
Elisha Otis (1811–1861), who was born in Halifax, Vermont. He improved his first lift of 1853 by devising a steam elevator in 1861.

Who invented the bunsen burner?
Robert Wilhelm Bunsen (1811–1899), a German physicist and chemist who became professor of chemistry at Heidelberg University in 1852.

Who invented the ophthalmoscope?
Hermann Ludwig Ferdinand von Helmholtz in 1851. An ophthalmoscope is the instrument used by doctors to examine the inside of the eye.

Who invented the spinning jenny?
James Hargreaves (1720–1788). The spinning jenny was a spinning engine which enabled a man to operate several spinning wheels at once. It was demonstrated in 1764 at Standhill in Lancashire. Hargreaves called it the jenny after his wife.

Who invented linoleum?
Frederick Walton, an English inventor, in 1860.

Who first produced the explosive mixture, nitro-glycerine?
An Italian chemist, Ascanio Sobrero in 1846.

Who invented celluloid?
The English chemist, Alexander Parkes (1813–1890). The transparent sheet was produced by the action of nitric acid on cellulose in a mixture of camphor and sulphuric acid.

Who invented the microphone?
David Edward Hughes (1831–1900), who spent several years as a music teacher in the USA and was also an experimenter with printing telegraphy. He invented the microphone in 1878.

Who invented the cotton gin?
This useful apparatus that separated the fibres from the seeds was invented in the USA by Eli Whitney in 1793. It produced a marked increase in cotton manufacture.

Who invented the flying shuttle?
This was a mechanically operated shuttle for a loom which enabled the loom to operate more quickly, and also enabled the user to make broad-cloth. It was a key invention in the Industrial Revolution, and was invented by John Kay in 1733.

Who invented the revolver?

Samuel Colt (1814–1862), in 1836. He came from Hertford in Connecticut in USA.

Who invented the flush lavatory?
Sir John Harington (1561–1612), an Elizabethan courtier, satirist and godson of the queen. During a period of banishment from court, he designed a water-closet with a reservoir and installed it in his own home near Bath in 1589. After his return to favour, two years later he constructed another for the queen herself in her palace at Richmond, Surrey. The design is to be found in his pamphlet, *The Metamorphosis of Ajax.*

Who invented nylon?
Wallace Hume Carruthers (1896–1937), an American chemist and director of research at du Pont. He invented this material which has properties similar to those of natural silk. It was moreover, the first fibre to be completely man-made.

Little Quiz 48
  Where are these waterfalls?
  1. Kalambo
  2. Niagara
  3. Sutherland
  4. Nevada
  5. Victoria
  6. Gersoppa
  7. Kaieteur
  8. Staubbach
  And these volcanoes?
  9. Villarica
  10. Cotopaxi
  11. Erebus
  12. Etna
  13. Pepee
  14. Nyamuragira
  15. Elbrus
  16. Fujiyama

What is the Pre-Cambrian era?
The first geological era in the story of the
Earth, from about 4500 million years ago
to about 2000 million years ago. There
are three main periods in the era, Azoic,
Archaeozoic and Proterozoic.

What is the Azoic period?
It is the period 4500–4000 million years
ago when there was no animal life on
Earth and the earliest rocks evolved.

What is the Jurassic period?
It is part of the Mesozoic Age, from about
180 million BC to about 130 million BC.
It was the age of dinosaurs and other
prehistoric animals, among them the
earliest birds.

What is the Abbevillian period?
A period at the beginning of the
Paleolithic Age (Early Stone Age). It is
named after a number of finds in the
estuary of the river Somme, around
Abbeville in France. The finds are dated
about 300,000 BC and include two-faced
stone hand axes.

Where is the Olduvai Gorge?
It is in Tanzania, East Africa. Here, in
the 1950s, Dr Louis Leakey and his wife
Mary, found fossils of Australopithecus
africanus (Southern Ape of Africa).

Who was Piltdown Man?
A remarkable forgery. Parts of a skull
found at Piltdown in Sussex in 1912 by a
Dr Dawson were said by him to be from a
hominid, but in 1953 Professor Sir
Wilfred Le Gros Clark exposed this as a
scientific hoax, for the skull was from a
modern man, and the associated jaw was
from an orang-utan.

What is potassium-argon dating?
A method devised in 1946 for dating
ancient remains. It is based on the
breaking down of radioactive potassium
into argon.

What was Australopithecus africanus?
It was an early ape, said for a long time
to have been the ancestor of man, but
now seen as an ape that lived alongside
another early but slightly different
ancestor of man. Australopithecus
africanus wandered about East Africa
between 2 and 5 million years ago.

Where is Taima-Taima, and what is it?
It is a site in Venezuela, South America,
which was occupied about 12,000 to
14,000 years ago. The inhabitants
produced two-faced stone axes, used
scrapers and other tools, and appear also
to have had some kind of horse.

Where did the first people in North America come from?
They are thought to have come from Asia
by wandering across the Bering Strait in
times when the strait was iced over,
which was about 25,000 BC or perhaps
earlier. The first men to appear in North
America were hunters.

When did human beings appear in Ireland for the first time?
During the Mesolithic period in Europe,
more specifically for Ireland about 7000
BC. Before that time, it is believed that
Ireland was uninhabitable, even though
there were early Stone Age people in
almost all other parts of Europe.

What was an aurochs?
The ancestor of present-day cattle. It
lived in forests in most parts of Europe,
in central Asia and in China. It appears
to have been domesticated as early as
about 4000 BC in south-east Europe.

Is it possible to say when pottery was first made?
Pieces of pots (sherds) have been found in
Anatolia (Asia Minor) which have been
dated to about 7000 BC.

Who was Cro-Magnon Man?
One of the closest of our ancestors, Cro-Magnon Man lived about 30,000 years ago. Remains of this ancestor were found at Cro-Magnon in France in the late 1860s, and after that time, very similar skull and skeleton remains were found in other parts of the world.

When was Siberia colonized by man?
Probably about 20,000 years ago, especially round Lake Baikal.

What was the Jomon period?
A Japanese early culture which lasted for many thousands of years, from about 12000 to about 500 BC, in which the people hunted and fished, and made pottery, but did not know about the use of metal.

When did European peoples begin to cultivate crops in fields?
About 10,000 years ago, in the period 9000 to 8000 BC. The first crops were not native to Europe. They were brought in from Asia Minor, particularly what is now Turkey in Asia. Settlers from this area reached south-east Europe, built small mud-brick villages, kept livestock and introduced the growing of cereals.

Which was the very first ancestral ape from whom we are descended?
The African ape, Proconsul, discovered on Rusuiga Island in Lake Victoria. It lived over 30 million years ago, dwelt in trees and walked on all fours.

What was the first animal to be intentionally domesticated?
The dog, which is first reckoned to have been domesticated about 16,000 years ago. This domestication would have been the work of late Palaeolithic hunters who, as farming gradually developed, recognized the dog's value as a guard as well as a hunting companion. While the dog's immediate ancestors were wolves, it gradually lost much of the wolf's characteristic behaviour.

When did the Magdalenian culture flourish?
The Magdalenians were an advanced hunting people who occupied parts of south-western Europe, between the Alps and the Spanish Cantabrian Mountains, some time between about 15000 and 10000 BC. They were late Palaeolithic (Stone Age) people who were highly inventive and who used a variety of stone tools. They produced much cave art, notably the animals in the famous Lascaux caves in France and the Altamira caves in Spain. The Magdalenians moved into central Europe, reaching as far as Czechoslovakia, and may also have come to Britain. They hunted reindeer, fished for salmon, and made their own clothes, cutting and stitching the garments with some skill.

What was a tylosaur?
A giant, scaly reptile which flourished about 80 million years ago in what is now Kansas, USA.

Little Quiz 49
Give the correct chemical name for these well known substances?
1. washing soda
2. common salt
3. epsom salt
4. glauber's salt
5. heavy water
6. caustic soda
7. slaked lime
8. aqua regia
9. potash
10. barytes

What is the difference between opéra comique and comic opera?
Opéra comique is opera in which there is a lot of spoken dialogue as opposed to sung dialogue. Comic opera is opera with a farcical plot.

What sort of operas did Gilbert and Sullivan write?
They wrote what is called classical operetta, which can loosely be defined as a play with overture, singing and dancing.

What is the libretto of an opera?
It is the book, or text, of the performance.

Who is the prima donna in an opera?
The phrase is Italian for leading lady, and in opera she is the leading singer in the cast. Sometimes the shorter term *diva* is used.

When is the intermezzo performed in an opera?
It is a brief musical interlude between two scenes or acts of an opera. But there are some early serious operas in which the intermezzo was a kind of mini-opera on its own, sandwiched between acts, and this was less serious, even humorous, and intended as a kind of light relief.

When is an opera a Grand Opera?
Usually, when the whole text is sung, not sung and spoken.

What is an aria?
The Italian for air, it means a song, and in opera it is a solo.

Where is the most famous opera house in the world?
La Scala in Milan, built in 1778. It was the leading opera house right up to World War II, when it was badly damaged by bombs. The building was reconstructed after the war and reopened in 1946.

When is the overture played?
At the start of the performance. It is an introductory piece of music played by the orchestra. Some composers introduced in their overtures the themes that they developed during the rest of the opera.

What is *Cosi fan tutte*?
It is an opera by Mozart. Cosi fan tutte means 'Thus they all do', which in modern terms is saying 'Everybody does it'. This opera is about two lovers who leave their ladies and later return disguised as Albanians, to test the faithfulness (or otherwise) of their deserted mistresses.

What was Offenbach famous for?
Jacques Offenbach (1819–1880), German born but brought up in France, composed some of the best operettas in the art. He is famous for the sensuality of his music, and among his best known works are *Orphée aux Enfers* (1858), *La Vie Parisienne* (1866) and the opera, *The Tales of Hoffman*, which was not performed until after his death.

Who is generally regarded as the greatest Italian opera composer?
Giuseppe Verdi (1813–1901). Born the son of a village innkeeper at Le Roncole, near Busseto in Parma, he failed to get accepted by the Milan Conservatoire. His first opera, *Oberto*, was put on in Milan at La Scala in 1839, and over the next half century he produced a string of the very finest operas, notably *Rigoletto*, *Il Trovatore*, *La Traviata*, *Aida* and *Otello*.

What is the *Ring* cycle and when was its first complete performance?
A series of dramatic operas based on the German legend of the Nibelungen and the hero Siegfried. They were composed by Richard Wagner and first performed as a whole in 1876 at the then new theatre at Bayreuth. The operas are *Rheingold*, *Walküre*, *Siegfried* and *Gotterdämmerung*.

Which was Kathleen Ferrier's most celebrated operatic role?
Orfeo, in Gluck's opera *Orfeo ed Euridice*. Kathleen Ferrier was born in 1913 and died tragically of cancer in 1953, a few weeks after a stupendous performance in the role at Covent Garden.

Who is the best known British composer of operas in this century?
Benjamin Britten (1913–1976), who composed several major operas that are, in the opinion of specialists, among the best of all 20th century compositions. His last great opera was *Death in Venice* (1973).

Where and what is Glyndebourne?
It is a large country house near Lewes in Sussex, owned by John Christie (1882–1962). He built a theatre at Glyndebourne in 1934, and founded the Glyndebourne Festival, an annual summer festival for operatic works, both new and well established.

In which role was Chaliapin perhaps best known in opera?
Feodor Chaliapin (1873–1938), the Russian bass, is probably best known for the role of Boris Godunov, in the opera of that title by Moussorgski.

Do you know what happened at the first performance of Rossini's *Barber of Seville* in Rome in 1816?
It was a disaster. To begin with, supporters of another composer who had written music to the same story filled the auditorium and began to barrack and whistle. One of the leading performers who was tuning his guitar snapped a string which made a loud noise. Another performer managed to fall through a trap door on the stage floor. And to cap it all, a stray cat wandered across the stage. The composer himself was booed and hissed and he went home before the end of the performance.

What have these three opera singers in common – Enrico Caruso, Beniamino Gigli, Placido Domingo?
They are or were all tenors.

What was the first real opera performed in Britain?
The Siege of Rhodes, in 1656, during the Protectorate of Oliver Cromwell who, far from being a kill-joy, loved music and patronized many musicians. This opera with music by several composers was put on by Sir William Davenant (1606–1668) who later became poet laureate.

When was Covent Garden Theatre, in London, opened?
The first theatre on the site was opened in 1732, but the present building erected in 1858 is the third on the site, the two earlier ones having both been burnt down.

What is *Tommy*?
This is the rock opera written by Pete Townshend of The Who in 1969 and performed initially by that group.

Who founded the Aldeburgh Festival?
Benjamin Britten, along with Eric Crozier, the producer and librettist, and Peter Pears, the tenor, in 1948. Some of Britten's operas were inspired by the history, scenery and literature of this part of Suffolk, and it is appropriate that the Aldeburgh Festival should have been founded, at least in part, to provide a vehicle for their production on 'home ground'. The purpose-built concert hall/opera house associated with this festival is in fact situated at nearby Snape. This building, a conversion of old maltings, was opened in 1968, burnt down in 1969 and rebuilt in 1970. Premières staged there have included *Death in Venice*, in 1973.

What is the correct length of a cricket pitch?
20.13 m (22 yd), and it has been so at least since the 1740s.

When did batsmen first begin to wear pads?
This is not known for certain, but one Robert 'Long Bob' Robinson, who played at Farnham in Surrey, is recorded as taking his stance in front of the wicket wearing a wooden shield round one leg. This was at the end of the 18th century.

How old is the game?
This is impossible to say for certain. There is a reference to cricket being played at a school in Guildford in the mid-16th century and another in 1654 at Eltham in Kent, for which the participants were fined. It was not until 1744 that the game was given its first proper set of rules.

What early form of cricket was played with a stone wicket?
Stonyhurst cricket, played by Roman Catholic exiles of the English College on the continent for two centuries up to 1794. This college was then set up in England as a school at Stonyhurst Hall near Preston, Lancashire, their cricket game accompanying the scholars who had been driven from *Liège*, their last refuge, by the French Revolutionary armies. Stonyhurst cricket continued to be played at the school until 1860, when it was displaced by the game played according to the MCC's regulations.

What is the origin of Lord's Cricket Ground?
One of the original members of the MCC was Thomas Lord (1755–1832), a Yorkshire born entrepreneur who leased the ground in Dorset Square to the MCC. The club moved from this ground to another nearer St John's Wood, but this was not popular among the players and

in 1814, Lord found a third site, costing £100 a year. This is the site occupied today.

What is the area of Lord's cricket ground?
About five acres, 2.025 hectares.

What is the I Zingari Cricket Club?
It is a wandering club, founded in 1845. The name is Italian for The Gypsies, and the club is still flourishing.

What is the John Player League?
A cricket league specifically played on Sundays among first class counties.

What were the first cricket rules?
They were the Laws of Cricket, drawn up in 1744 but not published nationally until 1752 when they appeared in the November issue of the New Universal Magazine. They appeared in booklet form three years later.

When was the MCC founded?
The Marylebone Cricket Club was founded in 1787, and its first headquarters was in Dorset Square, behind Baker Street in London. It cost 6d to watch one of the club's matches.

Who is still regarded as the most famous cricketer of all time?
Few would argue that it is W. G. Grace (1848–1915). William Gilbert Grace was a doctor, but his cricket career began in his teens when he made his debut at Lords and at the Oval aged only 16. During his career, Grace scored 54,896 runs in first class cricket, the highest score being 344 in the match between the MCC and Kent in 1876.

What other high score did Grace achieve?
Grace was also a top flight bowler, and in his career he took 2876 wickets in first class cricket. He captained

Gloucestershire from 1871 to 1898, and also captained 13 England test teams against Australia.

Which British test player became a Church of England bishop?
David Sheppard, Bishop of Liverpool.

What is a maiden over?
A full over during which no runs are scored by either batsman.

What is Wisden?
This is short for *Wisden's Cricketers' Almanack*. It was first published in 1864 by John Wisden (1826–1884) who played for Sussex and England. It is an annual containing well over 1000 pages with full details of all first class cricket matches of the previous year, with records, tours and so forth. From its earliest years of publication it has been accepted as the 'Bible' of cricket.

What was the Plunket Shield?
It was the leading cricket competition and trophy in New Zealand first class cricket. Originally presented in 1906 by Lord Plunket, then governor-general, it was awarded up to the 1974–75 season.

What was the body line controversy?
Harold Larwood (born in 1904), played for Nottinghamshire and England and now lives in Australia, was one of the fastest bowlers of his day. He was also one of the most accurate. In the England v Australia series in 1932–3, he concentrated on body-line bowling, that is, bowling directly at the leg stump in such a way that the ball often struck the batsman. This caused great offence in Australia, which was aggravated when the visiting team won the series.

Who is the greatest all-rounder today?
Sir Garfield (Gary) Sobers, the West Indian cricketer.

What is a 'googly'?
It is the term for a ball bowled as an off-break and sent down with a leg break action at the other end.

Who is generally regarded as the finest of all wicket-keepers?
Leslie Ames (L. E. G. Ames), born in 1905. He achieved 415 stumpings in first class cricket, which is still a world record. Ames was also a very skilled and dashing batsman.

Have any bowlers ever dismissed all eleven batsmen in a Test Match?
Yes, two: J. C. Laker for England versus Australia at Manchester in 1956; S. Venkataraghavan for India versus New Zealand at Delhi in 1964–5.

What was special about the first Australians to tour England?
These thirteen men, who toured England in 1868, were Aborigines coached by an English emigré, Charles Lawrence. Sadly, one of them, King Cole (native name Brippokei), died of tuberculosis during this tour, in which the visitors had 14 wins, 14 defeats and 19 draws. Apart from playing cricket, the tourists also gave exhibitions of their native skills, dressed in possum skins.

Little Quiz 50
   What do these units of measurement measure?
   1. ampère
   2. hertz
   3. watt
   4. ohm
   5. kelvin
   6. joule
   7. coulomb
   All are names of famous scientists: which of the seven were British?

What is the sea elephant's principal diet?

The sea elephant, also known as the northern elephant seal, eats octopuses and other cephalopods such as cuttle-fish and squids.

What is a cacomistle?

It is a curious nocturnal creature, related to the raccoon, and is distinguishable by the fact that half of its yard-long body is a thick, bushy, black and white banded tail.

What is a hinny?

It is the result of a cross-breeding of stallion and she-ass.

Rhinoceroses have been dying out as a family of mammals, largely through man's insatiable urge to hunt and kill them. Only a handful of species survive. Which is the most numerous?

The black rhinoceros, in central and East Africa. This creature seldom attacks humans unless roused.

Can you tell the difference between a leopard and a panther?

There isn't one. They are the same animal, and panther is the word used in India.

Which species of fox is most commonly found in Europe?

The red fox. Its Latin name is *vulpes vulpes*.

Which animal was the standard for the Roman legions?

The eagle, which was portrayed in several forms and carried by standard bearers. One form was as a gold model on the end of a pole.

Which is the only poisonous snake left in Britain?

The adder, which is a member of the viper family.

How does the humming bird hum?

By beating its wings extremely rapidly.

Why is the hoopoe so called?

The hoopoe is an attractive bird with golden plumage flecked with black and brown, and has a longish curving beak, like a scythe blade. Its call sounds like hoop-poop-poo, and its Latin name is *upupa epops*.

What is a bush baby?

A species of lemur (mostly nocturnal and tree dwelling), about the size of a squirrel, and generally grey-brown in colour. It has paws rather like human hands, with suckers on the finger ends.

How far can the Rana dalmatina species of frog jump?

Over 1.83 m (6 ft) in one leap.

Would you be safe in the presence of a broad-fronted crocodile?

Yes. It is a small crocodile from the equatorial region of west Africa, it seldom grows beyond about 1.83 m (6 ft) long and does not attack human beings.

Eagle

What is the mongoose well known for?
Killing snakes. It is a mammal with a longish tail, and it feeds on birds, small mammals and snakes.

How far can a gibbon leap in its progress through the forest?
At least 13½ m (45 ft) in one leap from one tree to the next.

What is the largest member of the deer family?
The European elk (known in Canada and the USA as the moose).

What is an alpaca?
It is a domestic species of llama which is found in South America. Its fine long coat, black or black and white, makes excellent wool.

Which of the big cats purrs?
The cheetah, or hunting leopard (*acononyx jubatus*). This splendid creature is also the fastest animal on earth, and can run at 110 mph (70 mph).

What is a tuatara?
This is a lizard-like reptile, found in the wild only on about 20 small islands in New Zealand. It is remarkable in that it is the only surviving representative of a reptile group which lived 170 million years ago. Its peculiar features include the possession of a rudimentary third or pineal eye on top of its head, and the lowest body temperature and incubation period of any reptile. It also exhibits an incredible indifference to pain. It is believed that wild tuataras enjoy a life expectancy of a century or even more.

Which birds build the smallest nests?
The Vervain and bee hummingbirds build nests which are, respectively, about the size of half a walnut shell and the size of a thimble.

What is the world's most common bird?
The red-billed quelea, frequenting the drier regions of Africa south of the Sahara. Its population may be as high as 10,000 million, and it poses a serious threat to cereal crops. The fact that about 1000 million of these birds are killed each year appears to have no real impact on this species' overall population and range.

In what part of Britain does a species of marsupial live in the wild?
A pair of red-necked wallabies escaped from a private menagerie in Staffordshire in 1939, and their descendants still thrive in the Peak District National Park.

What was the world's most dangerous 'big cat'?
This was a tigress accorded the title of the 'Champawat man-eater' and which lived in and around Nepal in India. In the eight years prior to its being shot in 1911, it had killed 438 people.

What is the largest member of the deer family native to Britain?
This is the red deer, which is found in Scotland, the Lake District and the West Country. One killed in Scotland in 1831 weighed 238kg (525lb).

Little Quiz 51
What are the metric equivalents of these?
1. acre
2. foot
3. cwt
4. gill
5. fathom
6. fluid ounce
7. peck
8. quart
9. square yard
10. pennyweight

What does a combine harvester do?
It is a large machine that plies up and down a corn crop field and cuts the ripe corn and threshes it, to separate the grain from the straw.

What is a forage harvester?
This cuts, chops and blows grass into a huge heap. The grass is fed to cows as silage in the winter.

What is silage?
It is food for cattle, in the form of hay or straw, stored in a silo and fermented with the help of molasses to preserve it throughout winter.

What is natural manure?
It is animal dung which is mixed with straw, and this is spread over land to fertilize the soil. The technique is as old as civilized man.

Why do farmers grow rape?
Rape is an annual plant grown chiefly in Europe and North America. It is grown particularly for food for sheep and pigs. It has a lovely yellow flower. When it is harvested, it is crushed to extract rape oil for a variety of uses. The residue is mashed into what is called rape cake, and given to the animals.

Hampshire Down sheep

What does a baling machine do?
A baling machine (or baler) picks up the loose straw dropped by a combine harvester and compresses it into tight bundles, which it then shoots out onto the ground to be picked up and piled into stacks. The baler is pulled by a tractor.

What are the principal corn-growing areas of Britain?
East Anglia and Lincolnshire. Norfolk produces the highest corn yields of any British county, and has done for centuries.

What is a harrow?
It is an iron frame containing a row of discs or spikes in echelon which is pulled by tractor (or in some places by horse) over ploughed earth, to break up the lumps into fine tilth.

Much farm machinery these days is huge and very expensive to buy. How does the small farmer overcome this problem?
He can hire the machinery from a special contractor who buys and maintains the machines for this purpose, or he can pay a contractor to bring the equipment to his fields and do the work for him.

What are a shepherd's tasks?
Basically, to care for the flock of sheep, building and keeping in good repair the fences round the fields on which the sheep graze, and seeing that the sheep do not get caught up in thickets or tree clumps, or fall into streams and ponds. Shepherds also are ready to help ewes giving birth to new lambs.

What is a cereal?
It is one or other of a number of plants of the Graminaceae family which included wheat, barley, oats, maize, rice and millet. The word is used to cover types of beans and peas as well.

Which animal provides veal?
Veal is the meat from calves. Calves are taken from their mothers two or three days after birth and reared in special calf pens, being fed on nuts and hay, until it is time to slaughter them.

What is seed drilling?
The seed-drill was invented in the early 18th century by Jethro Tull (1674–1741), a Berkshire lawyer and agriculturalist, and is a machine that makes a furrow in the ground, drops seeds into it at regular intervals (which can be adjusted) and then covers up the furrow.

Where is the Royal Show held?
At Stoneleigh Park, near Kenilworth in Warwickshire.

What is ley?
This is land which is temporarily sown with grass, being ploughed after one to three years (short duration ley), or after a longer period of up to ten years (long duration ley). Ley has the same meaning as the older English word, lea.

What is a Rhode Island red?
A breed of fowl which originated in and about Rhode Island in the north-eastern USA. It is a hardy, medium-sized bird, the hens noted for their large brown eggs.

What is foot-and-mouth disease?
This is an infectious viral disease of cattle, pigs, sheep and goats. The name derives from the characteristic blisters in the mouth and on the feet. While death would not always follow this infection, in Britain all diseased animals and their contacts are slaughtered as a matter of course.

What is a gilt?
A young female pig which has not produced a litter.

What is a mixed farm?
A farm where the farmer grows crops and keeps animal stock, such as cattle, pigs, poultry, etc.

What are broilers?
They are chickens reared in a special poultry house. The birds usually number several thousand to a house and they are reared to be killed and sold off as meat.

Where is dairy farming on the whole more productive in Britain?
In the western areas, where the grass grows well on gentle rolling hills and valleys.

Little Quiz 52

What is the feminine of?
1. gaffer
2. conductor
3. ogre
4. czar
5. wizard
6. cock-sparrow
7. man-servant
8. bridegroom
9. votary
10. testator

and the plural of?
11. dormouse
12. louse
13. house
14. man-of-war
15. court-martial
16. grotto
17. half
18. trout
19. dozen
20. veto

Are local councillors paid?

They get an allowance for attending meetings, plus allowances for travel and subsistence.

What is the role of a chief executive officer of a council?

He is the head of the council's paid service and has authority over all other officers so far as is necessary for efficient management and execution of the council's functions. In effect he replaces the old town clerk or clerk to the council, but has much greater responsibilities.

Can the Press attend meetings of local councils or their committees?

Yes, except if publicity would be prejudicial to the public interest by reason of the confidential nature of the business to be transacted. This covers nearly all meetings within local authorities and their committees.

Which of the local authorities is responsible for the library?

The county council. This means that a city library, which used to be under the city council, now comes under the county council.

What are rates?

They are an annual tax on property raised locally, the amount relating to the estimated annual value of the property. Rates contribute to the ability of the county and the district to provide public services for the inhabitants of the area concerned.

What is the Rate Support Grant?

It is a grant of money by central government, paid every year to local authorities to help them meet their expenditure. If it was not paid, householders and owners of industrial premises would have to pay much higher rates every year to their local authorities.

When was London's first mayor appointed?

As far back as 1191. The title Lord Mayor was first used in 1414.

Which were the first New Towns planned for England and Wales after World War II?

Basildon, Bracknell, Crawley, Harlow, Hatfield, Hemel Hempstead, Stevenage, Welwyn Garden City, Newton Aycliffe, Peterlee, Corby and Cwmbran. The first eight were all within 30 miles of London and were intended to relieve overcrowding in the capital.

Which were the first of the new towns planned for Scotland?

Cumbernauld, East Kilbride, Glenrothes and Livingston, which were to relieve overcrowding in Glasgow.

When was the old London County Council created?

By the Local Government Act of 1888.

When was the Greater London Council (GLC) formed?

In 1963, as a result of the Local Government Act. It consists of 92 councillors. The leader of the Council is elected from the political party which has the majority of the council seats.

At which time of year are local government elections supposed to be held?

In England and Wales, on the first Thursday in May or on such other days as may be determined by the home secretary of the time.

How often do county council elections take place?

Every four years, and the whole council retires altogether. Under the old system, the elections were staggered, that is, one third of the seats were contested every three years.

What is a county council?

It is the elected body governing the local affairs of a county and is the largest of the local government units. County councils were first created in 1888.

How many county councils are there in England and Wales today?

Before the Local Government Act of 1972, there were forty-six in England and thirteen in Wales. The reorganization left England with forty-five, six of which are called metropolitan district councils, and Wales with eight county councils.

Which old counties disappeared under the 1972 Act of England?

Huntingdonshire, Westmorland, Cumberland, Rutlandshire, Middlesex.

What are the names of the new Welsh counties?

Gwynedd, Clwyd, Powys, Dyfed, Gwent, West Glamorgan, Mid-Glamorgan and South Glamorgan.

What is a community council in Wales?

Briefly, it is the replacement for the old parish council which disappeared in the 1972 reorganization of local government.

How often must a parish council meet in a year?

At least four times, including one annual meeting in which local electors are allowed to take part.

What is the principal trade union of workers in local government?

NALGO, which used to stand for the National Association of Local Government Officers and was founded in 1905 by the merger of several smaller unions serving individual trades and professions serving the councils. In 1952, to widen the membership to include people working in nationalized industries and organizations such as the health service, it became the National and Local Government Officers Association, using the same letters.

What were county boroughs?

These were large towns in England and Wales which between 1888 and 1974, or for part of that period, were for local government purposes independent of the geographical counties they lay in. Initially, county borough status was conferred upon all towns with a population of over 50,000, and upon Canterbury which was somewhat smaller. Later, towns were not accorded county borough status unless their population had reached at least 100,000.

What local government area in England has a resident population of about 4,700 and a working day population of about 340,000?

The City of London.

Where in the British Isles are islands specifically entitled bailiwicks?

In the Channel Islands: the Bailiwick of Guernsey and the Bailiwick of Jersey.

In what English county are there district councils called Dacorum and Three Rivers?

Hertfordshire.

What is the most populous of the English metropolitan counties, and what are the others in descending order of population?

The West Midlands is the largest, with a population of about 2,667,000. Then follows Greater Manchester (2,605,000), West Yorkshire (2,063,000), Merseyside (1,511,000), South Yorkshire (1,312,000), and Tyne and Wear (1,149,000). Four non-metropolitan counties have in fact populations between those of Merseyside and South Yorkshire in size: they are Hampshire, Kent, Essex and Lancashire.

What is an anemometer?
An instrument for measuring the speed of the wind.

What is an anti-cyclone?
It is an area of high pressure in the atmosphere, which is as a rule accompanied by fine weather.

Where is the troposphere?
It is the bottom layer of the atmosphere over the Earth, about 8 to 16 km (5 to 10 miles) thick, and it contains most of the atmosphere's moisture.

What is humidity?
A term expressing the amount of moisture in the air.

How is dew formed?
Drops of moisture form on objects close to the ground when the air condenses, especially on cool surfaces at night.

What is hoar frost?
It is a white frost or rime which forms when dew freezes.

What is permafrost?
It is permanently frozen subsoil and bedrock, as in polar regions.

What is a sea breeze?
It is a current of cool air coming from the sea and replacing the rising warm air on land.

What was the most devastating hailstorm on record?
One in which hailstones reported to be as large as cricket balls fell in parts of India on 30 April 1888. About 250 people died, as well as over 1600 sheep and goats.

What is a depression?
It is a centre of low pressure that affects the weather and makes it unsettled, bringing periodic rain and winds.

200

What does weather-bound mean?
It means being delayed or confined by bad weather.

What are the cloud formations now accepted in the International Cloud Atlas?
High clouds – above 6000 m (20,000 ft) cirrus, cirrocumulus, cirrostratus; Middle – between 2000 m (8000 ft) and 6000 m (20,000 ft) altocumulus, altostratus, stratocumulus; Low – below 2000 m (8000 ft) nimbostratus, stratus; and ascending clouds – beginning as low as 500 m (1640 ft) cumulus and cumulonimbus.

What is a cloudburst?
A sudden and heavy downpour of rain.

What is Cloud-cuckoo-land?
An ideal kingdom in the air, invented by the Greek playwright Aristophanes (c. 448–c. 388 BC), in his play *The Birds*.

What is a stormy petrel?
Someone who habitually prophesies trouble, bad news and so forth, and seems to enjoy it. The phrase comes from a Mediterranean and North Atlantic bird, the storm petrel, which is traditionally a harbinger of storms and bad weather.

Who was the first person to describe weather conditions in Britain?
Julius Caesar, in the fifth volume of his famous work, the *Gallic War*, in which he describes his first invasion of Britain in 55 BC.

There is one place in the British Isles where the temperature has never dropped to freezing point since records began. Where is it?
Bishop Rock, Isles of Scilly.

Where is the Meteorological Office?
In Bracknell, Berkshire. It is an offshoot of the Ministry of Defence.

The Beaufort scale is a scale of numbers 1 to 17, indicating the strength of the wind. What does No 10 indicate?
Usually known as a Force 10 gale, it is of such strength that trees break and are blown down and ships are often compelled to heave to.

How do you convert Fahrenheit temperatures to Centigrade?
Take 32 away from the Fahrenheit temperature, multiply the result by 5 and then divide by 9, e.g. 70° F: $70 - 32 = 38 \times 5 = 190 \div 9 = 21.1°$ C.

When is a black frost likely to occur in Britain?
A black frost is most likely to occur in southern England, when there is an inflow of very dry, Polar continental air which has taken a short sea track from mainland Europe.

What is a frost hollow?
This is a location which experiences frost far more frequently than in adjacent areas. A frost hollow is determined by the configuration of the land and the nature of the soil: long narrow valleys draining large areas of high ground and sandy declivities are particularly associated with this phenomenon.

What became known as the 'Fastnet Storm'?
The depression which caused severe gales in the South-West Approaches on 13 and 14 August 1979. This was the occasion when the twenty-eighth Fastnet Race was taking place in that locality, and as a result fifteen yachtsmen lost their lives.

What is generally regarded as having been Britain's worst weather disaster?
This was the great gale and tidal surge which struck on 31 January and 1 February 1953. In the North Channel (between Scotland and Northern Ireland), the motor vessel *Princess Victoria* sank with the loss of 132 lives. A further 156 people died in the floods which affected Lincolnshire, Norfolk, Suffolk and Essex.

How do weather stations record the duration of sunshine?
This is done by means of a Campbell Stokes sunshine recorder, essentially a crystal glass sphere mounted on a pedestal which focuses the sun's rays onto a card. The length of the burn mark on the card is related daily to the duration of bright sunshine.

When is the latest date that snow has been reliably reported to fall in lowland Britain?
On 2 June, 1975, when it fell in amongst other places Edinburgh, Birmingham, Newark-on-Trent, Grantham, Peterborough, Norwich and Colchester.

Has there ever been a month in which the sun has not shone at all anywhere in Britain?
In December 1890 the sun was not seen at all in London.

What contrasting rainfall features were experienced in southern England in July 1955?
On 18 July, 279mm (11in) of rain fell at Martinstown in Dorset, the British record for a single day. Yet further to the south-west, at Camborne in Cornwall, no rain at all fell in the whole of that month. The fall at Martinstown exceeded the total for the whole of 1921 at Margate: during that year only 236mm (9.29in) was recorded at that resort, a British record.

Where is the crossing in a cathedral?
In a cruciform cathedral or church it is the space where the north and south transepts intersect with eastern and western arms, over which is usually raised a dome on a tower with or without a spire.

What is the origin of the term Gothic?
It was the term used by the Italian painter and art historian, Giorgio Vasari (1511–1574) who so described the architecture of the 12th to 15th centuries, because he and his contemporaries regarded the style as barbaric. The Goths were barbarian peoples who overran parts of Western Europe in the late 4th and 5th centuries.

What is an iconostasis?
It is a screen, usually of wood and/or stone, in an Eastern European cathedral, on which icons are placed. It divides the east end from the remainder of the building. The iconostasis at St Isaacs in Leningrad is 68 m (225 ft) wide, and is made of gilded marble and other stones.

What is a portal?
In cathedral or church terms it is an elaborate doorway with decoration. The portals of the Île de France cathedrals are almost breathtaking in their decorative and sculptural treatment.

Which famous sculptor wrote a book on the cathedrals of France?
Auguste Rodin (1840–1917). In 1877 Rodin made a tour of the French cathedrals, but it was not until 1914 that his book *Les Cathédrales de France* was published.

What is a *chevet* in a cathedral?
It is a word that describes a rounded or polygonal apse at the east end of a cathedral, when it is flanked inside by an ambulatory with chapels radiating from it. (An ambulatory is a covered walkway

202

behind the high altar, used for processions). The feature is of French origin and is to be found in many French Gothic cathedrals, such as Notre Dame de Paris, Chartres and Rheims. In England, there are chevets at Gloucester and Norwich.

What are the Ladies of the Vale?
This is the locally known phrase describing the three spires of Lichfield Cathedral, in Staffordshire, which from several angles appear all to be of the same height.

What famous riot took place in a Scottish cathedral?
In 1637, rioting broke out among the congregation in St Giles' Cathedral in Edinburgh, when the authorities introduced a new service book. This had been imposed by Charles I. The disorder began when a parishioner, Jenny Geddes, threw her stool at the dean.

What are the two most interesting facts about Salisbury Cathedral?
It was the only English cathedral to be built in one operation, in the 13th century. It has the tallest spire in England, viz 123m (404ft).

What are the most distinctive features of St Sophia's Cathedral at Kiev in the USSR?
Begun in the 11th century, this, the oldest cathedral foundation in Russia, has 21 domes of varying periods. Today it is no longer used as a church but is a museum.

Where is there a Gothic style cathedral that is very largely built of structural steel and concrete?
Grace Cathedral, in San Francisco, USA. It is built of these materials because of the city's liability to earth tremors. It was begun in 1910 and completed in 1964. (See also p 97.)

Why was Klaus Emil Julius Fuchs sentenced to 14 years' imprisonment in 1950?

Fuchs was a German-born physicist who was driven out of his native land in the 1930s when Hitler came to power. He sought refuge in Britain, and during World War II he worked with other British scientists on the atomic bomb project. For several years he was a senior figure in nuclear research, and during this time he leaked secrets about the research to agents of the USSR. He was eventually caught and sentenced to fourteen years in prison.

What were the Phoenix Park Murders?

Phoenix Park is in Dublin, Eire. Here in 1882 Irish extremists who called themselves The Invincibles, murdered Lord Frederick Cavendish, newly appointed chief secretary for Ireland, and his under-secretary, Thomas Burke, using surgical knives. The murderers were caught and hanged.

What sort of criminal was Eichmann?

Colonel Adolf Eichmann, an SS officer, was the Nazi war criminal responsible for exterminating at least two million Jewish people from various European countries who had been deported to German concentration camps as part of the Nazi programme to eliminate the Jewish race. Eichmann escaped justice after World War II and fled to South America. But in 1960 Israeli agents kidnapped him, brought him to Israel and in 1962 he was put to death after trial at Tel Aviv.

Who was Al Capone?

Alphonse Capone (1898–1947) was an American gangster who for some years dominated the criminal underworld of Chicago, but whom the police were never able to arrest and prove charges against. Then in 1931, it was found that he had deliberately evaded paying income tax. He was brought to court, found guilty and sentenced to ten years' imprisonment.

In which gaol was Oscar Wilde imprisoned for nearly two years?

Reading Gaol.

In a celebrated and still controversial murder trial held in Edinburgh in 1857 the verdict was 'not proven'. Who was the accused?

Madeleine Smith, daughter of a Glasgow architect, was on trial for poisoning her lover with arsenic. Although it was established that she had bought arsenic on three occasions, there was insufficient evidence to prove that she had seen the man during the last days before his death.

Little Quiz 53

Of which nationality were these artists?

1. Alfred Sisley
2. Van Gogh
3. Hieronymus Bosch
4. Mantegna
5. Rubens
6. Zoffany
7. Whistler
8. Jackson Pollock
9. Edvard Munch
10. Kokoschka
11. Kandinsky
12. Juan Gris
13. Fuseli
14. Klee
15. Chagall
16. Hans Arp
17. David
18. Raeburn
19. Van Dyck
20. Gwen John

What is a greenback?
It is a US bank note.

What are the seven colours of the spectrum?
When a band of white light is passed through a glass prism, it breaks up into seven colours, from violet through indigo, blue, green, yellow and orange to red. This was first demonstrated by Isaac Newton in 1672.

Where is the Black Country in Britain?
It is the part of the Midlands in England north of Birmingham and incorporating part of Warwickshire, Worcestershire and south Staffordshire. The name was given to the area because of the thick, grey-black atmosphere which shrouded it most of the time in the days before the Clean Air Acts.

What has the Black Market got to do with the colour black?
Nothing, really. The Black Market is a phrase describing unlawful trading in food and other rationed or hard-to-get products in time of war or shortage.

Where is Yellowknife?
It is the capital of the north-west territories of Canada, on the shore of the Great Slave Lake. The name comes from the gold mining activities there.

What is a sepia print?
It is a photograph, often an early one, produced in a brown tint that resembles sepia ink.

What is silver-gilt?
It is silver with a surface of gold applied to it. Today, the process is carried out by electrolysis.

What is a greenhorn?
A name for a simpleton, or for one who is new to some trade, skill or hobby.

Who were the Brownshirts?
They were para-military troops in Germany in the earlier days of the Nazis (1920s–1930s), led by Ernst Roehm. They wore brown uniforms and leather boots and were known as the *Sturmabteilung*, or Storm Troops.

Where is the Gold Coast?
Now called Ghana, it was the former colony of Britain in West Africa which was given the name Gold Coast because of the gold deposits found and worked there.

What were the Greys?
The 2nd Dragoons or Royal Scots Greys regiment, so called either because the horses or the uniform were grey.

Why is black pudding so called?
It is a kind of sausage made up from meat, suet, animal blood and other ingredients and encased in a dark skin.

Why is a greenstick fracture so called?
If you break your arm, or lower part of the leg, and only one side of the bone has fractured, it is called a greenstick, after the kind of break you sometimes get when you break a tree branch.

What are ultra violet rays?
They are rays which cannot be seen by the naked eye. They are in fact beyond the visible colours of the spectrum, at the violet end. These rays if directed with care on the human body produce the effects of sunburn.

What is greensward?
It is a carefully tended lawn or turf.

If someone offered you a cup of orange pekoe, what would you expect to be drinking?
A tea of high quality from India or Ceylon, although the term pekoe tea derives originally from China.

Would you benefit from being on anyone's blacklist?

Certainly not. It is a list of names of guilty or suspect people, or of people who may be considered undesirable for some reason.

Where is the Yellow Sea?

In the gulf between Korea and mainland China. It gets its name from the sediment that in parts gives it a yellowish appearance.

What kind of person would be classed as Cape Coloured?

Someone from a group of mixed white and non-white people living chiefly in Cape Province in South Africa.

Is a yellow-hammer a kind of hammer?

No, it is a bird of the bunting family with yellow feathers.

Where is the Black Forest?

This is a thickly wooded, mountainous district of south-west Germany, in the *Land* of Baden-Württemberg and east of the Rhine Valley. The trees of the Black Forest are mostly coniferous. It is probably the most popular tourist area of the Federal German Republic.

Where is the Black Sea?

This is an inland sea situated between Eastern Europe and Asia Minor. To the north and east it is bounded by the USSR, to the south by Turkey, and to the west by Turkey, Bulgaria and Romania. There is direct communication with the Mediterranean through the Bosphorus, Sea of Marmara, and the Dardanelles. A number of great rivers such as the Danube flow into the Black Sea, with the result that it is far less salty than most seas and oceans. It also experiences no discernible tides.

Is Greenland ever green?

Only along a narrow coastal strip during the short Arctic and sub-Arctic summer, when a profusion of grasses and other plants flourish. Even in summer most of this island is locked in ice and snow.

What is a greengage?

This is a small round plum which is green when ripe. It is mostly grown as a dessert fruit, although greengage jam is also widely produced.

What is a greenshank?

This is a medium-sized wading bird which breeds in the Scottish Highlands, but is otherwise mostly seen as a passage-migrant in Britain. Its name derives from its long green legs or shanks.

What is the House of Orange?

The ruling family of the Netherlands. William of Orange was a British monarch from 1688 to 1702.

Little Quiz 54

What are the monetary units of these countries?

1. Afghanistan
2. Sierra Leone
3. Nigeria
4. Malta
5. Iceland
6. Tunisia
7. Nepal
8. Czechoslovakia
9. Ghana
10. Ecuador
11. Singapore
12. Guatemala
13. Kuwait
14. Peru
15. Panama
16. Zaire
17. Senegal
18. China
19. Malawi
20. Argentine

What is tartare sauce?

It is a sauce made from mayonnaise, chopped capers, and chopped onion, well mixed and served with fried or grilled fish.

How is French dressing usually made?

The dressing is based on olive oil and malt or wine vinegar, two substances that don't mix and so have to be shaken or stirred every time before serving. Into the mixture you may add a pinch of pepper, a little salt and some dry mustard.

How do you make a champagne cocktail?

Take a lump of sugar and rub it against the outside of a soft lemon. Put the lump in the bottom of a champagne glass and pour a few drops of brandy over it, and then fill up the glass with champagne. The cocktail is rounded off with a dash of bitters and twist of lemon peel, and if you like, a tiny cube of ice.

What is a mint julep?

A cocktail that can be made in several ways. The commonest is to put a few crushed mint leaves into the bottom of a tall glass or silver cup, add a little sugar and fill it up with crushed ice. Then pour 2 or 3 ounces of Bourbon whisky into the glass, stir or shake the whole lot vigorously and drink.

What is James Bond's favourite cocktail?

A dry Martini, which is usually made from three or four parts gin to one part dry French vermouth, and a tiny squeeze of lemon. Bond always asks for it to be 'shaken, not stirred.'

What is porter?

A dark brown beer brewed from charred malt, produced and consumed widely in the 17th, 18th and 19th centuries.

What is a pink lady?

A drink consisting chiefly of gin, mixed with one egg-white and the juice of half a lime or lemon and a teaspoon of thick cream. This is mixed thoroughly and a drop or two of grenadine added according to taste.

What is mead?

One of the oldest known drinks, brewed as long as 2400 years ago in Britain, it is made by fermenting honey and mixing it with water and herbs and spices.

What is cider?

It is an alcoholic drink made from fermenting the juice of apples, and it has been drunk in both England and France (especially northern France) for at least 2000 years. (It is also drunk elsewhere.) Today, Britain and France are the principal areas of cider production. It comes in varying strengths and smoothness. One well known very strong variety, produced and sold in the West Country of England, is called scrumpy.

How is Gaelic coffee made?

Into a beaker of strong, hot coffee you put 1-2 teaspoonfuls of sugar, a single or double measure of Irish whiskey, then float some thick cream on top of the liquid. The sugar helps to create surface tension on the top of the liquid to let the cream spread without falling to the bottom.

How is macaroni grown?

Well, of course, macaroni is not grown. It is made from wheat flour in factories.

Which everyday fruits are particularly good to eat for Vitamin C?

Oranges, grapefruit and blackcurrants.

What is the source of the bitter taste in vinegar?

Largely, the diluted acetic acid.

What is a Bombay duck?
This is the name given to a salted and cured fish, known to zoologists as a harpodon, which is found in Indian waters. It is exported in great quantities and is usually served with curry.

What are truffles?
A truffle is an underground fungus that is regarded as a great delicacy. Normally, it is black or black-brown and is covered with warts. Truffles are enjoyed also by pigs and by some dogs, and dogs are often used to search for them. Some of the best truffles come from the Perigord district in France.

Where does sago come from?
It is the starchy substance in the pith of some East Indian palm trees. In Malaysia there is a sago palm tree that produces sago (from which the name comes).

Would you order *grenouilles* if you knew what they were?
Grenouille is the French for frog, and one French delicacy is frogs' legs. Normally, it is the hind legs that are cooked and served. The taste is not very distinctive but quite pleasant.

Are brown-shelled eggs better than white-shelled eggs?
No, the only difference between them is the colour. But there has long been a quite unsubstantiated belief that white-shelled eggs are in some way sub-standard, which is reflected in the gradual disappearance of white eggs from shops. The colour difference is entirely due to differences in the type of hen laying the egg.

What does it mean if vegetables are served 'macédoine'?
Strictly, it means they are diced and mixed.

What does *potage velouté aux champignons* mean?
Cream of mushroom soup.

What is Halal meat?
Meat used as food which has been killed in accordance with Muslim law.

What is a Welsh rarebit, and in what way does it differ from a buck rarebit?
A Welsh rarebit is a slice of toast covered with butter and melted cheese then seasoned to taste. For buck rarebit a poached or fried egg is added on top of the cheese.

What is Buck's fizz?
A mixture of champagne and fresh orange juice.

What is a simnel cake?
This is a rich cake, traditionally made at Easter in Britain. It has a raised almond crust, coloured with saffron, and filled with similar ingredients to a plum-pudding. It is prepared by boiling in a cloth for several hours, then brushed with egg and baked.

What is an Old Fashioned?
This is an American cocktail, consisting of rye or bourbon with sugar syrup, angostura and ice, then decorated with a twist of lemon, a slice of orange and a maraschino cherry.

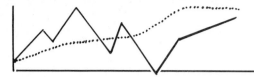

What is a telemeter?
It is a piece, or pieces, of apparatus for measuring physical changes from a distance. It has wide application in space technology.

What is a holograph?
It is the word used for any letter, document or paper written entirely by hand by its author. The word is used increasingly in an age of typed letters and photocopied documents.

What was a phonograph?
It was the earliest gramophone which operated by means of turning cylinders. It was invented in 1877 by Thomas Alva Edison (1847–1931).

What is iconography?
This is studying images, such as portraits, sculptures, brass rubbings, etc., examining their sources and determining what they mean.

What is a micrometer?
A special instrument with a screw and a scale, for measuring minute dimensions.

What is a chronometer?
It is the word describing a particularly accurate apparatus for measuring time, needed chiefly for navigation at sea.

What is chromatography?
It is a method of chemical analysis in which a mixture of liquids is split up according to the extent to which each constituent is adsorbed into a prescribed medium, such as chalk, paper, or other liquids.

What is a gravimeter?
An instrument for measuring the specific gravity of a solid or liquid.

What is an oscillograph?
It is an instrument that records changing electrical quantities, such as voltage.

What is radiography?
It is the process of taking and producing X-ray photographs.

What is an interferometer?
Interference is a phenomenon produced by the combination of waves, particularly sound and light waves. An interferometer is an instrument that can produce this interference, and thus allow measurement of the wavelengths.

What is a spectrograph?
It is an instrument for producing and photographing a spectrum.

What is a spectroheliograph?
It is an instrument for photographing the Sun.

What is an altimeter?
It is a dialled meter for showing how high an aircraft or spacecraft is above ground. Most altimeters work using air pressure.

Why do you use an exposure meter when taking photographs?
An exposure meter contains an electric 'eye' device that allows you to set the aperture of the camera and fix the speed, in order to get the best exposure for any light conditions.

What is a hydrometer?
A glass tube apparatus for testing the specific gravity of a liquid.

What is a magnetometer?
It records changes in the magnetism of the Earth.

What does a seismograph do?
This instrument measures earth tremors, how long they last, their magnitude and their direction.

What is a heliograph?
An instrument used for signalling by means of the sun.

What is a pictograph?
It is a picture employed to represent an object, idea, event, person, etc. The most obvious pictographs are the hieroglyphics from ancient Egypt.

What is a meter maid?
This is a jocular or facetious expression for a female traffic warden. John Lennon and Paul McCartney of the Beatles used it in their 1967 composition *Lovely Rita Meter Maid*.

What is a tachygraph?
This is a device fitted to commercial and public service vehicles for making a continuous record of the speed attained during a journey.

What is an electrometer?
This is the basic instrument used for measuring potential difference, depending on the attraction or repulsion of charges on plates or wires.

What is a polygraph?
This is another name for a lie detector, a device to indicate or record one or more functional variables of a person's body while that person undergoes the emotional stress linked with telling a lie.

What is graphite?
This is a mineral, one of the two natural forms of crystalline carbon, the other being diamond. It occurs mostly as a soft black lustrous greasy mass, or, less often, as shiny crystals. It can also be synthesized from petroleum coke. It is found in many parts of the world; in the Lake District of England its occurrence gave rise to a pencil-making industry. Other uses are in the manufacture of paints, polishes and lubricants. It is also known as black lead or plumbago.

What is a graphic formula?
This is the formula used in chemistry in which every atom is represented by its appropriate symbol, valency bonds being indicated by dashes. Thus water, H_2O, is represented by the graphic formula $H - O - H$.

What is usually meant by the word parameter?
In general terms it refers to an established or pre-set limit or condition within which any person, thing or abstract works or is worked upon.

What is a calligrapher?
One skilled in the art and practice of fine handwriting known as calligraphy.

What does perimeter mean?
It is the outside edge or boundary of a plane figure or the total length of its sides. A perimeter is also an instrument which is used to measure field of vision.

Little Quiz 55
What nationality were these Nobel Prize winners?
1. Niels Bohr   physics
2. Enrico Fermi   physics
3. E. T. S. Walton   physics
4. P. J. Kapitza   physics
5. Irving Langmuir   chemistry
6. Frederick Sanger   chemistry
7. Svante Arrhenius   chemistry
8. Odd Hassel   chemistry
9. G. von Bekesy   medicine
10. Sir MacFarlane Burnet   medicine
11. Corneille Heymans   medicine
12. Max Theiler   medicine
13. Henryk Sienkiewicz   literature
14. Rabindranath Tagore   literature
15. Gabriella Mistral   literature
16. Albert Camus   literature
17. Lester Pearson   peace
18. Carlos de Saavedra Lamas   peace
19. Tobias Asser   peace
20. Baroness von Suttner   peace

When was the first police force established in Britain?

Up to 1829, constables had been appointed by country parishes and watchmen by town councils to enforce law and order. In 1829, the Metropolitan Police Act established a regular police force for London. Borough forces were introduced in 1835 and county forces in 1856.

Why are policemen often known as 'Bobbies'?

They were nicknamed 'Bobbies' after the famous home secretary Sir Robert Peel, who was responsible for the Metropolitan Police Act. Policemen were also called 'Peelers'.

Who controls the Metropolitan Police Force?

The head of the Metropolitan Police is a commissioner, appointed by the home secretary to whom the commissioner is ultimately responsible.

Who controls the county police forces in England?

Police Committees consisting of local councillors and magistrates. The committees are often known as Watch Committees. Each county force is headed by a chief constable.

What is the principal job of a policeman or policewoman?

It is to prevent crime. The first commissioner of the Metropolitan Police, Sir Richard Mayne, stated that 'policemen should make it very difficult for anyone to commit a crime ... within that portion of the town under their charge.' Of course, the police have numerous other duties.

What are the principal qualities needed by a police detective officer?

They are dedication to the job, a sharp eye for detail, an excellent memory, the ability to judge character, a willingness to do much painstaking and sometimes unrewarding work.

What is the role of the police at political demonstrations, strike meetings, picketing of work premises and so forth?

It is the police's task to keep the peace and to uphold existing laws about demonstrations, picketing, marches and so on. Policemen and policewomen are expected to be impartial as to the points of argument and demonstration.

Do the police carry guns?

It is a long-established custom that British police forces are not normally armed, and in fact only in exceptional circumstances does any officer carry a firearm, and firearms are only issued on the authority of a very senior official. At the same time, the police are taught to understand all about firearms and to recognize every type of weapon that could be used in committing crimes of violence, and there are occasions when specialist training on the use of firearms is given for special duties.

How can the public help the police forces to prevent crime?

The most important thing the public can do is to cooperate with the police. One good way is for members of a community to make themselves more aware of the security of each others' homes, property and persons. This means agreeing to keep an eye on the house of a neighbour who goes away with his family for a holiday, and reporting at once anything suspicious to the police.

What happens when you dial '999'?

You get through to a special switchboard manned 24 hours of the day every day, whose operators ask which service you require, Fire, Ambulance or Police. The switchboard is linked to the most

convenient police stations, fire stations and hospitals, and can connect you immediately with whichever one you need.

Will the police mind if they are telephoned and the alarm turns out to be a false one?
No, not at all. They do not mind.

What are the main qualifications needed to be accepted as a recruit to the police force?
In the UK, police officers have to be ready to work shifts, must be at least 5 ft 8 ins tall (5 ft 4 ins tall if a woman), to be fit and have good eyesight, to be ready to accept discipline and responsibility, have personal integrity, be able to make decisions on their own and act quickly, be tolerant of peoples from a multitude of different backgrounds, and to work as part of a team. He or she must be a British citizen, a Commonwealth citizen whose stay in the UK is not a restricted one, or a citizen of the republic of Eire.

How long is the training?
Overall, it takes two years, during which time every recruit has to be prepared to serve in uniform as a constable. The period starts with ten weeks in residence at a police training centre (15 weeks for the Metropolitan Police, at Hendon). The candidates then return to their own force and spend another two weeks or so on a course on local procedures. Then the recruit is introduced to the 'beat', that is, the patrol of the streets, to begin with in the company of an experienced constable.

What are the ranks of the police forces in the provinces?
Upwards from the bottom, they are: constable, sergeant, inspector, chief inspector, superintendent, chief superintendent, assistant chief constable and chief constable.

Is there any difference in the ranks of the Metropolitan Police?
Yes, after the rank of chief superintendent upwards, the Metropolitan Police ranks are: commander, deputy assistant commissioner, assistant commissioner, deputy commissioner and commissioner.

How many police forces are there in England and Wales?
43, including the Metropolitan Police.

How many are there in Scotland?
Six regional forces and two combined forces.

What was the Scarman Report of 1981?
Basically, it was a report of a committee of enquiry held under the chairmanship of Lord Justice Scarman into the causes and effects of the rioting in areas such as Brixton and Toxteth in Britain in the summer of 1981, and the committee made a number of recommendations. Overall, the message was that efforts must be made for relations between police and the public to be improved, especially relations between police and immigrant communities.

Little Quiz 56

   Who followed as prime minister – ?
1. Benjamin Disraeli in 1880
2. A. J. Balfour in 1905
3. Herbert Henry Asquith in 1916
4. Ramsay MacDonald in 1935
5. Winston Churchill in 1955
   Who followed as president of USA?
6. John Quincy Adams in 1829
7. James Buchanan in 1861
8. William McKinley in 1901
9. Franklin D. Roosevelt in 1945
10. Lyndon B. Johnson in 1969

What does the clutch of a motor car do?

It lets the engine run without driving the wheels. It is basically two round plates between the engine and the gearbox: the engine end plate turns all the time the engine is running but the other (gearbox) end plate is stationary until you let the first plate begin to engage with it. Then, when the two are tight together, the engine is connected to the gearbox and the car can move forwards or backwards, according to which gear is selected.

What is synchromesh?

It is an arrangement of gears in the gearbox that synchronizes the driving and the driven parts before they engage, thus removing the noise and judder when the gears are engaged.

What is to double-declutch?

It is a process used in changing gear downwards when the gearbox is not fitted with synchromesh on all four gears. You have to do the matching of the gear speeds yourself, and this is done by depressing the clutch pedal twice during the movement of the gear lever from one position to the next lower gear.

How does overdrive work?

It is almost a separate gearbox providing a very high gear in addition to the others in the usual gearbox. It allows high speed cruising under easy conditions, the engine turning over at a slower rate than in normal top gear.

What is a universal joint?

It is a joint or coupling which can move in every direction.

What does the choke do?

It helps get the engine started when cold, by increasing the amount of petrol passing into the carburettor when the engine is being turned over by the starter motor.

What is the 'lollipop sign'?

This is the mandatory Stop–Children sign, carried on the end of a rod by school crossing patrols. It has black letters on a circular yellow background edged with a red border.

What is a box junction?

It is a road junction, on the road surface of which is painted a pattern of yellow criss-cross lines. The rules are that drivers must not go into the box with any part of their cars unless the way through is clear, except if you are intending to turn right in which case you may wait in the box until there is a gap in the oncoming traffic to let you through safely.

What is the differential gear?

An arrangement of gears connecting two shafts in the same line, enabling one of them to rotate at a rate faster than the other, if required. When a car turns the corner, the inner driven wheel travels for less distance than the outer wheel, and therefore slower. The differential gear in the rear axle (or front, if the car is front wheel drive) lets the two wheels turn at different speeds.

What are the advance warnings for a pedestrian crossing?

If it is uncontrolled, flashing yellow beacons. The crossing itself is also marked on the road surface by alternate black and white stripes – which explains its popular name, Zebra Crossing. There are also zig-zag white marks before the crossing on your left side, for several yards, and you should never park on these zig-zags.

What is the rule about distance between your car and the one travelling in front of you?

Leave enough space between you and the vehicle ahead, so that you can pull up safely if it slows down or stops suddenly.

What is the difference between cross-ply and radial tyres?

In crossply tyres, the cords making up the carcass run diagonally across the tyre, with alternate layers at opposite angles, forming a trellis. Radial tyres have all cords running at right angles across the tyre.

What is the hard shoulder on the left side of a motorway for?

It is for stopping in an emergency only, and not for picnicking, sight-seeing or any other non-urgent purpose.

When can a car be parked on a road without lights after lighting up time?

On roads subject to the 30 mph speed limit or lower speed limit, provided they are not parked within 15 yards of a junction.

What are disc brakes?

They are external contracting brakes where brake pads close like pincers onto a disc attached to the car wheel.

When is it illegal to use the horn?

When your car is stationary, or in motion in a built-up area between the hours of 11.30 pm and 7.00 am.

What is the MSM routine you should follow when approaching road junctions of any kind?

MSM = mirror–signal–manoeuvre: this means (i) use the mirror to see if your way ahead is not at risk from anything coming up behind and to check that you have enough time to make the next move, (ii) give the correct hand signal (or electrical signal if you have the right switches) and then (iii) move forward and turn left or right, or go straight ahead, whichever you wish, provided your path is clear.

What is a mandatory road sign?

It is a sign telling you what you must do.

Most have white symbols, with borders on a blue background.

Has there ever been a motor vehicle that could travel both on road and on rail in Britain?

The London Midland and Scottish Railway acquired a Karrier 26 seat railbus early in 1931. This was fitted with both road and rail wheels, the set not in use being locked clear. In 1931 this vehicle was used in the neighbourhood of Hemel Hempstead, Hertfordshire; in the following year it was used in and around Stratford-upon-Avon. While the wheels could be set from road to rail use or vice versa inside five minutes, the experiment was not considered worthwhile and it was abandoned before the end of 1932.

Is it true that a mail coach was once attacked by a lion in England?

What really happened to the Exeter Mail shortly after it left Salisbury one night in 1816 was that it was shadowed by an animal first thought to be a large calf. When it attacked one of the leading horses, it was discovered that it was really a lioness which had escaped from a travelling menagerie. The lioness which was being chased by its owners was caught before the horse was badly injured.

Austin 7 motorcar

What is First Aid?
First aid is given to sustain life and to help stop deterioration in the condition of someone who is sick or injured, until expert medical help arrives.

What is the Kiss of Life?
The simple term for mouth-to-mouth resuscitation, if an injured or collapsed person has stopped breathing. Take a deep breath, cover the person's mouth or nose with yours and blow steadily into the lungs.

How do you apply artificial respiration?
If the Kiss of Life does not produce the required result, turn the casualty so that he is lying on his stomach. Kneel at the head and lean over with your hands on his shoulder blades, throwing weight forward onto your arms. Rock backwards while holding the casualty's elbows. Raise these off the ground so that his chest expands and sucks in air, then lower the elbows again, and repeat the cycle every few seconds.

How would you stop bleeding from a wound?
Apply constant firm pressure to bleeding site or just above it with a clean pad of material such as cotton wool. The use of the tourniquet is not now regarded as advisable.

What do you do to help a child with a nose bleed?
Lift him or her onto a chair in front of a table, get a bowl and gently bend his head over the bowl, to catch the blood. Persuade him to breathe in and out through his mouth, and help him to pinch his nose, holding it at the softer, fleshy part near the nose tip for a few minutes.

If this fails, what do you do next?
If you can get some ice cubes, put a number into a handkerchief, lay the child down flat on his back, and place the pack gently on the bridge of the nose, taking it off from time to time.

What is a splint?
In first aid, a piece of wood or other rigid material for placing under or along a broken limb, to be anchored to the limb by means of handkerchiefs or lengths of string tied at intervals, though not at the actual injury site.

What action do you take if someone's clothes are on fire?
Soak the clothes in water as soon as possible, and if water is not available, roll the casualty over into a blanket or overcoat to try to smother the flames or smouldering. Don't attempt to remove the clothing once the flames are out.

What do you do if the casualty faints from the shock of an injury?
If the casualty appears to be coming back to consciousness and slipping out again, keep talking gently to him, to get him to respond, and that way he may stay conscious.

What is the normal temperature of the human body?
About 98.4 degrees F, 37°C.

What should you do about a blister?
Leave it alone until you can get to a surgery.

What should a first aid kit contain as a basic minimum?
Triangular bandages, large pieces of sticking plaster, some antiseptic cream, sterile gauze pads, antibiotic powder (a useful addition), and some safety pins. Probably a bottle of iodine would also be advisable.

What is the average pulse rate in the human being?
Anything between about 70 and 80 beats per minute is about normal.

What are the important things to remember when a person has been poisoned and you have sent for an ambulance?

You may not know what he has swallowed, and you should try to find out. It will help the medical team if you go with the patient to the hospital so that you can tell them when the poison was taken, what it was if you know, and how long the patient has been conscious or unconscious.

How does frost 'bite'?

Intense cold stops the blood circulating properly, and extremities like fingers and toes suffer skin damage. The pain is best eased by warming the whole body gently near the fire or radiator. Do not attempt to warm the frost-bitten hand or foot on its own in hot water.

What should you do if a diabetic suddenly complains of feeling faint?

He may be about to pass into a coma, in which case give him a little sugar as soon as you can; a lump or two or a boiled sweet would suffice in most cases. Then you should ring for an ambulance or get the local doctor to come as soon as possible.

What do you do to assist someone who has been injured by electric shock?

Do not touch the person if he is still in contact with the electrical appliance. Switch off the appliance, whatever it is, and remove the plug from the wall socket. Push the appliance away from the person, and then if he has been stunned, try to revive him gently with artificial respiration. You should also send at once for the doctor or ambulance.

How should you handle someone who appears to be suffering from amnesia?

There is no first aid treatment for this, which can be a serious medical problem. However, you should keep the person quiet and comfortable, then contact the police in case a reported missing person is involved.

What should you do if you find someone sleepwalking?

Do not waken the sleeper. If the person is not in danger, take him lightly by the elbow and lead him back to bed. Once in bed, the sleepwalker should be gently covered. It is then best to remain for a little while, in case he wakes and is confused.

How should you deal with someone suffering from hypothermia?

If it occurs indoors, place the patient between blankets. Allow the temperature to rise gradually, but do not force it up with hot water bottles or electric blankets. Warm sweet drinks should be given and the room warmed. If outdoors, get the person to rest in as sheltered a location as possible. Wrap in dry clothing, a sleeping bag or aluminium foil if available. Warm sweet drinks should be given if possible.

Little Quiz 1, page 11

1. *How they brought the Good News from Ghent to Aix* (Browning)
2. *The Revenge* (Tennyson)
3. *Kubla Khan* (Coleridge)
4. *Lepanto* (Chesterton)
5. *Elegy written in a Country Churchyard* (Gray)
6. *Cargoes* (Masefield)
7. *The Tiger* (Blake)
8. *The Jackdaw of Rheims* (Barham)
9. *The Burial of Sir John Moore after Corunna* (Wolfe)
10. *Bruce's Address before Bannockburn* (Burns)
11. *La Belle Dame Sans Merci* (Keats)
12. *Ozymandias* (Shelley)
13. *Henry V at the Siege of Harfleur* (Shakespeare)
14. *On His Blindness* (Milton)
15. *Daffodils* (Wordsworth)
16. *Silver* (de la Mare)
17. *The Soldier* (Brooke)
18. *Leisure* (Davies)
19. *The Ballad of Reading Gaol* (Wilde)
20. *The Destruction of Sennacherib* (Byron)

Little Quiz 2, page 13

1. Charlotte Corday, 1793
2. Sirhan Sirhan, 1968
3. Four knights of Henry II, 1170
4. Not known for certain, but Earl of Bothwell implicated, 1567
5. John Felton, 1627
6. His wife Isabella and her lover Roger Mortimer, 1327
7. James Earl Ray, 1968
8. Brutus, Cassius and other senators, 44 BC
9. Nathuran Godse, 1948
10. Dmitri Tsafendas, 1966
11. Sir Robert Graham, 1437
12. The Red Brigade, 1978
13. Dmitri Bogrov, 1911
14. Balthasar Gerard, 1584
15. John Wilkes Booth, 1865

Little Quiz 3, page 15

1. lawyer
2. tap
3. face flannel
4. sheaf of bank notes
5. petrol
6. braces
7. biscuit
8. policeman
9. dustbin
10. overshoes
11. roadway
12. illegal drinking house
13. bowler hat
14. banknote
15. underground railway
16. first rate
17. find fault with
18. tram
19. lift
20. sweets

Little Quiz 4, page 17

1. Burma
2. India
3. Italy
4. Portugal and Spain
5. Belgium
6. France and Switzerland
7. Scotland
8. Wales
9. Eire
10. England
11. Canada and USA
12. Australia
13. Russia
14. Peru
15. Brazil
16. Alaska
17. China
18. South Africa
19. New Zealand
20. Turkey

Little Quiz 5, page 19

1. Bonn
2. Rangoon
3. Pretoria
4. Quito
5. La Paz
6. Mexico City
7. Havana
8. Port of Spain
9. Belfast
10. Reykjavik
11. Montevideo
12. Santiago
13. Cairo
14. Jerusalem
15. Khartoum
16. Sofia
17. Valletta
18. Tirana
19. Lilongwe
20. Antananarivo

Little Quiz 6, page 27

1. Polish
2. Argentine
3. Spanish
4. Austrian
5. Greek
6. Ancient British
7. Dutch
8. Scottish
9. Italian
10. Red Indian

Little Quiz 7, page 29

1. Gold Coast
2. Northern Rhodesia
3. Nyasaland
4. Ellice Islands
5. Tanganyika and Zanzibar
6. Belgian Congo
7. British Guiana
8. part of French Indo-China
9. Ceylon
10. Madagascar

Little Quiz 8, page 35

1. Clive   India
2. Wolfe   Canada
3. William   Hastings
4. Cortes   Mexico
5. Pizarro   Peru
6. Caesar   Gaul
7. Montgomery   Alamein
8. Marlborough   Blenheim
9. Edward III   Crécy
10. Robert Bruce   Bannockburn

Little Quiz 9, page 37

1. Stirling
2. Bristol
3. Winchester
4. Oxford
5. Plymouth
6. Bosworth
7. Llanfair PG, Anglesey, N. Wales
8. Darlington
9. Glenfinnan
10. Portsmouth

Little Quiz 10, page 39

1. flute
2. trumpet
3. piano
4. violin
5. cinema organ
6. cello
7. harp
8. oboe
9. organ
10. saxophone
11. Delius
12. Percy Grainger
13. Debussy
14. Beethoven
15. Handel
16. Chopin
17. Bach
18. Mozart
19. John Bull
20. Elgar

Little Quiz 11, page 41

1. Soviet Union
2. Denmark
3. Rumania
4. Yugoslavia
5. Iceland
6. Great Britain
7. Switzerland
8. USA
9. Belgium
10. Brazil
11. Switzerland
12. Argentina
13. Vatican
14. Finland
15. Thailand
16. Liechtenstein
17. Sarawak
18. Guernsey
19. Poland
20. Uruguay

Little Quiz 12, page 49

1. 1360
2. 1814
3. 1801
4. 1898
5. 1902
6. 1878
7. 1739
8. 1895
9. 1783
10. 1917

Little Quiz 13, page 53
1. huit
2. trente
3. soixante-dix
4. drei
5. zwanzig
6. tausend
7. quaranta
8. cinque cento
9. otto
10. cinco

Little Quiz 14, page 59
1. Wales
2. Karakoram – India
3. India
4. USSR
5. Turkey
6. Canada
7. Greenland
8. USA
9. Ecuador
10. Japan

Little Quiz 15, page 61
1. Emperor Claudius
2. Alexander the Great
3. Prasutagus
4. Venutius
5. 1) Henry V of Germany
   2) Geoffrey of Anjou
6. Louis XIV
7. Thutmosis II
8. William III
9. Edward III
10. Richard I

Little Quiz 16, page 63
1. Texas, USA
2. India
3. New Hampshire, USA
4. France
5. France
6. West Indies
7. Switzerland
8. Germany
9. Lebanon
10. Belgium

Little Quiz 17, page 65
1. 871–900
2. 1504–06
3. 1740–1786
4. 1215–1270
5. 1016
6. 1310–1370
7. 1520–1566
8. 1762–1796
9. 1040–1057
10. 1194–1240

Little Quiz 18, page 71
1. Admiral Sturdee
2. Napoleon
3. Lord Kitchener
4. Arminius
5. Marlborough
6. Lord Wolseley
7. Ahab, king of Israel
8. Julius Caesar
9. Athelstan, king of England
10. Admiral Duncan

Little Quiz 19, page 73
1. Spain
2. Burgundy
3. England, Denmark, Norway
4. France
5. England
6. Wales
7. Haiti
8. China
9. Egypt
10. Zululand

Little Quiz 20, page 79
1. France
2. USSR
3. USA
4. Italy
5. Japan
6. Czechoslovakia
7. Holland
8. Germany
9. Britain
10. Sweden

Little Quiz 21, page 81
1. Deoxyribonucleic acid
2. Her Majesty's Stationery Office
3. Central Intelligence Agency (USA)
4. Schutzstaffel (Nazi secret police)
5. University College Hospital (London)
6. Baronet
7. Oxford University Dramatic Society
8. Cambridge University Press
9. National Union of Students
10. Doctor of Letters (Litterarum)

11. Lord Justice
12. Intercontinental ballistic missile
13. John FitzGerald Kennedy
14. Society of Jesus (Jesuits)
15. Royal Academy of Music.
16. National Society for the Prevention of Cruelty to Children
17. Master of Foxhounds
18. Isle of Wight
19. Tourist Trophy; tuberculin tested; teetotaller
20. opere citato (in the work quoted)
21. pages, or pianissimo (music, very soft)
22. leg before wicket
23. ounce (s)
24. cubic centimetre(s)
25. id est (that is to say)
26. instant (current month)
27. et cetera (and the others)
28. miles per hour
29. revolutions per minute
30. brake horsepower
31. circa (about)
32. hundredweight
33. auxiliary
34. non sequitur (it does not follow)
35. published, or public house
36. per annum (yearly)
37. delineavit (he or she drew it)
38. versus (against)
39. Criminal Investigation Department
40. Kentucky (USA)

Little Quiz 22, page 85
1. welder
2. stationer
3. ornithologist
4. campanologist
5. steeplejack
6. blacksmith
7. farrier
8. chandler
9. jockey
10. astronaut, or cosmonaut
11. purser
12. haberdasher
13. cobbler
14. cartographer
15. locksmith
16. psychiatrist
17. miller
18. quarryman
19. psephologist
20. stevedore

Little Quiz 23, page 87
1. form
2. earth
3. nest or bike
4. hive
5. set
6. drey
7. lair or den
8. eyrie
9. web
10. warren or burrow

Little Quiz 24, page 89
1. 5
2. 10
3. 3
4. 4
5. 3
6. 12
7. 5
8. 6
9. 5

Little Quiz 25, page 91
1. 1627–1628
2. 1347
3. 1648
4. AD 70
5. 1807
6. 1191
7. 1868
8. 1812
9. 1884–5
10. 1857
11. 1899–1900
12. 1689
13. 1453
14. 1649
15. 1799
16. 1814
17. 1899–1900
18. 212 BC
19. 52 BC
20. 1683

Little Quiz 26, page 97
1. 1789–1794
2. 1857–1858
3. 1922
4. AD 61
5. 1936–1939
6. 1917–1918
7. 1773–1781
8. 1642–1647
9. 49–48 BC
10. 1911

219

$2 + 5 \times 3 - 1 \div 2 = 10$

Little Quiz 27, page 99

1. or	6. vert
2. argent	7. purpure
3. gules	8. tenne
4. azure	9. sanguine
5. sable	10. murrey

Little Quiz 28, page 101

1. brood	6. gang or herd
2. clutch	7. plague
3. herd or drove	8. pride
4. host	9. school
5. nest	10. swarm

Little Quiz 29, page 105

1. Lothian
2. Mid-Glamorgan
3. Cornwall
4. Kent
5. Sussex
6. Lincolnshire
7. Hampshire
8. Derbyshire
9. Northumberland
10. Cheshire
11. Hertfordshire
12. Cornwall
13. Suffolk
14. Norfolk
15. Norfolk
16. Sussex
17. Berkshire
18. Clwyd
19. Dyfed
20. Strathclyde

1. France
2. Switzerland
3. Syria
4. West Germany
5. Switzerland
6. Italy
7. Syria
8. Belgium
9. France
10. Spain

Little Quiz 30, page 113

1. West Germany   2. Norway

3. Denmark
4. Sweden
5. USSR
6. Turkey
7. Sicily
8. Portugal
9. France
10. Hungary

Little Quiz 31, page 115

1. Jack Nicholson
2. Ben Kingsley
3. Vivien Leigh
4. Jennifer Jones
5. Charlton Heston
6. Laurence Olivier
7. Liza Minnelli
8. Henry Fonda and Katherine Hepburn
9. Robert Donat
10. Ingrid Bergman.

Little Quiz 32, page 121

1. Spain
2. Scotland
3. Kansas, USA
4. Turkey in Europe
5. Jordan
6. Switzerland
7. Denmark
8. Mexico
9. France
10. Northern Ireland
11. Belgium
12. Sudan
13. West Germany
14. India
15. USSR
16. China
17. Argentine
18. Japan
19. England
20. Italy

Little Quiz 33, page 123

1. West Sussex
2. Essex
3. Suffolk
4. Norfolk
5. Hertfordshire
6. Cleveland
7. Humberside
8. Hampshire
9. Surrey

10. Derbyshire
11. Lancashire
12. West Glamorgan
13. Gwynedd
14. Mid-Glamorgan
15. Clwyd
16. Gwent
17. Dyfed
18. Powys
19. Dyfed

Little Quiz 34, page 125

1. Earl of Clarendon
2. Baron Delamere
3. Earl of Portsmouth
4. Earl of Woolton
5. Marquess of Anglesey
6. Duke of Wellington
7. Viscount Scarsdale
8. Earl of Lichfield
9. Viscount Mersey
10. Marquis of Zetland

Little Quiz 35, page 133

1. Bragging or boasting
2. Attempting to achieve or obtain the impossible
3. Making plans that will never take effect
4. Trying to find out the value of a present that someone has given you
5. Showing off
6. Resolving to improve attitudes or behaviour, and sticking to it
7. Wasting energy trying to overcome obstacles that are not there
8. Wasting time trying to get people to keep up interest in something they are no longer interested in
9. Being realistic
10. Exaggerating

Little Quiz 36, page 135

1. 1.00 pm
2. 2.00 pm
3. 7.30 pm
4. 1.00 pm
5. 7.00 pm
6. 8.00 pm
7. 10.00 pm
8. 7.00 pm
9. 9.00 am
10. midnight

Little Quiz 37, page 137

1. Cantuar
2. Ebor
3. Oxon
4. Cestr
5. Petriburg
6. Roffen
7. Carliol
8. Sarum
9. Elien
10. Exon
11. Dunelm

Little Quiz 38, page 143

1. Harold I 1035–40
2. John
3. Edward 975–979
4. Richard I
5. Henry I
6. Henry II
7. Charles II
8. William IV
9. William II
10. Edward I

Little Quiz 39, page 149

1. violet
2. red
3. dark green banded
4. yellow
5. red and green
6. deep blue
7. green
8. bluey-white
9. green with red spots
10. all colours

Little Quiz 40, page 151

1. Epic Poetry
2. History
3. Astronomy
4. Song and Dance
5. Comedy
6. Lyric Poetry and Music
7. Love and Poetry and Mime
8. Tragedy
9. Sacred song

Little Quiz 41, page 153

1. skin	12. cutting
2. brain	13. outflow
3. blood	14. falling
4. hardening	15. eye
5. eye	16. gall bladder
6. muscle	17. liver
7. mind	18. kidney
8. chest	19. ear
9. intestine	20. nose
10. joint	21. bladder
11. inflammation	22. lung

Little Quiz 42, page 159

1. second son of Adam and Eve
2. one of the 3 faithful Jews who escaped from the fiery furnace
3. youngest of Joseph's brothers
4. king who entertained Abraham
5. last king of Babylon before it fell to Cyprus, 539 BC
6. mother of John the Baptist
7. great friend of King David
8. a king of Judah
9. high priest in time of both David and Solomon
10. nephew of Abraham
11. she was turned into a pillar of salt
12. one of the main sects of Judaism in Jesus Christ's time
13. nomads defeated in battle by both Saul and David
14. the original inhabitants of Jerusalem
15. interpreters of law
16. people who lived in tents and abstained from alcohol: praised by Jeremiah
17. Gallio
18. the prodigal son
19. Mary Magdalene
20. Joseph

Little Quiz 43, page 163

1. Vitus
2. Sebastian
3. Catherine of Bologna
4. Giles
5. Dunstan
6. Stephen
7. Bernard of Clairvaux
8. Joseph
9. Nicholas of Myra – Santa Claus
10. Giles
11. Antony
12. Gerard Majella
13. Andrew
14. Luke
15. Valentine
16. Ambrose
17. Jerome
18. Antony of Padua
19. Gabriel
20. Christopher
21. James
22. Christopher
23. Brigid
24. Drogo
25. Matthew
26. Gregory the Great
27. Peter of Alcantara
28. Paula
29. Francis de Sales
30. Anne
31. Genevieve
32. David
33. Isidore the Farmer
34. Gertrude
35. Olaf
36. Severino
37. Joseph
38. Barnabas
39. Nicetas
40. George

Little Quiz 44, page 167

1. Transport and General Workers' Union
2. National Union of Journalists
3. National Union of Teachers
4. Civil and Public Services Association

5. Union of Shop, Distributive and Allied Workers
6. National Union of Public Employees
7. Confederation of Health Service Employees
8. Associated Society of Locomotive Engineers and Firemen
9. Association of Scientific, Technical and Managerial Staffs
10. National Graphical Association

Little Quiz 45, page 171

1. Kenya
2. Cyprus
3. Argentina
4. Germany
5. Poland
6. USA
7. France
8. China
9. Eire
10. Israel

Little Quiz 46, page 179

1. Lugdunum
2. Lindum
3. Alexandria
4. Augusta Treverorum
5. Verulamium
6. Gades
7. Massilia
8. Lutetia
9. Segovia
10. Mediolanum
11. Genava
12. Byzantium
13. Colonia Agrippina
14. Aquincum

Little Quiz 47, page 185

1. Canada
2. Asia Minor
3. Tibet
4. Canada
5. Bolivia and Peru
6. USSR
7. USSR
8. Canada
9. Wales
10. Scotland

Little Quiz 48, page 187

1. Tanzania
2. Canada and USA
3. New Zealand
4. USA
5. Zimbabwe-Zambia
6. India
7. Guyana
8. Switzerland
9. Chile
10. Ecuador
11. Antarctica
12. Sicily
13. Martinique
14. Congo
15. USSR
16. Japan

Little Quiz 49, page 189

1. sodium carbonate
2. sodium chloride
3. magnesium sulphate
4. sodium sulphate
5. deuterium oxide
6. sodium hydroxide
7. calcium hydroxide
8. hydrochloric acid and nitric acid mixed
9. potassium carbonate
10. barium sulphate

Little Quiz 50, page 193

1. electric current
2. frequency
3. power
4. electrical resistance
5. thermodynamic temperature
6. energy, quantity of heat
7. quantity of electricity
   Watt, Kelvin, Joule

Little Quiz 51, page 195

1. 0.4047 hectare
2. 0.3049 metre
3. 50.80 kilograms
4. 0.142 litre
5. 1.8288 metres
6. 28.4131 cubic centimetres

7. 9.0922 litres
8. 1.1365 litres
9. 0.8361 square metre
10. 1.555 grams

Little Quiz 52, page 197
1. gammer
2. conductress
3. ogress
4. czarina
5. witch
6. hen-sparrow
7. maid-servant
8. bride
9. votaress
10. testatrix
11. dormice
12. lice
13. houses
14. men-of-war
15. courts-martial
16. grottos, grottoes
17. halves
18. trout
19. dozen
20. vetoes

Little Quiz 53, page 203
1. French
2. Dutch
3. Dutch
4. Italian
5. Flemish
6. German
7. American
8. American
9. Norwegian
10. Austrian
11. Russian
12. Spanish
13. Swiss
14. Swiss
15. Russian
16. Alsatian
17. French
18. Scottish
19. Flemish
20. Welsh

Little Quiz 54, page 205
1. afghani
2. leone
3. naira
4. pound
5. krona
6. dinar
7. rupee
8. koruna
9. cedi
10. sucre
11. dollar
12. quetzal
13. dinar
14. sol
15. balboa
16. zaire
17. franc
18. yuan
19. kwacha
20. peso

Little Quiz 55, page 209
1. Danish
2. Italian
3. Irish
4. Russian
5. American
6. British
7. Swedish
8. Norwegian
9. Hungarian
10. Australian
11. Belgian
12. South African
13. Polish
14. Indian
15. Chilean
16. French
17. Canadian
18. Argentinian
19. Dutch
20. Austrian

Little Quiz 56, page 211
1. William Gladstone
2. Sir Henry Campbell Bannerman
3. David Lloyd George
4. Stanley Baldwin
5. Sir Anthony Eden
6. Andrew Jackson
7. Abraham Lincoln
8. Theodore Roosevelt
9. Harry S. Truman
10. Richard Nixon

Little Quiz 57, page 215
1. Muriel Spark
2. Angus Wilson
3. E. M. Forster
4. L. P. Hartley
5. George Orwell
6. Carl Orff
7. Gustav Mahler
8. William Walton
9. Franz Joseph Haydn
10. Samuel Coleridge Taylor